Being Anti-Colonial

Jayan Nayar

Daraja Press

Published by Daraja Press
https://darajapress.com
Wakefield, Quebec, Canada

ISBN 9781998309016

Cover and interior design: Kate McDonnell
Cover photo: Motaz Abuthiab, taken in Qalqilya, Palestine

Library and Archives Canada Cataloguing in Publication

Title: Being anti-colonial / Jayan Nayar.
Names: Nayar, Jayan, author.
Description: Includes bibliographical references.
Identifiers: Canadiana 20240284356 | ISBN 9781998309016 (softcover)
Subjects: LCSH: Postcolonialism.
Classification: LCC JV51 .N39 2024 | DDC 325/.301—dc23

Jayan Nayar, revisiting a lifetime of intellectual and social, struggle, writes elegiacally that academic specialists(including himself) in decolonization and development 'have learnt to say plenty, without saying much at all', primarily because of 'the utter absurdity of what we have been colonized to understand, even accept, as the norm-ality of the World' (such as the thought that 'we' owe no 'duty' to rescue the globally impoverished). While colonies may have disappeared, colonialism, as a state of mind, and as a living presence, is everywhere. Jayan's work will continue to haunt and provoke us for a long time; rather than being miscellany of grievances, it urges us to seriously rethink the avatars of postcoloniality and to revisit the grounds of hope.

– **Upendra Baxi**, Emeritus Professor, University of Warwick, and Delhi

Being Anti-Colonial is a bold excursion into the philosophical premises of post-colonial, neo-colonial and decolonial discourses. Nayar argues that the declarations of independence did not mark a rupture; rather, they heralded a resettlement in which the colonial situation with all its ugliness continued to thrive while creating an illusion, in no small measure propelled by the "new" independence intellectuals, of change and breakthroughs.

In the example of Zionist settler colonialism that he chooses for a chapter-long treatment, no doubt, his thesis is borne out. The long, drawn-out colonial moment in Palestine is not only ugly and horrendous but a grotesque manifestation of the two inherent tendencies of imperialism, war and fascism. That is mine, not Nayar's thesis. Nonetheless, it bears out his basic argument. Being anti-colonial thus, is proving its credence in the most negative way in Gaza, where the European progenitors of zionist-Israel are hand in glove with the genocidal project. In sum, Nayar's argument is that the nature of the struggle is anti-colonial situated in the colonial situation. What we have, therefore, is not post-, neo- or de-colonial, all of which, in the last instance, are terms that are constitutive of the resettlement project of European imperialism, but a colonial situation originated by Europe.

Being anti-colonial, for Nayar, is therefore the true expression of the colonised's subjectivity challenging headon the reason and rationality of the colonial. Jayan Nayar's thesis is contentious but not frivolous, courageous but not adventurous, imaginative but not thoughtless. It demands attention beyond the world of philosophy.

— **Issa G. Shivji**, Professor Emeritus of Public Law & First Julius Nyerere Professor of Pan-African Studies, University of Dar es Salaam, Tanzania

When post-colonial critique becomes the "new normal" for intellectuals, where does that leave the critique of (neo)colonialism, oppression, and tyranny in the real world? Jayan addresses this question by posing penetrating questions about our times and does it with feeling, grace, and conviction. Easy to read and a lot to think about.

— **Radha D'Souza**, Senior Research Fellow, Leuphana Institute of Advanced Studies (LIAS), Leuphana University, Professor of International Law, Development and Conflict Studies, University of Westminster, UK

ACKNOWLEDGEMENTS

Kate, for everyday and everything, thank you.

Jasmin and Jyothi, for inspiring me with your courage to live your lives uncompromisingly, with beauty and creativity.

Amma, Achan, Chechi, Anu, Kimi and Meenu, Appachi, Suku Chettan, Sashi Chechi, Nirmala Chechi, Ian, Susan, Richard and Julia, for just being there, family.

This book is the outcome of the conversations and friendships of my many years being part of the community of the School of Law, University of Warwick, UK. My involvement in the postgraduate International Development Law and Human Rights Programme (originally, Law in Development) underpins the thoughts and perspectives articulated here. So many colleagues, and so many cohorts of students over the years, have shared in the evolution of this book. I could not have had a more inspiring intellectual home. For this I am truly grateful.

A few friends deserve special mention. Issa Shivji, for teaching me from the start the simple yet profoundly important lesson that 'theory is a site of struggle'. This has remained with me throughout. Corinne Kumar for showing me the power and beauty of words that speak truths and what it means to be in community, with love and solidarity. Upendra Baxi and Abdul Paliwala for insisting that I write this book, and for their comments on the various drafts over the years. Asad Farooq for our many conversations as the chapters took shape and for never allowing me to doubt that this was worth completing. Raza Saeed for his support through difficult times. Claire Denney, Andrew Williams, Solange Mouthaan and Clare Spiers for their care and friendship. Rohini Sen, for her encouragement and patience in listening to my many ramblings. Emily Phillips for her multiple roles of 'research assistant', proof-reader, all round sounding-board and friend. And Steve Adams and Dave Daguirda for dragging me away from my thoughts on the book, teaching me the ways of the East End of London, making me a member of the Leyton Orient Football Club community, and introducing me to the wonderful world of real ale.

And finally, to conclude this expression of gratitude, I'd like to thank Firoze Manji for his belief in this book.

INTRODUCTION

We[1] look at the immensity of world and see it, and understand it, as a *World*. That is, we see a World as a totality, named, emplaced, defined, enforced, a World whose meanings, structures, and strictures, serve as the points of reference with which to understand the conditions of human beingness, and the points of departure from which to imagine possibilities for human futures. Indeed, from the moment we are born, from the moment we are *legally* inscribed with our own names that present us as a *Being*-in-the-World, as 'subject' in/to the World, we are schooled into knowing *this* World, instructed in allegiance to its demarcated 'political-legal' geography, educated to recognise its inhabitants all, 'us' and 'them', through a common (but differentiated) register of names, to know our/their places in the (named) places of the World.[2] Simply, we are (b)ordered.[3]

How familiar we are with these ontological foundations of *being-in-the-world*: sovereignty and citizenship (in 'State' territory) as foundations of 'political belonging'; humanity and rights as foundations of 'equality'; law and justice as foundations of 'judgement'. Indeed, with these categorical inscriptions are we purportedly 'post-colonial'; thus are our subject-ed' rights/lessness defined and structured, our (b)ordered subject-beingness inscribed and experienced, our pasts, presents, and futures made sense of and given sense to, precisely because we have come to-*Be* defined by these foundational mythologies of political-legal philosophy. As we *are* (b)ordered, we are (made) *'subject-ed Beings'* within a totality that is *this* World.

This is not to say that we accept this World as it is. This is especially so for those of us who are inheritors of the rich traditions of struggles against subjugated, 'colonised' pasts. We understand that this *World* has been constructed out of unimaginable, and extensively documented, brutality, its History indelibly stained by the consciously inflicted suffering of the global majorities subjected to centuries of calculated oppression and cruelty. We understand

---

1 I use "we" throughout this work and it is used as an inclusive form which speaks to those of us who self-identify as 'critical thinkers, especially of the so-called. 'Global South'. I leave it to the reader to self-associate, or not, as judged appropriate.

2 This is not to say that there are not also, for some if not for all of us, socialisations into other worlds that form part of our beingness-in-the-world. This encounter between *worlds* and *this* World is very much at the heart of the matter that concerns this work.

3 I employ the terms (b)orders and (b)ordering to emphasise the co-constitutive operation of the normative architecture (orders) of the World as constructed, regulated, and enforced, and the assertion of discursive and technological regimes of differentiation (borders).

that this underlying brutality continues still to define the material conditions of human beingness, still to violently enforce the essential norm-alities of the present; we know very well that, as John Newsinger evocatively put it, 'the blood never dried'.[4] This is the context of the present that confronts us as critical thinkers of the 'Global South' as many of us like to call ourselves these days. So, we rage against the ravages and inflicted cruelties of imperial pasts and presents, against, as Ann Laura Stoler calls it, the ruination inflicted by the continuing 'duress' of 'imperial formations'.[5] Rightly, for there is abundant ruination, there is plenty to rage against.

To be clear, our angry voices are well rehearsed in calling-out what needs calling-out, in confronting 'coloniality' (in all its variants),[6] and upholding, as we see it, the causes of *justice*. Much of what we do now involves critique of the many colonial-imperial philosophers of the past and their philosophies. We analyse their Eurocentrism, their bigotry. We complain about their rationalisations of murderous brutality and plunder undertaken in the name of (their) King and God, about their legitimisations of the countless cruelties inflicted upon conquered and enslaved populations. We recount the ways in which the political-legal philosophies of so-called 'Modernity' and the 'Enlightenment' – of 'Man' (his 'property' and 'liberty'), of 'sovereignty' and 'citizenship', of 'civilisation', of (human) 'rights' etc. – were, and still remain, steeped in racism. We expose the truths of 'humanism' and 'universalism' as the means by which those named and deemed 'less-than' – for whatever reason of convenience and preference – were erased from the Earth, both philosophically and existentially, in order that lands and material riches may be appropriated and exploited through (purportedly legitimised) violence. We know that this is not simply a matter of the past. Our work also involves raising complaints against the present, against the continuing coloniality of globalised (neo-liberal, racialised, techno-militarised, surveillance)

---

4 John Newsinger, *The Blood Never Dried: A People's History of the British Empire*, (London: Bookmarks Pub 2nd ed., 2013)

5 Ann Laura Stoler, *Duress: Imperial Durabilities in Our Times* (Durham: Duke University Press, 2016)

6 On coloniality, see generally Anibal Quijano, 'Coloniality of Power and Eurocentrism in Latin America', *International Sociology*, 15(2), 2000, 215-32; Walter D Mignolo, *Local Histories/Global Designs: Coloniality, Subaltern Knowledges, and Border Thinking* (Princeton: Princeton University Press, 2000); Ramon Grosfoguel, 'Transmodernity, border thinking, and global coloniality: Decolonizing political economy and postcolonial studies', *Eurozine*, 4 July 2008, available at <https://www.ikn-network.de/lib/exe/fetch.php/themen/grosfoguel_2008_transmodernity.pdf> (last accessed 10 March 2020). I use the term *coloniality* to mean the operation and enforcement of power/knowledge as a totalizing structure of inscribed names and meanings that (b)orders, normalises and regulates the World (fully as *one* World) of enforced (differentiated) subject-beingness.

capitalism,[7] of the many actualities of imperialisms, racisms and sexisms that remain entrenched in the normalised structures of global 'regulation' that continue to define the operations of the World as a totality. All this we understand, all this we vehemently protest.

And so, from this understanding, we seek then to make corrections to such epistemologies of imperial design: by 'provincialising Europe',[8] and embarking on a 'post/decolonial turn' to reveal the geo/body-politics of power-being-knowledge that we identify as founding the global order of 'coloniality-modernity';[9] by excavating silenced voices of suffering, and phenomenologies and epistemologies of being invisibilised by colonial and post-colonial erasures;[10] by seeking to *think* liberation/freedom' and reinserting the 'postcolonial' or 'decolonial' subject' in politics and sociology;[11]

7 See generally, Jason Hickel, *The Divide: A Brief Guide to Global Inequality and Its Solutions* (London: Windmill Books, 2017); Vandana Shiva and Kartikey Shiva, *Oneness vs The 1%* (Oxford: New Internationalist, 2019), Kehinde Andrews, *The New Age of Empire: How Racism and Colonialism Still Rule the World* (Dublin: Allen Lane, 2021); Shoshana Zuboff, *The Age of Surveillance Capitalism: The Fight for a Human Future at the New Frontier of Power* (London: Profile Books, 2019); Didier Bigo, Engin Isin and Evelyn Ruppert (eds.), *Data Politics: Worlds, Subjects, Rights* (Abingdon: Routledge, 2019). It is interesting to me that while we are gripped with the daily news of the global pandemic, the 'critical theory' community appears little engaged with the various initiatives of the 'Great Reset' and the '4th Industrial Revolution' that are being coordinated under the auspices of the World Economic Forum. In these we see the actual implications of 'building back better' in the moves to integrate more completely the 'physical, biological and digital spheres as a systemic totality. For a WEF introduction to the initiative, see Klaus Schwab, 'The Fourth Industrial Revolution: what it means, how to respond', *World Economic Forum*, 14 January 2016, available at <https://www.weforum.org/agenda/2016/01/the-fourth-industrial-revolution-what-it-means-and-how-to-respond/> (last accessed 20 October 2020).

8 Dipesh Chakrabarty, *Provincializing Europe: Postcolonial Thought and Historical Difference* (Princeton: Princeton Uni. Press, 2000. Also, generally, Graham Duggan (ed.), *The Oxford Handbook of Postcolonial Studies* (Oxford: Oxford Uni. Press, 2013).

9 See Walter D. Mignolo and Arturo Escobar (eds.) *Globalization and the Decolonial Option* (Abingdon: Routledge, 2013); Maria Lugones, 'Towards a Decolonial Feminism', *Hypatia* 25(4), 2010, 742-59; Sabelo J. Ndlovu-Gatsheni, *Coloniality of Power in Postcolonial Africa: Myths of Decolonization* (Dakar: CODESRIA, 2013); Gurminder K. Bhambra, *Rethinking Modernity: Postcolonialism and the Sociological Imagination* (Basingstoke: Palgrave, 2007). I am not overly occupied by the differences between these two strands of thought – the postcolonial and the decolonial – as these have developed in the academy; Walter Mignolo, himself a self-declared 'decolonial' thinker, has taken troubles to draw the distinctions for our benefit. For my purposes – and I hope the substantive reasons for my conflation becomes clear as we proceed – I treat them collectively and will henceforth adopt the term generally as 'post/decolonial' theory/philosophy/thought/ without further distinction.

10 See for example, Ranajit Guha and Gayatri C. Spivak (eds.), *Selected Subaltern Studies* (Oxford: Oxford Uni. Press, 1988) 37-44; Gayatri C. Spivak, "Can the Subaltern Speak," in *Marxism and the Interpretation of Culture*, eds. Cary Nelson and Lawrence Grossberg (Basingstoke: Macmillan Education, 1988), 271-313. A particular strand of scholarship that has experienced a resurgence in this connection is 'Black Studies', especially with rise of the contemporary 'Black Lives Matter' movement; see in general; Gaye Theresa Johnson and Alex Lubin (eds.), *Futures of Black Radicalism* (London: Verso, 2017).

11 See for example, Enrique Dussel, E (trans. Aquilina Martinez and Christine Morkovsky), *Philosophy of Liberation* (Eugene: Wipf and Stock, 2003), Michael Neocosmos (2016) *Thinking Freedom in Africa: Toward a Theory of Emancipatory Politics* (Johannesburg: Wits University Press); Vivienne Jabri, *The Postcolonial Subject: Claiming Politics/Governing Others in Late Modernity* (Abingdon: Routledge, 2013).

by exposing the persistence of globalised colour-lines and racialized differentiation that define the norms and practices of international relations and law,
etc.[12] We are constantly on the alert and are ever ready to pen our denunciations of the utter inhumanity of the past and present, and of the philosophies, and philosophers, of continuing violence. We speak 'truth to power'.
Loud and clear. Unwaveringly. For some, a 'TWAILian' mission.[13] This, we
think, and we tell ourselves and each other, is important work, importantly
done. And we have come some way, this work we do no longer in the 'periph-
eries' of global academic production but now in its very heartlands; indeed,
there is much scope for such work to be hosted, even if not necessarily feted,
in these spaces found clustered here and there in the midst of imperial centres
of knowledge. We have had to struggle for this recognition, for sure, for these
'safe' spaces within which, from which, we protest the World. Notwithstanding the ongoing efforts of the 'mainstream' to question our 'rigour',
to doubt our full-worth in the institutional academic/scholarly hierarchies
of 'true' knowledge, we have nevertheless persisted. Here we are, make no
mistake, right in the thick of things, strident and confident. Let us acknowledge that we have become quite expert.

But still, the nagging realisation; notwithstanding all our critical analyses of problems and thoughtful suggestions of correction, despite all our
sophisticated 'epistemological' efforts of reimagination, we remain rebuffed
even as we are accommodated by the 'broad-churches' of geo/body-politics
of 'knowledge' systems. The philosophers of the norm-ality of *this* World,
while they may be polite in our company, if they deign to be in our company,
will have none of it; the materialities of appropriation and dispossession,
of obscene enrichment and abject impoverishment, of righteous imperial violence, of un-memorialised suffering and death, all these continue
as everyday normalities of *this* World in the *(post)colonial* present, just so,
rationalised and ever-justified in the purportedly 'post-colonial' present.[14]

---

12 See for example, Robbie Shilliam, *Race and Racism in International Relations: Confronting the Global
    Colour Line* (Abingdon: Routledge, 2015), Antony Anghie, *Imperialism, Sovereignty and the Making
    of International Law* (Cambridge: Cambridge Uni. Press, 2005).

13 On the evolution and rationale of the growing community of scholars self-identifying within the
    broad associative umbrella of 'Third World Approaches to International Law', see generally, Makau
    Wa Mutua, 'What is TWAIL?', *Proceedings of the 94th Annual Meeting of the American Society of
    International Law*, 2000, 31-40; Bhupinder. S. Chimni 'Third World Approaches to international
    Law: Manifesto', *International Community Law Review* 8, 2006, 3-27; Luis Eslava and Sundhya
    Pahuja,. 'Between Resistance and Reform: TWAIL and the Universality of International Law', *Trade,
    Law and Development* 3(1), 2011, 195-221; Mohsen Al Attar, 'TWAIL: A Paradox Within a Paradox',
    International Community Law Review, 22, 2020, 163-196.

14 It will be obvious that I repeat these counter-positions often, the 'post-colonial' to mean the settlement

But we persevere, for we feel we must; what else can we do after all in the face of our confrontation with inconsequentiality.

I have been part of this community of self-asserted 'South' intellectuals for close to three decades now, studying, 'teaching', and writing in the hope of contributing to this intellectual project to correct the ongoing injustice and violence still witnessed, still prevalent. However, with the passing of time, I find myself increasingly dissatisfied with this assumed shared project, viewing much of the abundant activity and prolific production of our current intellectual work – our practices, our critiques, the assertions we make about the world and our roles in it – with decreasing enthusiasm. It has begun to feel, to me, an unsatisfactory, rather complacent, and complicit 'project'. For whatever our stated and best intentions, our activities, it seems to me, find neat containment within the rationalities of rewards and inducements of corporatized 'scholarship'.[15] This is the hard truth of the matter. Whatever our claims, our 'critical' standpoints remain contained within the disciplinary and disciplined institutional boundaries of the permissible, a consequence – even if we might balk at this suggestion – of a *being-colonised* in the*(post)colonial* situation. Simply, it is not so easy to reconcile our critical, even radical, intellectual travelling through and in *mind-worlds* of (post/ decolonial) resistance, on the one hand, and our comfortable inhabiting of personal and professional neighbourhoods intimately implicated in the *life-worlds* of imperial networks, on the other. We endure this existential burden bravely, and for that we are more vociferous in our complaints of the many manifestations and enforcements of the 'imperial/colonial' present.

As an 'insider' as it were, this is what I observe. What we – professionalised critical ('South') thinkers – mostly do is assert a significance for *our* place in this World, and we have been seduced into this conceit. We have, quite frankly, become pretty mainstream. As members of 'critical/post/decolonial' global networks of scholarship no less, we have our journals, our academic 'departments' and our 'Chairs', our grant-funded research projects and international conferences, all not as a clandestine group operating in the margins, let alone in the shadows, of the academy, but proud and prominent, our scholarship,

of 'decolonisation' deemed to be effected following the 'declaration of independence', the (post) colonial to describe the actual continuity of coloniality that persists, indeed, flourishes, through the 'post-colonial' architecture of (b)ordering. See below, Chapters 1 and 2 for an elaboration of this frame of understanding.

15 I stress that I speak here of 'critical' academic scholarship, not of the diverse grounded intellectual labours of communities in material struggles against colonising forces for whom to think is less a matter of being-critical, and more of critical-beingness. We will return to this point later.

even if not wholly feted and equally rewarded, at least 'recognised' by and within the very imperial centres of knowledge-production that we make much to purportedly denounce. So, we busy ourselves, individually and collectively. Indeed, we have become 'entrepreneurs', ourselves peddlers of intellectual commodities, of 'pedagogies' and 'epistemologies', post/decolonial theory now equally a brand worthy of global markets governed fully by neoliberal rationalities. Of course, we complain about this incessantly, but operate within its strictures regardless. If once the burden of the anti-colonial thought was to think "clearly – that is dangerously" against the World, as Cesaire insisted,[16] we now have learnt to live radicality and revolution vicariously, celebrating and mediating the dangerous texts and thoughts of the past through the purifier of 'critical theory', marketing their 'terrorism' – as these insurgent and banned thoughts were quite explicitly considered in their time – via the safety of 'scholarship' in the academy. We are often heard to repeat to each other: "*Aluta continua*!". This we do, and it is cringe-worthy.

We have learnt to say plenty, without saying much at all.

Lest it be misunderstood, in all this that I say, I do not exclude or exonerate myself.

The (Absurd) Norm-ality of the ('Post-Colonial') Present

So, what of the World? By this question I don't simply allude to the 'harsh' realities and 'injustices' of the World, but to the very idea of the *World*, itself, fully as a totality, as *norm-ality*.

For all our complaints, for all our sophisticated ('post/decolonial') critiques and 'turns', exposes and denunciations, it seems to me that we nevertheless find this World, as (b)ordered, *sensible* even if inhumane, *meaning-ful* even if perverse. That is to say, we take as given the categories of political-legal philosophy that fundamentally defines the architecture of the *World*, as a totality of meaning, as being the 'terms' with which the conversation about the human condition may be entered into. This assumption requires examination and here is where I begin, by making clear the utter absurdity of what we have been colonised to understand, even accept, as the *norm-ality* of the *World*.[17] My purpose is to redefine the 'post-colonial' present as the problem of the (*post)colonial* situation.

---

16 Aimé Césaire (trans Joan Pinkham), *Discourse on Colonialism* (New York: Monthly Review Press, 1972 (2000)), 32.

17 Indeed, to be *colonised* is precisely to be inserted into the *norm-ality* of the coloniser, as 'subject'. See Chapter 2, below.

To explain what I mean by this, let us consider what might seem, initially, a bizarre question: *what do the 'global poor' owe 'us'?* My posing of the question is a deliberate inversion of a common philosophical enquiry undertaken on the scope and implications, if any, of 'global justice': "what do *we* owe the *global poor*?" We ask this question in order that we might interrogate the (in)justice present, to find solutions to the problem, as it were, of the 'global poor' as a normalised 'sector' within the totality of the global citizenry.[18] When this question is inverted however, we are able to see clearly the absurdity that underpins it, indeed, of the absurd *norm-ality* that we assume as the 'post-colonial' *World*. So, in all seriousness: what do the 'global poor' owe 'us'?

The answer is quite clear: *Everything!* The 'global poor' owe us everything. This is the irrefutable conclusion we reach when this *World*, as a totality of (b)ordered regulation and enforcement, is analysed in its brutal facticity. Let me explain.

The matter of *"what we owe to the global poor"* was considered by the philosopher Mathias Risse.[19] Following a long and meandering consideration of 'liberal' moral philosophy, and recognising fully the unfairness of fortune and fate and the very real human suffering that persists, Risse duly concluded that *we* – of the 'affluent' World – owe *them* nothing, save a very limited and conditional duty towards 'assistance' in promoting and developing 'liberal' governance institutions and capabilities. No alteration of the World as (b) ordered, regulated and enforced by the institutions and rules of 'international relations', no change to the everyday norm-ality of the World, so to speak, therefore, is deemed necessary by this reckoning, at least not by reason of any 'moral' or 'legal' duty of 'distributive justice' so to do. Risse, the philosopher of justice, considered the matter seriously and seriously determined so. And many others, equally seriously, have reached similar conclusions.[20] Indeed, we

---

18 Who are the 'global poor'? It is of note that when they have been invoked in 'development' or 'justice' discourses, there seldom is a clarification. It seems they simply are a meaningful category of the global population. For present purposes let us understand the 'global poor' as those global social majorities who have inadequate access to the main resources (or 'capabilities', if this this is the preferred discursive language of choice) for a healthy and secure life as frequently compiled by global 'development' and 'humanitarian' agencies. They are indeed the abject, the 'wretched' of the earth, disposable in their suffering, unwanted in their presence. And the 'us' that I speak of here; those who quite considerably have in excess of the average, let alone such baseline limits, of such necessities, for whom this World and its normalities provide us so.

19 Mathias Risse, 'What We Owe to the Global Poor', *The Journal of Ethics* 9(1-2), 2005, 81-117; Contra, Thomas Pogge, 'Recognized and Violated by International Law: The Human Rights of the Global Poor', *Leiden Journal of International Law*, 18, 2005, 717-45.

20 See for example Thomas Nagel, 'The Problem of Global Justice', *Philosophy & Public Affairs* 33(2), 2005, 113-147, Andrea Sangiovanni, 'Global Justice, Reciprocity, and the State', *Philosophy & Public*

can be sure many others will follow. No doubt, they will invite the engagement of dissenters for debate. Many of us, especially those from the 'Global
South', will duly present all manner of counterargument to refute such
uncaring conclusions. All this is little but distraction.

I have no intention to refute Risse's (or anyone else's) conclusions, nor to
demonstrate the errors of his understanding and analysis. My concern here is
to demonstrate the perverse absurdity that underpins the underlying assumptions that make possible the very asking of the question. What is at issue
here is the ubiquity of the idea of the 'global poor', and of the norm-ality
of the World in which the 'global poor' is a category – to repeat my earlier
refrain – that is *sensible* to us, even if we consider their condition inhumane,
meaningful to us, even if we might regard their condition perverse. It is this
assumption, and assertion of 'normality' that is at issue.

In enquiring about the 'global poor', we acknowledge *them* as present in
this World; indeed we acknowledge that this *World* persists both with *our*, and
their, presence as a given, as a normality of this World. The 'global poor' exists
(so incidentally do the 'global super-rich', the '1%' as they have been called).
The question that is being considered therefore is whether this normality of
opposition between the *us* and *them*, of 'our' affluence and 'their' abjection
as differentiated conditions of *subject-beingness* in the World, is demanding of
a readjustment of *this* World as is, requiring of a renegotiation of the 'moral'
parameters of ethical relationality, and thereby, of the institutional arrangements and rules of relations that operate to govern this *World* as a Totality.
This is the persistent norm-ality that the philosopher takes as a given, the
World as presently (b)ordered, a totality of meaning and imagination from
which continuity/change is (presumed) thinkable, possible, desirable. It
is from this assumed *normality* – that is the situation taken as a given, not
requiring further examination – that the question "what do *we* owe the *global
poor*" is posed.[21] Here, we pause.

Affairs 35(1), 2007, 3-39, Uwe Steinhoff, 'Why 'We' are not Harming the Global Poor: A Critique of
Pogge's Leap from State to Individual Responsibility', *Public Reason* 4(1-2), 2012, 119-38.

21 We see here a critical philosophical manoeuvre. The ascription of rights/less subjection following the
    debate on what *they* might or might not be 'owed', sets the baseline and benchmark of rationalised care
    or indifference to actualised suffering and subjugation. What the 'global poor' is 'owed' or not defines
    therefore the scope of response to any claim of (un)just suffering; the ('illegal') migrant, the (poten-
    tial) 'refugee', the (exploited) worker, for example, these ascriptions of (un)belonging are all subject
    therefore to the spectrum of (dis)regard following from the norm-alisations of abjection. Indeed, this
    is what 'philosophers' of 'justice' work so hard to do. For any such instance of appeal, therefore, it is
    that abstracted norm-ality of *just* deprivation and suffering that serves as a benchmark of justified care
    or abandonment; exactly such a determination is the work of 'justice'. What the 'global poor' is 'owed',
    or not, therefore, is fundamental to entrenching the (b)ordered ubiquity of *this* World. Indeed, the

To abide by the norm-ality of *this* World is to implicitly assume, if not to explicitly assert, that they, the 'global poor', owe 'us' *this* World, entirely so, as it is presently (b)ordered and enforced, subject of course to their 'right' to request measures for 'reform'. Put differently, within the norm-ality of *this* World, the 'global poor' owe us their continued abjection in the presence of our affluence, again subject only to whatever justifiable claim to reform 'we' might concede. Bluntly, what we are fundamentally acknowledging when we recognise *this* World as norm-ality is this: they, the 'global poor', owe us their continued silence in the face of their suffering; they owe us our peace of mind as we shrug our shoulders at their 'misfortune'; they owe us their uncomplaining 'collateral' deaths – be it through our righteous 'economic sanctions' or our 'surgical' drone strikes – as a 'price that is worth it' for *our* 'security' globally; they owe us their wretchedness, their continued destitution and death in this norm-ality of the *World*.[22] They owe us precisely this norm-ality, just so, and for that reason they owe us their compliance, their supplication, indeed, their *obedience* to this *World*, to *this* World as (b)ordered and enforced in the 'post-colonial' present. This is what the 'global poor' owe 'us' when all is said and done. This is, as things are, the only conclusion we might reach. *They* owe *us* Everything.[23]

Let us take in this proposition fully. It is worth re-stating it in full to make clear its full implication: the global communities of the impoverished, the destitute and dispossessed, the 'wretched of the earth' all, are duty-bound to remain subject-to, and abide by, *this* World as norm-alised through political-legal regimes of regulation and enforced through all the means of legalised violence necessary. By this account, what fate then the 'global poor' following this assertion of norm-ality? Precisely the pitiful fate that is their due, due that is to their perverse *debt* to this World in which theirs is deemed a condition entirely *just*. Owing *this* World everything as they do, they are entitled to nothing but hope in the 'philanthropy' of the affluent, and at a stretch, for

---

norm-ality of *the World* is fully revealed when we consider its implication from the reverse perspective, that is when we ask: "what the global poor owe us"?

22 See Mbembe's notion of necropolitics for a fuller elaboration of this norm-alised condition of contemporary (in)humanity; Achille Mbembe, *Necropolitics* (Durham: Duke University Press, 2019).

23 This demand of obedience was seen starkly in the face of the Covid-19 'lockdown' measures enforced globally. Purportedly to secure the 'health' of all the population and to 'save' national health services, reports indicate once again the increasing evidence that, notwithstanding the claims that 'we are all in it together', populations of the impoverished and of marginalised and exploited labour – the 'global poor' as it were – everywhere bore the full brunt of both vulnerability and policing violence and still continue to bear the entrenched consequences of dispossession that thereby resulted.

our due consideration in the calculations and reckonings of 'global justice',[24] their due place to remain in their assigned places, or if they must, outside of the hallways of erudite deliberations on 'moral' and 'political' philosophy, or the grand chambers of judicial proceedings if they might be so admitted, arms folded in appropriate deference, heads bowed, compliant to whatever judgements of 'just' norm-ality that might be rendered. Thus is the under-lying norm-ality of cruelty that defines, still, the philosophical orthodoxy of 'post-colonial' time; the World as we know it, as we think it, as we speak it, entirely the artefact of (post)colonial (b)orders.

There is nothing natural or inevitable about all of this, of course. Yet so we have it. A norm-ality of the 'post-colonial' World philosophically rationalised by the affluent of the World, for all 'Humanity'. I am not so concerned to carry on an argument about the perversity, or the 'injustice' of the situation for that is all too obvious and well understood. No, it is the absurdity of *norm-ality* that is of relevance, for it is this that we must see clearly, and understand. 'Post-colonial' norm-ality as (post)colonial situation: this is the problem that demands our attention.

But first, we consider a question, seldom asked.

Why Blame the (Post)Colonial Philosopher?

This much is clear. Much of our attention – as 'critical scholars' of the 'South' – is invested in arguments against the positions and the rationalisations of the 'mainstream' protagonists of *this* World as (b)ordered and enforced. It seems we take offence with what they think and say and do. But, what is that we assume when we make such complaints? Simply, why do we blame the 'philosophers of domination' – let us for present purposes call them that – for their offensive philosophies?

Why, for example, should the philosophies of the 'White-Man' be anything but the rationalisation of the World as imagined by *White*-ness, of the Right and Justice of this World so imagined and enforced against all that is (thought) 'non/un-White', 'non/un-European', 'non/un-Christian', 'non/un-civilised'? Why should such thinking, as worlds of 'Others' were variously encountered, serve anything but the purpose of (b)ordering the *World* such that Whiteness is sought to be norm-alised as that which is Right-ful, as righteous? Let us be fair to those philosophers whom we might consider to be racist, misogynist, imperialist (or even, just plain 'liberal') etc, past or present,

---

24 See Monique Deveaux, 'The Global Poor as Agents of Justice' *Journal of Moral Philosophy* 12, 2015.

it is not his (and it has been and remains largely his) 'problem' the wretchedness of the dispossessed, the abjection of the conquered, the 'subalternisation' of the other-ed. However repulsive *their* thoughts might be to *us*, it is, quite simply, not their burden to take us into account, not their responsibility to think the World on 'our' behalf. We appear to assume it to be so. But why?

It seems to me that our complaints against these philosophers, advocates and apologists of domination are predicated upon some perceived abrogation of their responsibility to be concerned with the fate of the World as a whole – of the wretched, their encountered-'Other' as they might regard 'us' – rather than to pursue their partial, partisan interests through their philosophical rationalisations of superiority, power and right. We protest that the thoughts they have thought, and continue to think, become into the world at our expense, indeed that they subjugate and violate 'us' in their rationalisations of 'White/imperial' norm-alities. We insist on holding them to account as if our interventions would engender a philosophical turn true to a universal humanity against 'lazy reason',[25] as if what was lacking was a better, more pluralistic, 'pluriversal', inclusive, democratic quest for knowledge that would bring about a more humane civilisation. And so, we continue to engage in a critique of their positions, to reveal limits, biases, false assumptions, so on and so forth. We repeat our discoveries of oppression, our repudiations of domination, our epistemologies of liberation, our arguments increasingly sophisticated, and we do this, again, and again, and again. Aside from being useful as a conversation amongst the 'converted', so to speak, we do this in the belief, I suppose, – as it might assuages our self-perception to so do – that *they* would have real interest in what *we* might have to say by way of post/decolonial corrections and insertions, that thereby they might be convinced and recant the errors of their thoughts, that thereby our arguments, our truths, our hope, may abide. Of this our hope seems perpetual. An example might be useful to illustrate the point.

As he introduces a series of collected essays on *International Relations and Non-Western Thought*, Robbie Shilliam asks the following question:

> Why is it that the non-Western world has been a defining presence for IR scholarship and yet said scholarship has consistently balked at placing non-Western thought at the heart of its debates?[26]

25 See Boaventura de Sousa Santos, *Epistemologies of the South: Justice Against Epistemecide* (Abingdon: Routledge, 2014). We might rather regard the Reason of subjugation that has constructed and enforced *this* World as anything but 'lazy', being quite on the contrary utterly diligent and focussed in its propagation and management.

26 R. Shilliam (ed), *International Relations and Non-Western Thought: Imperialism, colonialism and*

The question is put to explain the urgency of the work. Recognising the colonial history of the discipline of IR and its complicity in rationalising the enslavement and subjugation of 'non-Western' peoples, Shilliam continues to explain the 'project' undertaken:

> Over the last twenty years a project has emerged that seeks to critically reinvent the comparative tradition of the Western academy. Scholars associated with this project have sought to 'provincialize' thought on the Western experience of modernity heretofore taken as a universal reference point... Primarily the project seeks to give *legitimate standing* to the traditions and figures of non-Western thought.[27]

And as to the point, and intention, of this 'project', Shilliam is hopeful:

> The retrieval of this global context to the knowledge production of modernity in IR might help to provide deeper insights into the contested nature of a global modernity shaped so fundamentally by colonialism and Western expansionism. Now, as ever, these insights are desperately needed for a discipline that is closely implicated in Western foreign policy-making and *yet has such a myopic horizon of inquiry.*[28]

Shilliam's scholarship demands respect; he has repeatedly exposed the racialized and imperial underpinning of international relations theory and practice. But this is precisely the point at which we need to take stock. We know that this kind of correction has been repeatedly done. Many times over. The literature, as we know, is rich. We consistently engage in deliberations of such rigorous critical work. And yet, each time we repeat the exercise, we appear to act as if we make some new discovery, that some new critical pathway is now charted for transformation this time, and we congratulate each other for it. We have become rather accustomed to celebrating repetition; as sophisticated as our 'new' discoveries and expositions of the wrongs committed by the (post)colonial philosopher undoubtedly are, much of our work remains repetitions of complaint all the same. For sure, the academic publishing industry has thrived on all this effort, and careers have so been built. But what effect our fixations with (post)colonial philosophers and their philosophies of (in)justice on the realities of the matter? For, we see, *their* World remains as *norm-ality.*

---

investigations of global modernity (Abingdon: Routledge, 2011), 2.

27 Shilliam, *International Relations and Non-Western Thought*, 3 (emphasis, mine)

28 Shilliam, *International Relations and Non-Western Thought*, 4 (emphasis, mine)

Let us be clear: there is no contradiction between the implicatedness of IR (or international law, or economics, or sociology or anthropology etc. etc), as a 'discipline', of its imperial pasts and presents of 'Western' foreign policy-making, on the one hand, and its abiding absenting and neglect of 'non-Western' traditions and insights, on the other. IR as a discipline has a 'myopic horizon of enquiry' precisely because its original and continuing function is to absent those conquered, to norm-alise the 'universality' of the 'parochial', to rationalise the present as normal, and good, and just, a 'garden' of *civilisation* in the midst of a vast and oppressive 'jungle'.[29] Our repeated injunctions for corrections, our appeals for 'deeper insights', all of this, worthy as our intention may be, simply misses the point. And the point is significant.

The fact is quite plain. We remind ourselves that colonial philosophers were nothing but utterly unabashed in asserting their *Right*, in total righteousness, to "exterminate all the brutes" that came to be in the way of their desires.[30] There is no equivocation on the matter. 'Black-ed lives', as it were, under the rationalised brutalities of the 'racial contract', were indeed regarded and enforced as nothing but 'White'-matter.[31] The same continues today; there is little embarrassment or hesitation on the part of contemporary philosophers of 'White' righteousness in asserting the Right to violence in the face of any perceived threat to civilisational supremacy. This is not by reason of mis-education or mis-information on the 'humanity' of the 'Other'. It is the way it is, fully as the way of *this* World. Our assumption that our 'corrections' of their 'myopia' is what is lacking to rectify the horrors of this reality is simply foolish.

Bluntly, it is our weakness that is revealed by our protests for philosophical accountability on the part of the imperial White-philosopher. What if not weakness prompts a perception that 'we' need to attain, or seek recognition for, a 'legitimate standing' with respect to 'the traditions and figures of

29 For a recent re-statement of this view, see Robert Kagan, *The Jungle Grows Back: America and Our Hostile World* (New York: Alfred A. Knopf, 2018).
30 For a simply presented yet, for that, powerful treatment of this fundamental philosophy, see Sven Lindqvist (trans., Joan Tate), *Exterminate All the Brutes* (London: Granta, 2018). The literature on colonial atrocity is abundant, of course, but strangely, seemingly non-consequential in any material way in thinking about the matters of the World. The implications of this inconsequentiality I think bears critical reflection. We have thus far failed to do so and instead persist in the perpetual restatement of the record of atrocity.
31 See Charles W. Mills, *The Racial Contract* (Ithaca: Cornell University Press, 1997). Also, Kathryn Yusoff, *A Billion Black Anthropocenes or None* (Minneapolis: University of Minnesota Press, 2018). For further discussion of this point, see below, Chapter 3.

non-Western thought'?; in whose eyes?; by what terms of judgement?; as if such a correction was what is lacking in solving the problem of the imperialism and expansionism of 'Western foreign policy-making'. It is our error to assume that the philosophical endeavour – particularly in matters pertaining to the material issues of power and its right-ful/less distribution – is ever intended to attain an inclusive all-encompassing thinking-for-humanity. We have swallowed whole, it would appear, that most potent of (post)colonial philosophical deceits that laid down the original totalising onto-epistemology of colonisation: the assertion that the philosopher (of domination) speaks for, on behalf of, and towards, a *universal* 'Humanity'. Now we are fully aware that the 'universality' of the conquerors was a partial one, the claim simply rationalising the power and the right of some to name and define the (Hu) Man of Humanity as universal Human-Beingness. This assertion has long been repudiated of course, and for so long our struggle was to 'decolonise' the Human of Humanity so defined. This, it would appear, we have done successfully, at least as a matter of philosophical etiquette even if not experiential actuality; the 'proof' is in the unequivocal expression that all *human beings* are born equal in rights and dignity, and with it, in the affirmation of the equal sanctity of 'life' whereby we might demand that (all) lives matter, etc, all this frequently repeated mantras of the 'Human Rights' community of believers. But the actuality is something quite the opposite. While some may insist on the importance of such affirmations of an *ideal* notwithstanding the *actual*,[32] I see it rather as an *untruth*, not only obscene in its lie, but in that it functions as a potently disabling philosophical deception.[33] My interest does not lie in the metaphysics of the matter, but in the material and experiential actualities of the *World*.

Better we recognise and come to terms with the truth of the *vocation* of 'philosophers' and 'historians' of imperial dominance. It is not their job to right the wrongs of (in)Humanity; quite the opposite, it is precisely theirs to assert, as Right, the normality of the wrongs *we* protest and suffer, to normalise *this* World as it is (b)ordered, to claim the mastery of the Master's truths, the truths of their (in)justice, and the justice of their rights.[34] It is their place in the world to define the World, to name us Negro, Red, Black, Brown and

---

32 For an example of this argument, see Alan Norrie, *Dialectic and Difference: Dialectical critical realism and the grounds for justice* (Abingdon: Routledge, 2010).

33 See Jayan Nayar, 'The Non-Perplexity of Human Rights', *Theory & Event* 22(2), 2019, 267-302.

34 The various historical celebrations of Empire as a good and essentially progressive force in human civilisation is exactly to point; for a recent a classic of this genre, see Niall Ferguson, *Empire: How Britain Made the Modern World*, (2003).

Yellow, savage, native, uncivilised, the undeveloped to be developed, the terrorist to be killed, the victim to be saved, it is their philosophical labour to rationalise the violence of the world as civilisation and development, *their* violence as humanitarianism, their oppression as order, their demarcations of incarceration, exclusion and negation as borders. The philosopher thus rationalises their construction of the *World* as a coherent totality, and propounds this basic knowledge of the World so imagined, constructed, and enforced, as the normality from which all others are prescribed, to think. And it appears this *we* do; even as we vociferously protest the White-imperial-patriarchal-World that has come to be constructed and continues to be enforced, even as we repudiate the onto-epistemological violence of their philosophies of negation, we remain enchanted, *colonised*, by the authority of their 'Words' by which the World has been named, imagined and (b)ordered.

Enchanted, we might even say entranced, ours is a complaint of injustice, an insistence on correction, as if justice and correction were immanent, a truth of Humanity awaiting discovery, awaiting recovery even, a hope held out that it is indeed the destiny of Humanity to attain that ideal of *justice, equality, freedom*. As such, against *this* World, we assert, rightly that "Other Worlds *are* Possible". And against their philosophies of negation, we protest that "We also think"! This is all right and good, to an extent. It is right that we are outraged by the thoughts of the thinkers who have rationalised, justified, and normalised – as abiding universal Truths and Right – the utter brutalities of conquest, industrialised commercial slavery, colonial subjugation, all. It is imperative that we are outraged by on-going continuities of predatory appropriation and dispossession, violence and oppression, and the structurally enforced normalities of global inequalities of power and wealth as presumed Right. It is right we are outraged. But then, what? Towards what consequence? Do we continue to seek 'legitimate standing' for our pasts, our thoughts, our experiences, our imaginations? Do we continue to presume, to harbour hope, that the philosopher of (post)colonial domination pays regard to this appeal of/to Humanity in any way other than as conceit? What exactly is our intention, our aspiration, as we do this, repeatedly? Here is the stark truth, and we know it: global coloniality is quite able to abide comfortably with post/decolonial critique, with TWAILian pedagogies of International Law and Human Rights, with excavations of 'epistemologies of the South', etc. It is no surprise therefore that *they*, the philosophers of domination, of imperial Whiteness, of (post)colonial 'nationalist' order, simply put, couldn't care less. We delude ourselves if we think otherwise.

Sven Lindqvist is correct:

You already know enough. So do I. It is not knowledge we lack. What is missing is the courage to understand what we know and to draw conclusions.[35]

This Book and My Intention
To understand what we know and to draw conclusions.

So, about this book as I envisage it. I write it from the conviction that the present *norm-ality* of this *World* as (b)ordered and enforced is absurd, and untenable. And that to abide by the underlying terms of this manifest global actuality as we engage in 'being critical' is just so much useless chitter-chatter, a safe and self-congratulatory *non-thinking*. We must, I believe, begin with this harsh self-criticism.

This book, therefore, is not intended as a work that strives to speak 'truth to power'. Power is fully aware. I am not concerned with correcting the philosophers of domination. They will continue to think as they wish. They will rationalise the present as they will. I am not concerned to demonstrate the necessary corrections to the errors, or injustice, or silences or neglect of conventional thoughts so as to make true and complete the visions of a universal Humanity. The views I present do not seek affirmation from conventional philosophical wisdoms, nor to find a niche of belonging within extant (permitted) thinking to justify their validity. My intention is rather to see clearly the actuality of the present and to understand it as it is, not as a reification or fantasy of a 'post-colonial' possibility 'to-come',[36] but as actuality, fully of 'imperial durabilities' as Stoler calls it,[37] a reconfigured totality of regulation and enforcement, (b)ordered and enforced as 'post-colonial' *resettlement* of global (post)coloniality. In light of this actuality of the *(post) colonial* present, my interest is to return the *anti-colonial* to philosophy and to present implications that follow from such anti-colonial praxes.

The book is divided into two parts.

Part One undertakes the task of explaining what I mean by 'returning the anti-colonial to philosophy'. My argument begins with an understanding that the 'post-colonial' – both as a philosophical manoeuvre and '*World*-making' architecture – is fully the global resettlement of the *Reason* of

---

35 Lindqvist, *Exterminate All the Brutes*, 2
36 See Jabri, *The Postcolonial Subject*.
37 Stoler, *Duress*.

coloniality. Briefly, what I call 'methodological post-colonialism' operates as a closure of imagination that marks the philosophical rupture from 'colonial' pasts of sins and depravity to a 'post-colonial' present promising universal 'humanitarian' virtue and 'justice'. I present a different view of the discursive and regulatory architecture of the *World*: not 'post-colonial' rupture, signalled by the 'declaration of independence', but (post)colonial totality. Understanding the present as a (post)colonial resettlement thus is to be neither entranced by a mythology of the 'post-colonial' nor be fixated with simplistic fixations of the continuities of some 'external' imperial, so-called 'neocolonial', impositions. Instead, we understand the (post)colonial in its context, as a resettlement, a reconfiguration of (b)ordering and enforcement, a self-reflexive, ever-malleable, and adaptable systemic organisation of coloniality. If the 'post-colonial' pushes for a philosophical obscuration of global coloniality, the (post)colonial reopens it fully to view. This is the actual situation from which the perspectives and arguments of this book begin. Against the actuality of the (post)colonial present, the *anti-colonial* is here reaffirmed as a philosophical situation and praxis of struggle to *(re)make worlds*.

At the heart of the 'anti-colonial' recovery of imagination therefore is an overturning of the fundamental assertions of 'methodological post-colonialsm'. Simply stated, this is the opening to question the norm-ality of (post)colonial *(b)orders* as fully, still, the unresolved situation of anti-colonial *frontlines*. No finality to the colonial situation is thus assumed, the 'declaration of independence' returned to its historical moment as a significant, but open and incomplete, assertion of anti-colonial repudiation of colonial designs of *World*-making. Indeed, this is to make explicit that the *World*, both as *word* and as *matter*, itself remains fully subject to judgement, no convenient settlement deemed conclusive of the colonial problem. The task is both philosophical and material, of imagination and life-places.

Part Two then provides arguments of the substantive application of anti-colonial praxis to some prominent matters of worldly contention. The various chapters that follow suggest, perhaps uncomfortably for some, the implications of extending an anti-colonial philosophy to the presumed norm-alities of the (post)colonial present. Here, we consider such issues as 'Black-ed' lives as White-d matter, the Lie of *Europe* and *Postcolony* as World-(b)ordering categories of intimate-separation, the situation of Palestine and the problem of *Zionist-Israelism* as a manifestation of (genocidal, yet utterly fragile) *White*-supremacy, and inevitably, the question, and implications of 'un/violence' that inheres in the *encounter* marked by the incommensurable situation that is (post)colonial *(b)order*/anti-colonial *frontline*. In all these situations, we see the significance of the *words* that norm-alise *this* World. These indeed are colonial remnants, deeply entrenched, requiring repudiation. Against all these, I suggest an anti-colonial position of praxis.

An important caution is due. The thoughts that follow in this book might not offer security or promises of better futures. As we will see, the *(post)colonial*, and *anti-colonial* situations are mutually present as *(b)orders* and *frontlines*. But in saying this, it is necessary to emphasise the point that there is nothing fixed or determined by this assertion of a philosophical situation. There is nothing inevitable or even wondrous in being-anti-colonial in the sense of any grand 'historical' unfolding, nothing capable of abstraction as some essential content to an *anti-colonial beingness*. The *anti-colonial* in this understanding does not pertain to any imagined totality either of oppression or liberation. The *anti* here is entirely contingent upon the materialities of coloniality in their specificities of time, place, and experience; these are matters we cannot know in isolation nor in the absolute. What we do know is that the struggle against colonial rule in the past – the ordinary, everyday uprisings and refusals to be-subject to regimes of impoverishment and degeneracy – dared imagine otherwise so as to be conjoined in a collective articulation and action towards greater dignity, solidarity, and material security. These actualities of refusal and regeneration, as projections of imagination and hope, can only be understood and appreciated in their specific historical contexts. What we might say by way of generalisation is that such refusals were an assertion of beingness in the *frontline,* that is as a presence – in full Beingness – that claims voice and author-ity in the denunciation of asserted (b)orders of subjection as rationalised and enforced in place and time.

So, I return to the terminology of the 'anti-colonial' very intentionally. Precisely to remind us of the outrageous and impertinent responsibility to think being-anti-colonial against the assumption and assertions of (post) colonial normality. Especially for those of us who originate from the *Post-colony*, as descendants of the 'post-colonial' settlements that have come to normalise (post)coloniality, this historical legacy is a fundamental burden of intellectual responsibility to be carried. In this connection, with this connection, 'critical' thought is not simply a matter of sophistry and sophistication, be it of pedagogies or epistemologies. It is a matter of matter itself, and, so being, directly answerable to all the ghosts of anti-colonial struggles past who imagined otherwise to make different worlds. In this respect, the legacy of our anti-colonial past is an important and heavy responsibility we must bear.[38]

As a result, what is revealed and what is provoked may not, to many, appeal. I make no apologies for this unease or discomfort. From the point of view of a professionalised intellectual, writing from my location – and I suspect a similar location is shared by most who might read this – there is an obvious conflict of interest, however fervently we might object. The truth of it is that we are implicated in this World as it is (b)ordered and enforced, we have a stake in its continuing security, indeed we benefit from it being so whether we like it or not. It is unsurprising therefore that we are mostly inclined to think in ways that perpetuate our relevance, as 'critical intellectuals', to think futures in ways that impinge little on our beingness, as such. I see no reconciliation however between this World that we occupy and the anti-colonial positions I advance here; no 'safe spaces' for our continued significance. I do not speak of the World as it should hopefully be in some imagined future, but as it brutally is in this, the present, (post)colonial time. What becomes of this World is a matter to come, if so. My intention is simply to draw out the implications of what an unfinished and necessary anti-colonial responsibility to think might entail as we contemplate *this* World as it is. On this point, we might well recall Fanon's insight:

> Decolonization, which sets out to change the order of the world, is, obviously, a programme of complete disorder. But it cannot come as a result of magical practices, nor of a natural shock, nor of a friendly understanding ... Decolonization is the meeting of two forces, opposed to each other by their very nature...[39]

With this in mind, and taking seriously the implications of 'complete disorder', let us return to that earlier question: *what do the 'global poor' owe 'us'?* This question provides a simple point of entry with which we might re-view the *World*, with which we might begin to know *this* world differently; against the implicit assertion that 'they' owe 'us' everything, a different

---

38 On this point, it also bears stating that I adhere to no conventions of 'academic' lineage bar a commitment to an anti-colonial spirit; I have therefore no 'stake' in perpetuating any particular 'brand' of 'critical' intellectual thought. The implication of this 'indiscipline' is that my use of relevant citations, references, authorities, may appear idiosyncratic, I may omit to give regard to any particular favoured doyen assumed to be a compulsory point of reference, I might in this way disappoint readers accustomed to occupying identified terrains of the critical philosophoscape. For all of this, I offer no apology, save to acknowledge the fact. Any discomfort is the reader's, I feel none.

39 Frantz Fanon, (trans. Constance Farrington), *The Wretched of the Earth* (London: Penguin Books, 1967 (2001 reprint)), 27-28

answer – we might regard this a fundamental assumption – ground my views expressed here. What do the 'global poor' owe 'us'?

The 'global poor' – the violated, subjugated, impoverished 'subjects' of (post) colonial norm-ality who were previously dignified by the names and hopes of anti-colonial struggle – owe this World, (b)ordered through the 'post-colonial settlements of contemporary global coloniality, Nothing!

PART ONE

How is it that we have come to abide by the 'post-colonial' norm-ality of impover-ishment amidst splendorous enrichment? How is it that we appear accustomed to this pervasive actuality of the global human condition so acutely differen-tiated even as the grand assertions of universal 'post-colonial' Humanity and the equal sanctity of all Human life are ever frequently repeated? How is it so normalised that we find it a reasonable inquiry to ask 'what we owe the global poor' as if this were somehow a progressive gesture?

We might ask, what's in a name: the 'global poor'? A great deal. We recall that those who have now been so reduced as a matter of technocratic, biopolitical, 'developmental' concern – a global 'developmental/humanitarian' business no less – are the embodied descendants of past anti-colonial struggles, their ongoing misery the normalities of brutality now resettled into the (b)orders of the perverse 'post-colonial' present. From the anti-colonial insurgent to the global poor, this transformation of 'name' is profoundly meaningful. Simply, through this name is completed the resettlement of global coloniality. It is an abomination of memory that we have philosophically abandoned communities of struggle to be re-inscribed with the names of norm-alised depravity, permitting therefore their re-(b)ordering, their re-subjection, back into the frames of rationalised dispossession and subjugation as ubiquitous populations of 'poverty'. Indeed, it is 'post-colonial' (b)ordering, that names and emplaces the 'global poor' as norm-alised subject-being in the World. What effective colonisation this, to have made, and Worded, the World so.

What is at stake is precisely the meaning attached to the World, this World, made, enforced, normalised, the entrenchment of perverse human inequality rendered, apparently, the normal Order of (in)Humanity. This, indeed, is a matter of philosophy: the conceit and deceit of the 'post-colonial'. Against this absurd norm-alisation of perversity, we return the 'anti-colonial' to philosophy.

1

On the Deceit, and Conceit, of the 'Post-Colonial'

It was not so long ago that the world was consumed by an intoxicating hope: 'decolonisation' as the complete 'disordering' of the world and the birth of the 'new man', exhorted Frantz Fanon;[1] the 'resistance will win', affirmed Tru'ò'ng Chinh;[2] and even as he guarded against claiming 'easy victories', Cabral demanded everything:

> "At the end of the day, we want the following: concrete and equal possibilities for any child of our land, man or woman, to advance as a human being, to give all of his or her capacity, to develop his or her body and spirit, in order to be a man or a woman at the height of his or her actual ability. *We have to destroy everything that would be against this in our land.*"[3]

Such was the 'revolution' imagined, the 'post-colonial' as a portend for a new humanity and the overturning of the colonial order, completely, utterly. Perhaps the burden was simply too great, to 'destroy everything'. Now, this great dream of 'decolonisation', as it has unfolded through the actualities of the 'post-colonial' state, and the politics of the 'Third World', is commonly spoken of in terms of disappointments if not betrayals.[4] After Fanon's

---

1 Frantz Fanon (trans. Constance Farrington), *The Wretched of the Earth* (London: Penguin Books, 1967 (2001 reprint)), 255.
2 Trường Chinh, *The Resistance Will Win* (Miami: University Press of the Pacific, 2001).
3 Amilcar Cabral (trans. Dan Wood), *Resistance and Decolonisation* (London: Rowman & Littlefield, 2016), 77 (emphasis mine).
4 Basil Davidson, *The Black Man's Burden: Africa and the Curse of the Nation State* (Woodbridge: Boydell & Brewer, 1992); Partha Chatterjee, *The Nation and Its Fragments: Colonial and Postcolonial Histories* (Princeton: Princeton Uni. Press, 1993); George B.N. Ayittey, *Africa Betrayed* (New York:

premonitions of the 'pitfalls of national consciousness', and Nkrumah's warnings of 'neocolonialism', the actualities of the 'post-colonial' have since been plentifully described and analysed.[5] To cut many a long story short, this we understand of the present: the 'post-colonial' state exists within a 'global' systemic totality, at best as a 'cunning' state that mediates the interests of the national capital in competition with the transnational,[6] and at worst, as a dependent state – in the 'comprador' phase of the 'Second Scramble for Africa' as Issa Shivji put it – functioning as a contemporary 'native authority' subservient to the demands of global capital and its security imperatives.[7] Simply stated, liberation – Cabral's 'concrete and equal possibilities' – for the social majorities never quite came to pass; land, bread, freedom, never quite their 'national' inheritance. Instead, 'post-colonial' duress and imperial durabilities.[8]

All this so far from the hope invested in the 'tryst with destiny' invoked in so many 'midnight hours', from the exaltations of new beginnings portended by the 'declaration of independence', the flag, the anthem and the 'constitutional' document that marked the birth of the post-colonial into the global imaginary, so distant that is from the intoxicating promise of 'decolonisation'. From the hope of the 'post-colonial' moment, now how differently is evoked the 'unhappiness' of the Postcolony:

> Having set out to discover what remains ... of the African quest for self-determination, we find ourselves thrown back on the figures of the shadow, into those spaces where one perceives something, but

Palgrave Macmillan, 1994); Mahmood Mamdani, *Citizen and Subject: Contemporary Africa and the Legacy of Late Colonialism* (Princeton: Princeton Uni. Press, 1996); Albert Memmi, *Decolonization and the Decolonized* (Minneapolis: Uni. of Minnesota Press, 2006); Achille Mbembe, (2001) *On the Postcolony* (Oakland: Uni. of California Press, 2001); Sabelo J. Ndlovu-Gatsheni, *Coloniality of Power in Postcolonial Africa: Myths of Decolonization* (Dakar: CODESRIA, 2013).

5 In addition to the previously cited literature, Vijay Prashad provides further insights on 'post-colonial' actualities in his two volumes, *The Darker Nations: A People's History of the Third World* (New York: The New Press, 2007) and *The Poorer Nations: A Possible History of the Global South* (London: Verso, 2015), where the multiple factors, temptations and betrayals that drove to the ground the 'Third World' projects of the New International Economic Order (NIEO), The Non-Aligned Movement (NAM), and the Group of 77, are extensively presented. From the ashes of the Third World as a 'project' of global transformation, and from the failures of 'economic delinking' from global capitalist structures of dependency and imperial dominance, now the neoliberal phoenix of BRICS and the global prescriptions for a (de)regulated 'race to the bottom' is taken as norm-ality. We consider the absurdity of this situation below.

6 Shalini Randeria, "The State of Globalization: Legal Plurality, Overlapping Sovereignties and Ambiguous Alliances between Civil Society and the Cunning State in India", *Theory, Culture & Society* 24(1), 2007, 1-33.

7 Issa Shivji, 'Pan-Africanism or Imperialism?: Unity and Struggle towards a New Democratic Africa', *African Sociological Review* 10(1), 2006, 209.

8 Ann Laura Stoler, *Duress: Imperial Durabilities in Our Time* (Durham: Durham University Press, 2016)

this thing is impossible to make out – as in a phantasm, at the exact point of the split between the visible and the graspable, the perceived and the tangible. In many respects, this conclusion is frightening. It suggests that Africa exists only as an absent object, an absence that those who try to decipher it only accentuate. In this logic, our power to state the thing is reduced to our capacity to create shadow effects – literally, to lie – so great is the contradiction between the discourse we produce, and experience as one "fabricates" it from day to day. Thus we must speak of Africa only as a chimera on which we all work blindly ... to the point that we may evince toward it the kind of disgust we feel on seeing a cadaver.[9]

These are telling evocations. With grand dreams, such deep disillusionment. I repeat these indictments of betrayed hope not as a precursor either to lament the 'injustices' of the present, nor to reveal in ever more insightful terms the corrections necessary to return 'justice' to (in)Humanity. I do so – and this is a point I will repeat – rather to consider how such realisations impinge on *our* (self-assumed) responsibilities to think in the present.

Perhaps the dreamers of the past had it easier, theirs was a simpler world to describe, analyse and imagine otherwise: the coloniser and the colonised, the settler and the native, the oppressor and the oppressed, a world 'cut in two', as Fanon famously described it. It's not so straightforward now. The coloniser/colonised, oppressor/oppressed, these old categories of 'them' and 'us' no longer readily hold. With the demise of the 'post-colonial' state as a force for liberation having morphed into Mbembe's *Postcolony*, with the post-colonial 'middle-classes' finding the lures and enchantments of being incorporated and integrated into 'European memory' – as wa Thiong'o put it – it is not so easy to demarcate now the World of the present into the Manichean duality that inspired earlier thinkings against the colonial.[10] The 'post-colonial' as actuality appears to be just too mired, a totalitarian whole that engulfs the world as an entirety, integrated, networked, a complex system of 'distanced', yet structurally-relational, 'un/violence'.[11] Grand dreams of decolonisation didn't translate so well to the actualities of the 'post-colonial' we now know. In this 'post-colonial' present, (b)ordered as a (post)colonial

9 Mbembe, *Postcolony*, 241.
10 Mbembe, *Postcolony*, 44. See Ngũgĩ wa Thiong'o, *Decolonising the Mind: The politics of Language in African Literature* (London: James Currey, 1986). On this point, I expand on what I call the intimacy of belonging-separation in Chapter 4.
11 See Chapter 6, below, for the significance and implications of my use of the term 'un/violence'.

totality, the contemporary critical thinker finds habitation.

It is necessary instead to understand correctly the situation of the *World*.

On Methodological Post-Colonialism

As we look upon the actualities of the World, , we see it, understand it, speak of it, as a 'post-colonial' World.

The *World* as we know it, its words and its meanings, its geographies and its subjects, its possibilities and limits as a totality, even as we denounce its perversity, we understand it, speak of it, and assume it to be a 'post-colonial' World. We do so the result of a *methodological post-colonialism*.[12] The significance of this assumption must not be under-estimated; it marks after all, as a fundamental tenet of the global order, a radical departure from a prior 'colonial' norm-ality of *Right*-ful domination. To claim the 'post-colonial' is to fully adhere to a 'universal' Humanity. Or so we assume. So, we continue to believe. But the truth of the *World* is quite different.

For all the repeated celebrations of the sanctity and primacy of Human Rights and the universal dignity of the human-person in the plethora of 'post-colonial' international legal pronouncements, the 'post-colonial' actuality has been the normalisation of the perverse: it is in the settlement of 'post-colonial' norm-ality, after all, that the 'global poor' find habitation as 'subjects' in their complete wretchedness. Clearly, liberation from 'White Man's Rule' did not quite mean freedom from imperial desire and subjugation for the social majorities of the World. Instead, the 'post-colonial' settlement has enforced the differentiated conditions of unimaginable wealth for a small minority of the global elite, and existential precarity, or utter destitution, for the global majorities; such is the absurdity of the situation that it is almost trite this complaint. How has this come to pass? Especially so if we recall the suffering and sacrifices, refusals and repudiations, imaginations and promises of past anti-colonial struggles which purportedly underpin the contemporary affirmation of a global 'post-colonial' settlement for 'Humanity'. I do not accept that this present actuality of the *World* fulfils the aspirations of

---

12 We are familiar of course with the idea of 'methodological nationalism'. First employed by Andreas Wimmer and Nina Glick Schiller, the term is now ubiquitous in critical social and political-legal theory to open up analytical optics to wider 'cosmopolitan' global connections and connectedness; see Andreas Wimmer and Nina Glick Schiller, "Methodological Nationalism, the Social Sciences, and the Study of Migration: An Essay in Historical Epistemology", *The International Migration Review*, 37(3), 2003, 576–610. Also, Ulrich Beck, 'The Cosmopolitan Condition: Why Methodological Nationalism Fails' *Theory, Culture & Society*, 24(7-8), 2007, 286-90. My argument extends the analytical lens to situate 'methodological nationalism' within a broader, and deeper, totalising structure that assumes the givenness of what I name the 'post-colonial settlement' in the 'International/Global' order.

anti-colonial struggles, or that the abject condition of human-beingness in *this* World can be regarded as the culmination of the struggles and hopes of *being-anti-colonial*. The philosophers of (post)colonial norm-ality might not agree. This they are bound to, as it is their vocation, after all, to normalise *this* World as a totality, 'post-colonial', fully. It is our obligation, those of us who regard ourselves critical thinkers of the 'South', to address this problem. We begin with the matter of philosophy.

The Declaration of Independence as Philosophical Manoeuvre

We are 'post-colonial' due to a constitutive singular event that is understood to have marked a reconfiguration of global norm-ality: the 'declaration of independence'. Thus, those previously 'anti-colonial' became anew into the World as 'post-colonial' *subject*, birthed in that moment of 'liberation'. No matter all the regrets since, the disappointments and recriminations, the betrayals and disillusionment, even the very collapse of various 'post-colonial' dreams of early visionaries of the emergent 'independent nations' – and indeed there were many a revolutionary spirit whose intentions were to "dare to invent the future" as Thomas Sankara proclaimed[13] – we 'post-colonials' are indelibly marked by this moment which birthed our politico-juridical Beingness as fully belonging to, and in, *this* (post-colonial) World. We cannot escape its inscription upon our 'selves'; that coming-into-Being, acquiring of a 'name' of belonging to a 'representative' collective – the national political community – heralded by the raising of flags, the singing of anthems and the exaltations of Constitutions. What intoxicating redemption, this 'becoming', through 'citizenship' under 'sovereignty', into a World of politico-juridical Humanity, a moment forever to be cherished no matter what else is taken from 'us' in unforetold futures.[14] This moment will remain as proof that we are more than 'native', no longer without name, meaning, memories, futures. There is no doubting the powerful and persistent seductiveness of the 'national consciousness' so birthed by the 'declaration of independence'. Take Vivienne Jabri who is eloquent in stating this assumption:

---

13 Interview with Jean-Philippe Rapp, in Michael Praire (ed.), *Thomas Sankara Speaks: The Burkina Faso Revolution 1983-1987*, (New York: Pathfinder, 1988.2007), 189.

14 It is interesting to note that there have been many recent retrievals along these lines that emphasise the historic achievements of the anti-colonial past; see for example, Sundhya Pahua, *Decolonising International Law: Development, Economic Growth and the Politics of Universality* (Cambridge: Cambridge University Press, 2013); Priyamvada Gopal, *Insurgent Empire: anticolonial resistance and British dissent* (London: Verso, 2019); Luis Eslava, Michael Fakhri, Vasuki Nesiah (eds), *Bandung, Global History and International Law: Critical Pasts and Pending Futures*, (Cambridge: Cambridge University Press, 2017); Jochen von Bernstorff and Philipp Dann (eds), *The Battle for International Law: South-North Perspectives in the Decolonization Era* (Oxford: Oxford University Press, 2019).

[D]espite this persistent and continuing presence of the past in the present, there is at the same time, and constituted by the prefix 'post' in the postcolonial, the assumption of a break, a limit, *a borderline in time that hails forth a moment of emergence, of presence* – an *interjection into time of a significant and signifying moment that inaugurates a rejection of the past*; a *culminating moment* registering the place of resistance in the colonial experience and a claim to a future free of colonial subjection. There is, in this moment what we can refer to, looking back historically, as a 'declaration of independence', a declaration that clearly asserts rejection of foreign rule and hence a *symbolic claim* to the cultural and material resources of a political community constituted through anti-colonial struggle. *This declaration of independence is the defining moment that places a break, that defines the limit dividing the colonial and postcolonial despite the persistence of the colonial legacy in the present.* This moment is *as constitutive of the postcolonial subject as is the colonial past and its ongoing power in shaping the present.*[15]

Jabri's description fully encapsulates the assumption of the 'post-colonial' transformation of global norm-ality. Beginning as it does with a perceived rupture of global (b)ordering marked by the 'declaration of independence' as the 'culminating moment' which brings into being the 'postcolonial', a new ontology of the 'political' and the 'subject' is assumed, this notwithstanding the "persistent and continuing presence of the past in the present". But what precisely is newly 'defined' by the 'borderline in time' as the 'defining moment' of the declaration of independence?; what exactly is the substance of the 'break?; what is understood as the 'limit' that divides the colonial and the postcolonial? How do we think through the perplexing situation of the *persistent* problem of (post)colonial subjugation under the purported 'post-colonial' becoming-into-the-International? Recalling our previous discussion on the 'global poor' who, as we have concluded, owe 'us' everything with respect the norm-ality of the *World*, what meaning this 'borderline in time' that hails forth a moment of emergence and a claim to a future free of colonial subjection'?

Jabri's account is useful – we see here clearly the entrenched norm-ality of methodological post-colonialism. The implications are significant.

---

15 Jabri, *The Postcolonial Subject,* 18-19, emphasis mine.

Let us examine the question of 'subjection' more closely.[16] To be clear, the 'global poor' are (persistent) *subjects* of the 'post-colonial' World, their enduring fate in *this* World not simply the consequence of intransigence by philosophers of the 'Global North' to recognise and effect the claims of 'global justice', but rather quite the consequence of a settled 'post-colonial' global order. While political-legal philosophers might ruminate over the philosophical implications of ruptural becomings of postcolonial subjectivity etc, everywhere, as the 'post-colonial' normal, persist the actualities of splendour in squalor; Ngũgĩ wa Thiong'o:

> From Asia to Africa to South America, a prosperous middle class, a global middle class, with shared values and lifestyles, is currently being touted as exactly that [the measure of progress]. It does not matter that millions of working people – the worker, the small farmer – are sinking in misery.
>
> The splendour of the middle class blinds us to the squalor of the working class. The very visibility of the middle and upper classes makes the poverty of the working and underclass invisible.[17]

Everywhere, citadels of extravagance amidst ghosts of destitution; Arundhati Roy:

> In India the 300 million of us who belong to the new, post-International Monetary Fund (IMF) "reforms" middle class – the market – live side by side with spirits of the netherworld, the poltergeists of dead rivers, dry wells, bald mountains and denuded forests; the ghosts of 250,000 debt-ridden farmers who have killed themselves, and of the 880 million who have been impoverished and dispossessed to make way for us.[18]

These are two descriptions of a very familiar present; we are accustomed to looking out onto the World and observing these actualities of inequality, to lament and criticise their perpetuation, to proffer all manner of suggestions for correction to alleviate the cruelties of ever increasing 'post-colonial' misery. We are familiar with such accounts and efforts. Too familiar. Little time however is spent to pause, and to seriously think about what such

---

16 I say more on the implications of *subjection* in relation to our understanding of 'violence' in Chapter 6.

17 Ngũgĩ wa Thiong'o, *Secure the Base: Making Africa Visible in the Globe* (London: Seagull Books, 2016), 34-35.

18 Arundhati Roy, *Capitalism: A Ghost Story* (London: Verso, 2015), 8.

descriptions of the World implicate. We seldom take in the scene fully as it is, and then to ponder the meaning of the purported 'break' of the 'post-colonial' within which these actualities of enforced beingness perpetuate.

The descriptions above reveal something fundamentally significant in my view.

Thiong'o and Roy tell not of aberrations or oversights but of a global structuring of (b)ordered and enforced 'subject-ed beingness'. All that we accept as the everyday normalities of law, politics, and economic, all the inducements and profits, the costs and suffering, all coherently are the actuality not of any prevailing *dis*order or error but of the proper workings of global *(post)colonial* norm-ality. Not just by the mind of the philosopher of (in)justice – recalling Risse and his ilk – this actuality of continued global enrichment and impoverishment, not solely by the actions of the 'White' master this perpetuation of globalised domination and subjugation, but fully, and unapologetically now, the 'global poor' remain (post)colonial subjects of abjection by the desires of many 'post-colonial' champions of the South, championed as they are, by the so-called 'middle-classes' of the South, in complete cohesion of intent with the transnational agents of appropriation/dispossession. We are mistaken if we regard such inequalities of *human beingness,* such enforced conditions of *differentiated* beingness in the World, as deviations from 'justice'. Precisely the opposite. In this global totality of the 'post-colonial' organisation of *(post)colonial* (b)ordering, there is little regard for the 'global poor', little comfort for them the much vaunted 'post-colonial' *becoming-into-the-International.* The 'post-colonial' settlement is precisely the efficient technology of (b)ordering that enables and sustains the materiality of coloniality in the present. And for this norm-alisation of global coloniality, the 'declaration of independence' is utterly pivotal as a constitutive manoeuvre of *resettlement.*

I see the 'declaration of independence' operating differently than Jabri, not as a 'borderline in time' but as a portal for the resettlement of coloniality; we might better understand it as a philosophical manoeuvre that presents an ontological shift from the 'colonial' – as an abomination that had to be dismantled – to the 'post-colonial', now as an architecture of global normality that commands (enforced) universal acceptance and obedience.[19] As such, it is both a point of departure and of origin; we consider it properly as ruptural and constitutive, the dialectic of continuities and ruptures informing

---

19 Sundhya Pahuja, 'Corporations, Universalism, and the Domestication of Race in International Law' in Duncan Bell (ed.), *Empire, Race and Global Justice* (Cambridge: Cambridge University Press, 2019) 74-93.

much of what goes under the general theoretical/philosophical orientations we familiarly refer to as 'post/decolonial' thought. The full significance of the 'declaration of independence' as a *resettlement* of international/global (b)ordering therefore can be described as follows:

- the 'colonial' and the 'post-colonial' are marked as distinct temporalities, and ontologies, of global (b)ordering;
- the 'National' and the 'International' are demarcated as distinct, and categorically opposed, territorialised 'political' rationalities of regulatory and enforcement regimes/structures/technologies of global (b)ordering.
- the 'citizen' is inscribed as a new and universal subject-being under 'post-colonial' *sovereignty*, a beingness purportedly liberated in philosophy from colonial subjection, and materially from colonial subjugation-subjection.

This is the conventional understanding, the view of the World as seen through the lens of methodological post-colonialism. A different view sees the 'post-colonial' settlement as a resettlement of the Reason of global coloniality:

- there are not two distinct ontologies and realities of colonial pasts and post-colonial present/future but, instead, a coeval, contingently adaptive and evolving actuality of diverse and differentiated (post)colonial presents;
- there are not two spheres of (in)justice demarcated as 'National; and 'International', but a coherent 'global' worldscape of variously (b)ordered differentiations of Rights/lessness; and
- there is not an historical emergence of a 'post-colonial', *universal* subject in the 'International' but the global-ised regulation and enforcement of differentiated (post)colonial subject-beingness – of *licence, containment and a(ban)donment,* I call them – within a global totality.

We see from this that with the 'declaration of independence', a global geography of coloniality is resettled.First, a little back-story.

The Reason of Coloniality

All that is asserted of the *World*, that has come to make *this* World (as norm-alised) a totality of commensurable inscriptions of names and meanings of human-beingness, is the outcome of an audacious and impertinent philosophical invention: of 'discovery'. The *conquistadors* 'discovered' the 'Americas' and named her inhabitants 'Indios'. With this begins the Colonial-Modern story of the World in 'History'. We know this story well. Its relevance for my purpose here is to reveal how this story as such invents the *World* as a *(post)colonial* artefact. These are indeed philosophical matters. But more importantly, they in turn reveal the underlying matter, that is to say, the *materiality*, of philosophy as it has come to be norm-alised.

The philosophical invention of discovery was essentially an act of naming and rationalising an *encounter* of appropriation/dispossession; the assertion of discovery inscribed name and meaning upon a place encapsulated – the New World – and a population defined – Indios. This was nothing less than a feat of magic, this act of transforming the materiality of conquest into philosophical authorship. To assume the Right to name was in this context an act of creation out of the facts of cruelty; by inscribing the encountered peoples into a regime of imposed meaning were they made-subject to the philosopho-scape of the 'discoverer', accounted for, made *commensurable*, this the original performative act of coloniality. Through this manoeuvre of 'discovery' was the actuality of presence negated into philosophical absence precisely by a gesture of naming the purportedly *nameless* – as *Non-Being* – who *becomes* now (b)ordered and *made-subject* to a rationalisation of ontological differences – as heathens/children of god, savage/infantile – all dependent upon an imperial, colonising ascription of inside/outside, inclusion/exclusion, belonging/non-belonging, and enforced by the material structures of physical delineations of differentiation – fences, cages, churches, schools, territories. So were situated, inscribed, and emplaced the *named-negated*, the now *Other-ed*, within regimes of invented subjection-subjugation. All this we know and has been much repeated.[20] I point to this past in order to recall the underlying *Reason* of so much 'European'[21] philosophical labour: the negated 'Other', inserted into philosophy as *Non-Being*, were not excluded from the 'European' World, their subjection not an expulsion into an Agambenian 'state of exception',[22] quite the opposite, theirs an intimacy of *belonging-separation*.[23]

---

20 These insights are much discussed in recent 'decolonial' literature in terms of the 'coloniality of being'; see for example, Sylvia Wynter, 'Unsettling the Coloniality of Being/Power/Truth/Freedom: Towards the Human, After Man, Its Overrepresentation – An Argument', *The New Centennial Review* 3(3), 2003, 257-337; Nelson Maldonado-Torres, 'On the Coloniality of Being: Contributions to the Development of a Concept', in Walter D Mignolo & Arturo Escobar (eds), *Globalization and the Decolonial Option* (Abingdon: Routledge, 2013) 94, 98-103; Maria Lugones, "Toward a Decolonial Feminism", *Hypatia* 25(4), 2010, 742-759.

21 As an interesting aside, a different reading of 'Europe' is provided in Boaventura de Sousa Santos, *Epistemologies of the South: Justice Against Epistemecide* (Abingdon: Routledge, 2014), Also, Boaventura de Sousa Santos, *The End of the Cognitive Empire: The Coming of age of Epistemologies of the South* (Durham: Duke University Press, 2018). In contrast to such attempts to recover a radical orientation for the invented category of 'Europe', I present a different understanding, of *Europe-Postcolony*, in Chapter 4

22 Giorgio Agamben, *Homo Sacer: Sovereign Power and Bare Life* (Stanford: Stanford University Press, 1998); and Giorgio Agamben, *States of Exception* (Chicago: University of Chicago Press, 2005).

23 See below, Chapter 4, for an elaboration of this argument.

The subject-ed *Other* was fully *thought-into-(non)being* – in response to, and in consequence of, a material desire for appropriation – as subjected-being within a World of differentiated subject-beingness thus *norm-alised*.

By this we see that the *Reason* of coloniality is wholly mundane, indeed, for all its metaphysical and liturgical profundity, utterly profane. "Discovery" was first and foremost an assertion of appropriation as Right, norm-alised thus through the inventions of the 'natural right' to 'travel' and 'trade', and to receive in turn, due 'hospitality'. When divested of the sophistry of medieval liturgical and doctrinal pontifications, what is revealed by this *Right* to name and author the World is simply the rationalisation of the crude desires of appropriation and domination. As Patrick Wolfe put it in the context of 'settler colonialism',

> [w]hatever settlers may say—and they generally have a lot to say— the primary motive for elimination is not race (or religion, ethnicity, grade of civilization, etc.) but access to territory. Territoriality is settler colonialism's specific, irreducible element.[24]

We see here plainly the material foundations of the 'colonial' encounter, and of the colonial-modern philosophies of 'sovereignty' and 'Humanity' thereby invented and norm-alised.[25] I call this the original assertion of *licence*: the Right to enfettered enrichment. We remind ourselves of Cesaire's response to the question, "what is colonisation":

> To agree on what it is not: neither evangelization, nor a philanthropic enterprise, nor a desire to push back the frontiers of ignorance, disease, and tyranny, nor a project undertaken for the greater glory of God, nor an attempt to extend the rule of law. To admit once for all, without flinching at the consequences, that the decisive actors here are the adventurer and the pirate, *the wholesale grocer and the ship owner, the gold digger and the merchant, appetite and force, and behind them, the baleful projected shadow of a form of civilization which, at a certain point in its history, finds itself obliged, for internal reasons, to extend to a world scale the competition of its antagonistic economies.*[26]

---

24 Patrick Wolfe, 'Settler colonialism and the elimination of the native', *Journal of Genocide Research* 8(4), 387-409, 388.

25 I have elaborated on these arguments in Jayan Nayar, 'The Non-Perplexity of Human Rights', *Theory & Event* 22(2), 2019, 267-302.

26 Césaire, *Discourse on Colonialism*, 32-33 (emphasis mine). Césaire's description conflates two distinct

This is no revelation of some deep secret.[27] My interest here is not simply to excavate capital's original motivations as such; from the teachings of Marx onwards we are familiar with such excavations as a matter of historical telling of colonial pasts. It is necessary however to extend understandings of the *Reason* of Capital with the *Reason* of *Coloniality*.[28] A more general, and prior desire thus comes to view. My concern is to recall and emphasise how this underlying *Reason* of *licence* to unfettered predatory appropriation (and its associated exigencies of *containment/a(ban)donment*) underpins the totality of the Colonial-Modern political-legal philosophoscape to this day.

As a preliminary to appreciate fully the norm-alisation of this assumption of *licence*, we recall that the motives of plunder and subjugation were far from the cause of any embarrassment in the time of their enunciation, indeed such motives were explicitly and proudly the rationale for policy-making. Take the exemplary clarity of the British 'colonial administrator' Edward Gibbon Wakefield pointing to the errors of 'philanthropists':

> It is strange that it should never have come into the head of philosopher or philanthropist to ascertain the causes of the revival of slavery by all the nations of modern Europe, which have engaged in colonisation. Political economists were bound to make this inquiry for without it their science is incomplete at the very foundation; *for slavery is a*

---

aspects of the 'colonial' relationship that are the material and what might be described as the cultural or civilisational. I think it is useful to understand these separately as pertaining to 'colonialism' as the institutional and relational norm-alisation of *conquest-subjugation*, on the one hand, and 'colonisation' as the norm-alisation of onto-epistemological *subjection*, on the other. The distinction matters when we consider the implications of the *anti-colonial* in the present; I return to this in Chapter 2.

27 As we know, Karl Marx was brutally clear in revealing the underlying logic of capitalism as he saw it; to repeat an oft-quoted passage:

> The discovery of gold and silver in America, the extirpation, enslavement and entombment in mines of the indigenous population of that continent, the beginnings of the conquest and plunder of India, and the conversion of Africa into a preserve for the commercial hunting of blackskins, are all things which characterize the dawn of capitalist production.

Karl Marx, *Capital: A Critique of Political Economy*, Volume 1, trans. Ben Fowkes (Harmondsworth: Penguin Books, 1976), 915.

28 This point has been variously made by 'decolonial' thinkers; for example, see Anibal Quijano, 'Coloniality of Power and Eurocentrism in Latin America', *International Sociology*, 15(2), 2000, 215-32; Walter D Mignolo, *Local Histories/Global Designs: Coloniality, Subaltern Knowledges, and Border Thinking* (Princeton: Princeton University Press, 2000); Nelson Maldonado-Torres, "On the Coloniality of Being: Contributions to the Development of a Concept," in Walter D. Mignolo & Arturo Escobar (eds), *Globalization and the Decolonial Option* (London: Routledge, 2013) 94. For a specific demonstration of this more general colonial Reason underpinning the appropriation of indigenous lands and the dispossession and containment of 'native' populations in Canada, see Glen Coulthard, *Red Skin, White Masks: Rejecting the Colonial Politics of Recognition* (Minneapolis: University of Minnesota Press, 2014).

question of labour, 'the original purchase of all things.' Philanthropists, however, have treated it as a moral and religious question, attributing slavery ... to the wickedness of the human heart ...[29]

So was Carl Schmitt clear in explaining the foundational premise of modern 'European International Law':

> Not only logically, but also historically, land-appropriation precedes the order that follows from it. It constitutes the original spatial order, the source of all further concrete order and all further law.[30]

These are clear and truthful statements that point to the material, and not some 'moral' or metaphysical, foundations for the making of *this* World. In them we find the underlying matter of philosophy laid bare, devoid the sophistry that characterises much of the elaborate nonsense that we indulge in when we meditate upon 'political-legal' thought. But this indulgence in philosophical sophistry is entirely useful; incessant rumination of and discussion on rationalisations of *universal Right* perfectly obfuscates the assertion of *particular Might*, the abstracted, idealised and reified categories of political-legal philosophy perfectly suited to cleanse thought from its bloody underbellies. Cast aside these metaphysical adornments, however, and we see clearly appropriation/dispossession and domination/subjugation as the coherent Reason of colonial-modern political-legal thought and practice. *Licence* to violence founds Right: from the brutalities of predatory ('primitive') appropriation, and the attendant enforcement of subjugated obedience, all else that we know and speak of the *World* follows.[31] Appropriation, subjugation, enslavement, expulsions and massacre, these then are the actual '"accidental and historical reasons" which founds the 'Modern' architecture of 'international' (b) orders,[32] and that originate the normative categories of 'racialised capitalism'

29 Quoted in Bernard M. Magubane, *Race and the Construction of the Dispensable Other* (Pretoria: University of South Africa Press, 2007) 37 (emphasis, mine). Magubane provides a detailed account of the evolution of 'White' supremacist thought in their material contexts. Similarly, see also, Theodore W. Allen, *The Invention of the White Race* (London: Verso, 2012 (2nd edition)).

30 Carl Schmitt, *The nomos of the earth in the international law of the Jus Publicum Europaeum*, trans G L Ulmen (New York: Telos Press, 2003), 48.

31 Enrique Dussel's correction of *ego conquiro* (the conquering *I* that precedes the sovereign *I* who thinks) to the Cartesian *ego cogito* is precisely correct; the mythological *I* that "thinks," of colonial philosophy, is founded upon the material *I* that conquered; see Enrique Dussel, *Philosophy of Liberation*, trans. Aquilina Martinez and Christine Morkovsky (Eugene: Wipf and Stock, 2003). See also Maldonado-Torres, "On the Coloniality of Being: Contributions to the Development of a Concept", 98-103. (mentioned above)

32 "Every state has the boundaries and population it has for *all sorts of accidental and historical reasons*"; by this flippant gesture Thomas Nagel dismisses the very idea of global 'injustice' as a 'politically meaningful concept' see Nagel, 'The Problem of Global Justice', 121.

that defines still the essential 'political' structures of global norm-ality.[33]

We return to the present. I have argued that the 'declaration of independence' serves to resettle and reconfigure the (b)ordered norm-ality of coloniality. It does so by entrenching the *Reason* of coloniality in the structural DNA of the 'post-colonial' Inter/National institutional order. And thus, the crux of the manoeuvre; what is regarded as the prize gained from the repudiation of colonial norm-ality – 'Sovereignty' – is precisely that which, through the *formal*, we might say performative, termination of 'conquest', completes *colonisation*. Two consequences follow. First, through the investiture of 'Sovereignty', the 'post-colonial' State *becomes-into-the-International* as a node of global coloniality-governmentality. And secondly, the locations regulated by 'post-colonial' state-jurisdictions thereby serve as institutional sites for negotiation and contestation over the regulation of imperial intentions of appropriation/dispossession, and as a surveilled geography of enforcement for the containment and a(ban)donment of populations. Whilst unceasing labours of sophisticated philosophical meditations on sovereignty have persisted, this simple and essential truth of its materiality appears largely obscured. Strip away its metaphysical adornments and we see the invention of 'sovereignty' in all its profane worldliness.

Bluntly, there is no such *thing/power/being* as Sovereignty. It is nothing but a rationalisation, an apology even, invented and enforced – through all manner of convoluted argument, ancient and contemporary – to rationalise an utterly mundane desire. Sovereignty is an assertion of *license*, simply that, relying entirely upon the *colonised* obedience of 'subjects' for its worldly effecting. It is therefore nothing else than a claim, but one founded upon, and maintained by, the very material fact of violence, of the *Right* to demarcate the (b)orders of domination/subjugation – and this is crucial to its function – based on a territorial rationality. In this way, sovereignty (b)orders and regulates the systemic operation of 'national' geographies of violence, and 'national-ised' subject-ed bodies-in-territory, within a global structural and discursive totality. It is important here not to confuse a *technology,* with the *Reason* of (b)ordering; there is nothing interminable or inevitable about the sovereign arrangement of global (b)ordering. What appears ubiquitous is merely the operation of a particular and contingent expedience, contingent

---

33 For a recent reflection on the pasts, presents and future implications of racial capitalism, see Gargi Battacharyya, *Rethinking Racial Capitalism: Questions of Reproduction and Survival* (London: Rowman & Littlefield, 2018). See below, Chapter 3, for a further elaboration of the philosophical, material and experiential durabilities of 'racialisation'.

that is to its efficacy in regulating and enforcing the primary *Reason* of coloniality.[34] All that we regard as the foundational categories of a political-legal
theory/practice – 'State' and 'Citizenship', 'subjectivity' and 'political
belonging', 'rights' etc. – are similarly rationalised and adapted to implement
this original *Reason*, to enforce the differentiated subject-beingness of *licence,
containment, and a(ban)donment*.[35]

    To be sure, there is no doubting the power of these categories that have
come to make and name the *World*; indeed, the true success of *colonisation*
is that the 'post-colonial subject' has been properly schooled to speak the
World in such *(post)colonial* tongues.[36] But for all its apparent ubiquity, this
we note: none of the aforementioned names and categories of purported
human-beingness pertain to any inherent truth as such; sovereignty, state,
citizenship (investor/corporation/refugee/migrant), for example, none of
these have intrinsic or interminable meaning. They are but invented names
ascribed with meaning to satisfy the particular exigencies of (b)ordering, thus
to materialise the desires of the 'discoverers', 'colonisers', 'governments' – the
grocers, the ship-owners, the gold-diggers and the merchants – as these are
inflicted upon the bodies and territories of the conquered, the *made-subject,*
the *made commensurable, made 'post-colonial'*, named and duly (b)ordered.[37]
Their significance lies not in their truth, not in their essential meaningfulness, but in their repeated rationalisation and violent enforcement. The
norm-alisation of Right/violence was the work of colonial-philosophies to
do. And so it remains in the (post)colonial present, now to tell the story of
the *past* cleansed of its sins, to rationalise the 'post-colonial' norm-alities of
Right-ful appropriation/subjugations, to name anew *subjects*, to define again
the universal terms of 'civilisation' ('development') and 'Humanity', and,
crucially, to set the possibilities and limits of critical imagination and action
for glorious, prescribed, futures.[38]

    Thus, we see the proper effect of the 'declaration of independence' in

34 I have previously expanded on these arguments in Jayan Nayar, 'On the Elusive Subject of Sover-
     eignty', *Alternatives: Global, Local, Political* 39(2), 2014, 124-147; and in 'The non-perplexity of
     human rights', *Theory and Event* 22(2), 2019, 267-302.
35 Adaptability is one of the defining features of legal categories after all. As we have seen, originally
     rationalised through the languages and semantics of racialised colonial civil-isation upon the bodies,
     consciousness, and imaginations of the conquered, then by the sanitised semantics of *post-colonial*
     political-legal rationalisations, our understanding of Rights and Citizenship, Humanity and Sover-
     eignty etc. have all undergone substantial revision, all the while retaining its core *Reason*.
36 We will return to this point in Chapter 2.
37 Césaire, Discourse on Colonialism, 32-33.
38 I speak more on this point as a configuration of *Europe-Postcolony* in Chapter 4.

its global systemic context, as a manoeuvre of resettlement and *norm-alisation* of the Reason of coloniality. The new 'sovereigns', that is the emergent 'nationalist' elites of the *postcolony*, were granted *the* author-ity to dispense – or in Schmittian terms, 'decide' – *life* and its 'resources'.[39] Materially, this entailed the following 'post-colonial' *privileges* as the gains of *becoming-into-the-International*: 1) of 'treaty-making' (the dispensation of transter-ritorial 'Rights'/licence; 2) of 'borrowing' and 'trade' (the assignation of inter-generational profiteering and indebtedness) and; 3) of the 'monopoly of (national) violence' (the *constitutive* (re)distribution of brutality). And the global outcome of this heady mix of 'post-colonial' International polit-ical-legal re-settlements? Not the early aspirations and assertions of a post-Bandung 'New International Economic Order (NIEO),[40] but the following: the renegotiation of the 'international property order' which renewed the global Rights to resource extraction and expropriation for private profit; the re-norm-alisation of 'civilisational' interventions now 'humanised' through the categorical reformulations of 'humanitarianism', 'human rights' and 'democracy', and; perversely, the violent suppression of challenge and opposition through the re-instatement of old colonial logics of 'emergency' and 'sedition' within the 'post-colonial' territorial jurisdictions of mili-tarised containment. The *Reason* of global coloniality is now, we see, fully rationalised through the categories and vocabulary of the 'post-colonial' in the 'International'. With the 'post-colonial' settlement – the (re)insertion of the *postcolony*-in-the-*International* – was *colonisation* as the transmogrifica-tion of being-ness structurally entrenched under the (b)ordering imaginary of 'sovereignty'. This is 'sovereignty' not as a philosophical problem raising perplexities of ontology but as an expedient of continued *coloniality*, of the (b)ordering of imperial desires now purportedly cleansed of its sordid pasts.[41]

Such are the actual features of the *(post)colonial* worldscape under 'post-colonial' World-making. Contrary to the juridical reification of the state as a realm of 'sovereignty-citizenship' in colonial-modern mythologies, we

39 Schmitt, *Political Theology*.
40 Vijay Prashad provides a compelling telling of the ins and outs of this resettlement in *The Poorer Nations: a possible history of the Global South* (London, Verso, 2012). Particularly informative is Prashad's account of the conflicts and tensions within the South Commission, as the 'post-colonial' relationship with global capitalism was negotiated. For a recent account of the operation of extractive licence in the way I describe it, See 'Report of the UN Panel of Experts on the Illegal Exploitation of Natural Resources of the Democratic Republic of the Congo', *UN Security Council*, 12 April 2001, available at <https://reliefweb.int/report/democratic-republic-congo/report-panel-experts-illegal-ex-ploitation-natural-resources-and> (last accessed on 12 February 2022).
41 Nayar, 'The Non-Perplexity of Human Rights', 277.

see the (post-colonial) state, as good 'international citizen', operating quite blatantly as a 'cunning' participant in the distribution of unequal enrichment and impoverishment.[42] Not the Schmidtian fantasyland of the 'political', defined by the territorialised boundedness of *national* 'friends' against *international/foreign* 'enemies', the actuality of the *postcolony* is defined rather by differentiations and enforced inequalities premised on corrupt transnational 'economic' mutualities of profit, privilege, and the accommodation of predatory desires, this the *(post)colonial* reality of 'postcolonial citizenship', so far from the exalted 'liberation' anticipated by the 'declaration of independence'. This is as it is, the way of *this* (post)colonial World.

A (Post)Colonial Totality

To repeat, we are familiar with the *World* described and analysed through the 'post-colonial' lens; our frames of understanding are largely constructed by the onto-epistemologies of 'methodological post-colonialism'. And so, we look at the *World* and see a 'post-colonial' worldscape, of distinct state-formations, international organisations and treaty-bodies, transnational corporations and 'non-governmental' organisations. We understand the separation of 'politics' and 'law' as marked by territorial (b)orders, and perceive their operations as dictated by the opposing rationalities of the 'public' and 'private' spheres. We see a *World* that is of many distinctly (b)ordered parts, 'co-existing' in perpetual tension between conflict and cooperation. Perhaps, on a rare occasion, we might experience a coming together of separated 'Humanity' in expressions of solidarity. But it is not a coherent totality that we perceive, this remains a view of the *World* as a complex architecture of *borders* that mark separation, disorder rather than order is understood to be the defining feature of the 'International/global'. The norm-ality of 'order', instead, is understood to be the domain of the 'national', governed by the relationalities of 'sovereignty-citizenship', of 'political-belonging', giving meaning to an *us* contra *them*. No doubt, this has been a powerful imaginary, a view, an understanding, an assumption, of the *World* as a tapestry of separated territorial geographies, (b)ordered as distinct spaces of knowing-being such that an essential incoherence prevails.

But, for all the 'normative' strictures of 'sovereignty' and the assumption of separation projected by the regime of names and meanings that follow,

---

42 For an elaboration of 'cunningness' as an operation of 'post-colonial' states, see Shalini Randeria, 'Cunning States and Unaccountable International Institutions: Legal Plurality, Social Movements and Rights of Local Communities to Common Property Resources', *European Journal of Sociology* 44(1), 2003, 27-60.

the real-world operation of a (b)ordered geography of 'territoriality' is less defining, less determined and determining, than is usually assumed. This we have increasingly come to realise and document. The evidence and analyses of so-called 'trans/supra/de-territoriality', of the permeable and fractured opera-tion of territorial borders, and of the privileges and exclusions thereby differ-entiatedly regulated, are plentiful, long recognised as complicating the neat assumptions of 'separation'. Take Zygmunt Bauman's descriptions of 'liquid modernity' and the supersession of the 'transfixed imagination' associated with territoriality by a globalised 'disengaged imagination' associated with the fears and possibilities of 'individualised' lives.[43] Or Saskia Sassen's anal-yses of 'global assemblages' constituting global-ised geographies that disrupt the presumed fixity and boundedness of territoriality, authority and rights within 'state'-spaces.[44] Or the various theorisations of 'global law' that have been identified to operate through the modalities of fractured, fragmented and dispersed territorial and regulatory loci of transnational sectoral global relationalities.[45] Or the many exposes of the blatant assumptions, and asser-tions, of violent *Right* to impose 'civilisational' and 'humanitarian' orders of neoliberal *freedoms*.[46] Or the analyses of the ubiquity of what Derek Gregory has called 'everywhere war', and of the biopolitical regimes of freedoms and containments, of 'global mobility', of 'human security', of surveillance, 'counter-terrorism', and the global 'management of unease', etc.[47] All are so many examples, from some while back already, of much agonising on the problematics, paradoxes and incongruences of a purportedly 'post-colo-nial' *World* variously and manifoldly (b)ordered. What is less recognised, as

43 Zygmunt Bauman, *Liquid Modernity* (Cambridge: Polity Press, 2000); and *The Individualized Society* (Cambridge: Polity Press, 2001).

44 Saskia Sassen, *Territory, Authority, Rights: From Medieval to Global Assemblages* (Princeton: Princeton University Press, 2006). Also 'Bordering Capabilities Versus Borders: Implications for National Borders', *Michigan Journal of International Law* 30, 2009, 567-597. For a description of a more chaotic, locally grounded, and contingent operation of transnational capital, see Anna L. Tsing, *Friction: An Ethnography of Global Connection* (Princeton: Princeton University Press, 2005).

45 Andreas Fischer-Lescano and Gunther Teubner, 'Regime-Collisions: The Vain Search for Legal Unity in the Fragmentation of Global Law', *Michigan Journal of International Law* 25(4), 2004, 999-1046; Catá Backer, (2012). The Structural Characteristics of Global Law for the 21st Century: Fracture, Fluidity, Permeability, and Polycentricity', *Tilburg Law Review* 17(2), 2012, 177-199

46 Naomi Klein, *The Shock Doctrine: the rise of disaster capitalism* (London: Penguin Books, 2008); Jessica Whyte, *Morals of the Market: human rights and the rise of neoliberalism* (London: Verso, 2019).

47 See Derek Gregory, 'The Everywhere War', *The Geographic Journal* 177(3), 2011, 238-250; Barry Hindess, 'Neo-liberal Citizenship', *Citizenship Studies* 6(2), 2002, 127-143; Mark Duffield and Nicholas Waddell, 'Securing Humans in a Dangerous World', *International Politics* 43, 2006, 1-23; Didier Bigo, 'Security and Immigration: Toward a Critique of the Governmentality of Unease', *Alternatives* 27 (Special Issue), 2002, 63-92; Henry A. Giroux, 'Totalitarian Paranoia in the Post-Orwellian Surveillance State', *Cultural Studies* 29(2), 2015, 108-140; Patrick Petit, '"Everywhere Surveillance": Global Surveillance Regimes of Techno-Securitization', *Science as Culture* 29(1), 2020, 30-56.

these identifications of tensions and complexities are considered, however, is the reality that these re-viewings of the *World* speak essentially of a totality, coherent even in its apparent 'anarchy'. This is not to claim that there are no conflicts, that territorial locations governed by regimes of 'national' law and 'politics' do not throw up particular and specific tensions and contestations, merely that such apparent conflicts notwithstanding, the 'post-colonial' architecture operates as a whole, its diverse constituent components, territorial and otherwise, and its seemingly opposed rationalities of 'public' and 'private', all cohere as an identifiable totality of *Reason*. This is my argument.

It is important to make clear the point. While the many analyses of the 'global' and its various impacts on the Inter/National frame is bread and butter to the critical commentator, still the fundamental assumptions of *methodological post-colonialism* maintain their defining obscuring hold. I say this because in these analyses, the *global* – and all its perceived novel characteristics and innovations – is understood as a categorical disruption, if not rupture, of some original 'national-international' imaginary of territorialised political-legal (b) ordering. What these critical analyses set out to do, therefore, is highlight and problematise the perceived tensions between territorial norm-ality and trans/supraterritorial novelty. Even the more nuanced understandings of the complementarity of the national/global actuality, such as Bauman's and Sassen's, retain, as a problematic of analysis, the apparent novelty of these identified spheres of 'liquid' beingness and 'global assemblages' which reveal a primacy of *private* Reason over the assumed *public* Reason of national/international regulatory imaginaries and regimes; the dualities and oppositions of the perceived 'new' and the assumed 'old', of the novel 'global' and the traditional 'inter/national', define still the underlying frame that informs critical interrogations of the present. With a focus clearly on the reified features of metropolitan colonial/capitalist states as viewed and theorised from within its (b)orders, these assertions of 'novelty' from a prior stable condition of the 'national' are far removed from the experiences of (post)colonial state formations; theirs have been, from the very onset of the imposition of colonising *Reason*, a 'liquid', 'disaggregated', 'permeable', and 'porous' domain of desire and profit. No 'transfixed imagination' originated the (b)ordering of the *postcolony*.

No, perceptions of 'novelty' often obscure prevailing and persistent continuities; we might read the evidence of the World differently. Not as revealing novel disruptions of, or challenges to, the 'post-colonial' norm-ality but as demonstrating the very coherence of a global (post)colonial architecture constituted by multiple geographies of differentiatedly regulated socialities. We might understand the actuality of enforced differentiation better if we shift our attention from the philosophical fixation with the 'political' domain of 'subjectivity' to what might be properly termed the 'social' domain of lived subject-beingness; the 'political' has concerned itself with the performative and the form, with questions of political inscriptions and institutional formalities, with interpellations and subjectivities, with *becomings* and *Events*,[48] the 'social' would focus on the relationalities of appropriation/dispossession, protections/abandonments, material 'friendships/enmities' that condition the actualities of subject(ed)-being-ness as actual being-in-the-World. To have obscured the experiences of the 'social' with the ceremonial and performative rituals of the 'political' has been a major effect (and success, we might add) of methodological post-colonialism.

A different view of the *World* as a global (post)colonial totality is this. The essential *Reason* that defines the global architecture of the 'post-colonial' is, not the juridical affirmation of the 'Sovereign' equality of 'decolonised' Humanity, not the making of citizen-subjects of previously negated 'Non-Beingness' in the 'exteriority. Instead, it is that of the organisation and management of a global disciplinary and biopolitical regime of differentiated "subjected"-beingness – of licence, containment, and a(ban)donment. What are perceived as the dualities of the 'national-territorial' and the 'global-supra-territorial' are but the contested and negotiated settlements through which the primary *Reason* of coloniality is regulated and enforced. When viewed and understood as a coherent totality, we see clearly the actual conditions of a (post)colonial global order.[49]

So, let us return to the question posed by Vivienne Jabri: "[w]hat does it mean conceptually and theoretically to talk of the subject of politics in post-coloniality?"[50] Setting aside the 'conceptual' and 'theoretical' reifications of colonial-modern' mythologies of the 'political', and returning our view to the 'social' actualities of beingness in the *postcolony*, we might answer as follows: for some of us, (post)colonial sovereignty and 'citizenship' mean privileged access to the global competition for (the 'Rights' of) *licence* and protection from

---

48 We see the worst tendencies of this fixation with the 'political' in the vast corpus of Eurocentric 'critical', 'poststructuralist' literature mired in this utterly self-indulgent, and inconsequential gazing upon the World.

49 An interesting example of this is the mapping project of global environmental injustice as seen through the geographies of global commodity chains – EJAtlas; see Leah Temper, Daniela del Bene and Joan Martinez-Alier, 'Mapping the frontiers and front lines of global environmental justice: the EJAtlas', *Journal of Political Ecology* 22(1), 2015, 255-278. It is interesting that the term 'front line' is used here, aptly so, even if its implications are not fully considered.

50 Jabri, *The Postcolonial Subject*, 58.

regulatory encumbrances; for some, they mean the regulation of the rights and duties of *containment* where the discourses, technologies and disciplines of precarious belonging-citizenship are enforced; and for most, they mean a fate of rightless *abandonment* – of disposability and superfluity – that remain the material condition of subject-ed beingness so acquired by the meaningless moniker of 'citizen' under 'sovereignty'. Thus we see, the licence to unencumbered enrichment, the domestication and pacification of compliant labour and consumptive economic participation, and the expulsion or eradication of 'disposable' or 'dangerous' bodies continue to operate as the material *Reasons* of global (post)coloniality and its complex and rich heritage of philosophical rationalisations.[51] For this *Reason* does the territorialised architecture of 'political-legal' (b)ordering – of 'Constitutions' and 'citizenship' enforced through both militarised policing (both public and private) and a 'general biopolitical' (b)ordering of differentiated populations – sit coherently with the supraterritorialised regimes of 'global assemblages' and 'global law' which maintain structural and persistent actualities of global enrichment and impoverished suffering.[52] There is no contradiction here, no perplexity; such is the coherent norm-ality of the (post)colonial World resettled, a World made commensurable as a totality of inscriptions and emplacements, meanings and rationalisations, a 'post-colonial' redemption of global coloniality. All following the 'post-colonial' resettlement, the *World* of licence, containment and a(ban)donment restored, splendour in squalor as business as usual.

To conclude this chapter, I suggest a corrective to the categorical deceptions of *methodological post-colonialism*:

- the 'colonial' and 'post-colonial' operate as an onto-epistemological reset-

---

51 'Global flows' – of capital, labour and 'commodity chains' – now are the new euphemisms that disguise the violence of norm-alised structural exploitation of contemporary licence, containment, and a(ban) donment; see Intan Suwandi, R. Jamil Jonna and John Bellamy Forster, 'Global Commodity Chains and the New Imperialis', *Monthly Review* 70(10), 2019 at <https://monthlyreview.org/2019/03/01/global-commodity-chains-and-the-new-imperialism/> (last accessed 30 April 2020).

52 The radically differential experiences of 'citizens' under the enforced restrictions of movement and work resulting from the global Covid-19 pandemic again reveals this structural disjuncture between the actualities of subject-beingness and the rationalising ideologies and rhetoric of mutuality and interdependence; the hard truth is that 'we' are not all in it together! Naomi Klein has rightly named the current effects of the pandemic as portending a 'coronavirus capitalism'. See 'Coronavirus Capitalism – and How to Beat it', *The Intercept*, 16 March 2020, available at <https://www.filmsforaction.org/watch/coronavirus-capitalism-and-how-to-beat-it/> (last accessed 30 March 2020). Also, Rob Wallace, Alex Liebman, Luis Fernando Chaves and Rodrick Wallace, 'Covid-19 and Circuits of Capital', *Monthly Review* 72(1), 2020, at <https://monthlyreview.org/2020/04/01/covid-19-and-circuits-of-capital/> (last accessed 4 May 2020); and Didier Bigo, Elspeth Guild and Elif Mendos Kuskonmaz, 'Obedience in times of COVID-19 pandemics: a renewed governmentality of unease?', *Global Discourse*, 11(3), 2021, 471-489, at https://bristoluniversitypressdigital.com/view/journals/gd/11/3/article-p471.xml (last accessed, 15 June 2022)

tlement of temporalities and consciousness which, through the signal of rupture, entrenches and internalises the Reason of coloniality – the differentiated inscriptions of rights/lessness of appropriation/dispossession and its attendant regulatory and enforcement regimes – within a totalising global 'post-colonial' institutional order;

- the 'national' and the 'international' operate as a coherent, even if contested, regulatory regime that together regulate 1) the inscriptions and emplacements of bodies-within/out-territory, and 2) the enforcement of differentiated rights/lessness consequently ascribed.

- the 'citizen' operates as a category of containment and pacification of subjection – imposing precarious rights of belonging and absolute obligations of obedience – in the face of the actualisation of differentiated socialities of licence, containment, and a(ban)donment.

We see here clearly the work of the 'post-colonial', operating, as it does, both as a philosophical manoeuvre and technology of material (b)ordering. The fixation and the fetishization of the 'declaration of independence' – the purported ruptures of the 'before/after' and the 'inside/outside' – ignores crucially the abiding *Reason* of coloniality which persists through to the 'post-colonial' resettlement of global norm-ality, precisely enabled and entrenched by it. In this resettlement, the 'declaration of independence' serves as the philosophical rationalisation for the re-(b)ordering of the state-in-the-international within the global geography of coloniality. Granting fully the momentous achievement and the psychological significance of 'self-determination' from racialised rule, the resulting operation of the 'post' in 'post-colonial' has, in this connection, served as both an exoneration and an alibi. With the 'declaration of independence' is the 'colonial', as a governmental modality of material subjugation, marked as 'past'. With it, the materiality of continuing coloniality becomes resettled as (legitimately) 'post-colonial'. And as a final manoeuvre, the *anti-colonial* as a praxis of refusal and transformation is thus deemed terminated. This, the ultimate perversion of methodological post-colonialism: the liberation brought about by the 'declaration of independence' was not that of the conquered, but of the 'coloniser', now cleansed of the sins of the past and redeemed for impending futures.

2

On the Anti-Colonial as Situation and Praxis

In being schooled into the ways of *wording* the World, we have become accustomed to the rationalisations of colonial philosophy which define and emplace, as a commensurable totality, all conditions of subject-ed beingness in *this* World. To *be-subject* in/to the *World* is to be commensurable to the (b)ordered categories of the World, now morm-alised as 'post-colonial'. No other imagination is to avail, no 'other Worlds' are to be permissible. So, it would seem. With the 'post-colonial' settlement is the category human(beingness) thus asserted as finalised, redeemed and completed, out of the 'colonial' past into the 'post-colonial' present/future. The proper 'end of history' one might say. But not quite.

The story of the *World* as (b)ordered is not all of the story of the world, not the only story of *this* World. This *World* is but one assertion and materialisation of the present, but one rationalisation of a philosophical situation enforced as a totality.[1] There is obviously much to be gained through this assertion of 'post-colonial' (b)ordering for those who have appropriated the

---

1 The assumption of the 'sovereign' (b)ordering of the World is illustrative. Much is made of Schmitt's first sentence in his *Political Theology: Four Chapters on the Concept of Sovereignty* (Chicago: University of Chicago Press, 2005), 5: "the sovereign is the one who decides the exception." But this, I suggest, is not the most important line in the work. It is the second line that is more instructive when Schmitt qualifies his initial assertion: "only this definition can do justice to a borderline concept." Indeed, what is interesting to me is that the first line has proved to be precisely the distraction that has beguiled critical thinking and prevented a clearer view of the (post)colonial manoeuvre at play. That Schmitt was thinking a 'borderline' concept – of the limits, or the 'outermost sphere' (p.5) – is relevant not because it pertains to the 'border' of the imagined nomos, but because it is from this outermost limit of meaning that the entire theory of the political-state, and its foundational philosophical invention/ assertion of 'sovereignty', is constructed. Let us remember that this explicitly borderline concept is the fundamental philosophical ground from which the entire architecture of the (b)ordered World as a totality of meaning is constructed.

author-ity to so name (b)orders; indeed, it is profitable precisely to insist upon this settled-totality as a truth of the World. All such efforts notwithstanding a different philosophical situation still maintains, other than (post)colonial assertions, *anti-colonial* repudiations, other than the situation of *(b)orders*, one of *frontlines*. This, I elaborate here.

Anti-colonial philosophies are articulations of a confrontation which open to incommensurability the opposing locations and experiences of think-ing-being in the World. They articulate the seditious rejections of commu-nities of resistance and recovery of the extant *Wordings* of *this* World, not simply as a matter of epistemological repudiation, but more importantly as a consequence and reflection of material beingness in the World. Understood thus, the *anti-colonial* is a praxes of thinking-being-otherwise-than-subjected – we might call it a praxes of *desubjectification* – by which are the (b)orders of (post)colonial norm-ality de-named, de-reified and transformed into sites and imaginaries otherwise than prescribed by the names and emplacements of 'post-colonial' settlements, properly, to borrow from Ariella Aisha Azoulay, an opening up of 'potential history'.[2]

In saying this it is necessary to emphasise the point that there is nothing fixed or determined by this assertion of a philosophical situation, nothing capable of abstraction as some essential content to *anti-colonial beingness*. The *anti-colonial* in this understanding does not pertain to any imagined totality either of oppression or liberation. The *anti* here is entirely contingent upon the materialities of coloniality in their specificities of time, place, and experience; these are matters we cannot know in isolation nor in the absolute. What we do know is that the struggle against colonial rule in the past – the ordinary, everyday uprisings and refusals to be-subject to regimes of impov-erishment and degeneracy – conjoined in many a collective articulation and action towards greater dignity, solidarity, and material security. These actu-alities of struggle are commonly assumed to be the historical foundation of

---

2 Ariella Aisha Azoulay, *Potential History: Unlearning Imperialism* (London: Verso, 2019). Azoulay's description of 'potential history' is close to my assertion of the anti-colonial position, and provides a rare statement, unlike so many critical commentaries, that takes head on the assumption of (post) colonial totality:

> Potential history is not an attempt to tell the violence alone, but rather an onto-epis-temic refusal to recognise as irreversible its outcome and the categories, statuses, and forms under which it materializes. Potential history refuses to inhabit the position of the historian who arrives after the events are over, that is, after the violence was made into part of the sealed past ... the work of potential history is to argue that this violence can be reversed ... Potential history is a commitment to attend to the potentialities that the institutional forms of imperial violence – borders, nation-states, museums, archives, and laws – try to make obsolete or turn into precious ruins. (286)

the 'national' anti-colonial imagination which translates into 'post-colonial' author-ity and legitimacy.[3] Memorialisations are important. But these are incomplete and contingent; the actualities of refusal and regeneration, as projections of imagination and hope, can only be understood and appreciated in their specific historical contexts and cannot be taken as a termination of imagination. It is necessary therefore to revise our understanding, or more accurately, our assumptions, regarding the 'post-colonial' situation. This is more than a task of empirical correction. It is one of fundamental philosophical significance.

We consider this question posed by Aimé Césaire.

So, "What, Fundamentally, is Colonization?"[4]

It seems to me, we have confused colonialism, as a regulatory technology and discourse of 'subjugation', with *colonisation* that is an onto-epistemological and material transmogrification of beingness-in-the-world; the latter we properly understand as *subjection*. To conflate the two is a fundamental philosophical error, the result of a reification of the category 'colonial' in rationalisations of 'Modern' political-legal philosophy.

The 'Colonial' in/and the 'Post-Colonial'

The *World*, as we know it, is entirely invested in the prior onto-epistemological assumption of 'colonialism'. Upon this category, as a situation in History, are innumerable arguments still waged, numerous investments still sought to be protected or challenged; we see all around in contemporary political contestations the struggle over the memory/History of 'colonialism'. Purportedly, what is at stake is the 'post-colonial' World itself. My view is that much of this argument is misleading and distracting.

We know that following what is conventionally regarded as the 'world-making' events of 'decolonisation',[5] there has been a great deal of attention given to understanding the many possible implications of the problematic 'post' in 'post-colonial'. There has also been a great deal of attention given to retelling rich histories of 'colonial' pasts from the ground up by excavating 'colonised' experiences from historiographical silencings. But in all this, it is notable that the idea of the *colonial* itself seems to have escaped scrutiny. That there exists

---

3 A significant corrective to this assumption of historiography is the contributions of the 'subaltern studies group'; see Ranajit Guha and Gayatri Chakravorty Spivak (eds.), *Selected Subaltern Studies* (Oxford: Oxford University Press, 1988)

4 Aimé Césaire, *Discourse on Colonialism*, trans. Joan Pinkham (New York: Monthly Review Press, 1972).

5 Adom Getachew, *Worldmaking After Empire: the rise and fall of self-determination* (Princeton: Princeton University Press, 2019).

a situation as such, a categorically essential point of departure as such, appears to have been simply taken as given. While we readily utilise the word, there is, it needs emphasising, no essential meaning to 'colonialism'; indeed, it might be said that 'colonialism' itself is a categorical reification. We have simply accorded primacy to a particular category of (b)ordering and assumed it to be of fundamental ontological worth. This has been a defining error.

While we assume understanding, what existed under this generalised 'political' category of the 'colonial' situation were manifold structural relationships of domination/subjugation, accumulation/dispossession, enrichment and abjection, that were, in the specificities of time and place, contextually rationalised, specifically inflicted and contingently enforced through particular institutional modalities. 'Colonialism' therefore serves as a general term based on a certain conception of 'foreign rule', premised on a particular view of 'racially' differentiated and territorialised 'political' structure of institutional relations.[6] While there is a certain utility in simplifications of this sort, the problem arises when the category 'colonialism' is then reified into a foundational onto-epistemological point of departure that has come to define both the philosophoscapes and temporalities that constitute the *World* as a totality. Its effect is to obscure the substantive and material relationalities of actual appropriation/dispossession, domination/subjugation by a preoccupation with the formalised 'inter/national' framing of 'political' relations, and of its discourses and rituals; we have seen the effects of this philosophical bifurcation of the actualities of the 'social' and the reified formal rituals of the 'political' previously in Chapter 1.

Let us briefly recall. In meaningful terms, the category 'colonialism' explains little of actual substantive significance, that is, it reveals little of the content and structure of the social relation of domination/subjugation in any particular emplaced and embodied context. This emptiness is precisely useful to deflect attention from substance to form.[7] Importantly, as we have

---

6 When we concentrate on the specific nature of 'colonial' (b)ordering, we see a whole range of 'social' relations and institutions of domination/subjugation. We might see, for example that British 'colonialism' manifest in Kenya as compared to India, were distinct regimes of (b)ordered enforcement, as were the French 'colonial' regimes of Algeria as compared to Indochina. Common usage of the term aside, the point is that the 'colonialisms' of the British, French, Dutch, Portuguese, German, Italian, North American, Russian, Japanese, in all their various particularities of time and place, shared little in common in the specificities of their 'social' organisation of relations except in their shared racialised rationalisation of differentiation. As a convenience however, based on an inherited territorialised and 'nation-alised' conception of right-ful 'political' subjection encapsulated through the mythologies of 'sovereignty' and 'citizenship', the 'colonial', as an ontological category of political-legal (b)ordering has now come to stick as a catchall category of analysis and understanding.

7 The effect of this subterfuge is particularly insidious in the rationalisations of 'un/violence' that are

seen, the category colonialism enabled a formal demarcation of past and present that served to resettle the norm-ality of global coloniality. While the rationalisations of coloniality have observably changed its *Reason* remains consistent and coherent; from the 'colonial' to the 'post-colonial' what has remained unchanged is the underlying rationality of (b)ordering to regulate and enforce the differentiated conditions of *licence, containment,* and *a(ban) donment.* In these messy entanglements of differentiated social relations are the materialities of (post)coloniality maintained and enforced, no matter the ceremonial and ritualistic invocations of (colonial-)modern mythologies of sovereignty, nationalism, citizenship, human rights etc. In these entanglements also are enmeshed the actualities of differentiation now considerably more complicated than what was previously understood as defined by divisions based on 'class'.

As I have argued, the implications of the necessary disentangling of the 'social', in this respect, from its subsumption into the 'political' are significant; it necessitates a departure from categorical comforts thus far assumed. By this I mean that the categories that have come to articulate both the aspiration of 'liberation' and the condition of 'political-belonging' no longer sustain. Specifically, we refer here to the understandings of 'state-sovereignty' and 'citizenship'. The former fetishises a sphere of territorial organisation (of regimes of justifications and enforcements) that is premised upon a Schmittian mythology of friendship and enmity; as we have seen, the friend and the enemy are rather more materially, and non-territorially, (b)ordered. The latter reifies an abstract 'subjectivity' of belonging-in-political under a 'constitutionally' ordained juridical 'equality'; instead, sophisticated structures of differentiated subject-beingness regulate the actual access to, and realisation of, (b)ordered rights/lessness. Together, these operate to entrench the 'post-colonial' deceit, seductively so, its hold, undoubtedly powerful. Consider this claim by Achin Vanaik's, which Neil Lazarus cites in agreement, on the "exceptional character of nationalism" which lies,

> in its unique combination of politics and culture, of civic power (e.g. the importance of citizenship) and identity. The nation-state for the first time invests ordinary people (through the principle of equal citizenship rights) with an authority and importance that is historically unique. To date the zenith of popular individual empowerment is

---

routine under the global 'post-colonial' settlement; see Chapter 6, below.

political citizenship, whose frame of operation is the nation-state or multinational state.[8]

Here we see in essence the 'post-colonial' deceit. Such sentiments, we might appreciate it as an adherence to a conviction, are appealing but simply wrong, entirely premised on an idealised and reified categorical assumption, precisely the work of *colonisation* – and I will return to this point shortly. Let us first note that notwithstanding the philosophical rationalisations of *methodological post-colonialism*, the 'nation-state' does not in actuality invest 'ordinary people' with any semblance of 'authority and importance'. No amount of repetition of this 'constitutional' platitude is able to relieve us of the weight of evidence to the contrary. Such views which celebrate the laudatory assertions of 'equal citizenship', derived no doubt from past anti-colonial assertions of transformatory imagination, simply do not account for the actuality of 'post-colonial-nationalism' and 'citizenship'. While the entire architecture of colonial-modern structures of state power has been built on these repeated promises of becoming/belonging, the empirical actualities of embodied life experiences across 'post-colonial' geographies reveal a very different truth of containment within the (b)ordered inflictions of 'citizenship'. It is foolish to think that this is simply a matter of oversight or aberration.

All this said, the question remains: what do we make of this difficult realisation? How do we contend with the problem of 'colonisation', separated from its 'colonial' vestiges, properly understood?

Achille Mbembe observes that there does not exist a 'theory of decolonisation' as such.[9] On this he is correct. He is mistaken however to follow this observation with the assertion that "decolonization signalled a planetary reappropriation of *the ideals of modernity and their transnationalism.*"[10] This is already to have fully internalised the categorical reifications of colonial philosophy, to see the World through the frames of meaning purportedly universal. What we understand as the 'post-colonial' political-legal order, born out of the 'event' of 'decolonisation', is no creation of some 'Modern', 'Enlightenment' philosophy come to final fruition, it is no gift of 'modernity' upon the wretched of the earth, finally to have been granted. By all reckoning, it was attained fundamentally in opposition to the rationalities and convictions of the great (philosophical) spirits of the 'Enlightenment', for whom

---

8 Quoted in Lazarus, *Nationalism and Cultural Practice in the Postcolonial World*, 138.
9 Achille Mbembe, *Out of the Dark Night: Essays on Decolonization* (New York: Columbia University Press, 2021), 45.
10 *Ibid,* 49 (emphasis mine).

the Enlightenment Spirit was a spectre that oversaw the regimes of cruelty and despoilation of slave ships, *frontier*-lands, plantations, 'settlements' etc. It is essential that we understand this. The spirit of struggle of innumerable peoples behind those great *moments/events* of 'decolonisation' that birthed the 'post-colonial' Inter/National order, originates not from the rationalities of 'Modernity', not from any treasures redeemed from the 'European archive';[11] it is of an altogether different *Reason,* fully a future only made possible by insistent repudiatory *anti-colonial* imaginations focussed, not on the prize of becoming-into-the-International out of 'colonialism' but, on the specificities of *colonisation'*. When seen through the light of *anti-colonial* philosophy, therefore, we understand that the insurgent Third Word 'nationalist' response to past subjugations must be understood as a contingent manifestation of struggle, born as it was out of a particular historical context of capitalist/imperial (b)ordering: the 'colonial' mode of global coloniality.

Context is everything. In a moment in time, with the philosophical and ideological resources at hand, we know that this imagination translated into articulations of, and actions toward, 'post-colonial nationalism'. Of its time, this was an imagination and aspiration of beingness-in-the-World informed by the discursive registers and institutional forms of 'nation-statehood' considered as vital and expedient, the manifestation of anti-colonial possibility as envisaged and desired largely by the *European-ised* elites who fronted the 'decolonisation' movements. In this regard, the 'declaration of independence' does indeed herald a significant articulation of Beingness against the closures of a *colonial* philosophy that presumed the Right to *colonise* Beingness and (b)order the World. But not as a completion of imagination or possibility. How could it be so? The underlying *Reason* of coloniality as discussed previously, remain fully operative, the desires of predatory licence to appropriate and consume the World remain fully evident, the illogics of capitalism remain firmly entrenched as global (post)colonial norm-ality; a continuity of depravity and cruelty - "from colonialism to the coup" as Jason Hickel put it in exposing the coherence of 'the divide' that is global inequality – thus, we see, remains entrenched, little disturbed by 'post-colonial' formalities of 'sovereignty'.[12] It does not seem credible to me to assume that a rebellious affirmation of being-otherwise-than-subjected – that which

---

11 Achille Mbembe, *Necropolitics* trans. Steven Corcoran (Durham: Duke University Press, 2019), 188. I will return to this notion of 'Europe's archive' in Chapter 6.
12 Jason Hickel, *The Divide: A Brief Guide to Global Inequality and Its Solutions,* (London: Windmill Books, 2018), 104.

was ascribed the *Reason* of being-anti-colonial – can be so terminated upon an instant, however momentous and ceremoniously encapsulating of the liberatory spirit the 'declaration of independence' as that moment of instantiation might appear to be. The 'declaration of independence' thus represents a point of reference for anti-colonial *Reason*, not a marker of termination; it is, I argue, a 'declaration' of a *frontline*, not an affirmation of a resettled *(b)order*.

So, I repeat the correction I want to affirm. An *anti-colonial* perspective understands the 'colonial' – as form and discourse – as a particular regime of (b)ordering which served the rationalisation of the *Reason* of coloniality. As such, *anti-colonial Reason* is less fixated with reifications of 'post-colonial' grand designs. Instead, it would open to question precisely this assignation of the post-colonial moment of the becoming-into-the-international as a categorical rupture. The *anti-colonial*, I argue, exceeds *colonialism*. It survives the 'post-colonial' resettlement. Underpinning anti-colonial Reason, therefore, is a repudiation of the desire towards *colonisation* whatever might be the institutional architecture of coloniality that is thereby sought to be norm-alised. This distinction between *colonialism* as a particular institutional structure of conquest/subjugation – that is, of licence, containment, and a(ban)donment – and *colonisation* as *subjection* – a transmogrification of (already-)Being into enforced subjected-Beingness – is critical to understanding what I mean by 'post-colonial' distractions and the continuing urgency of anti-colonial praxis in the present.

On Colonisation and the Colonised?

For the sake of clarity, let me restate my position. Colonialism is a general description of an historical institutional architecture of (b)ordering which makes-subject(ed) the encountered 'other' *to* a racialised structure of rule/govern-ment. As a matter of subjugation, the colonial order may dominate, even exterminate, but it does not necessarily subsume the encountered 'Other' into commensurability with the 'Self'; there is a fundamental difference between *conquest/subjugation* and *colonisation-subjection* when we speak of the 'colonial' encounter and experience. We can agree that 'colonialism', as a particular institutional modality of global (b)ordering, is past following the 'event' of the 'declaration of independence'. Colonisation on the other hand, I want to stress, is something quite different. More than merely a political-legal inscription of domination-subordination, it entails a penetrative and consuming relationality of transmogrification; this is the manoeuvre of *subjection*. Colonisation properly understood is the closure of (the meaning-of-)beingness within a bounded Totality; it involves first the destruction of (already-)Being through the philosophical negation and material subjugation of the encountered *Other-Self* as Non-Being – without name, meaning, cosmologies, pasts – and subsequently, its reinscription into an imposed *culture* as subject-being, 'assimilated' that is into the onto-episte-mology of the coloniser.[13] It is in this respect that colonisation is properly to be understood as *World*-making, as a process that *makes-subject* the encoun-tered 'other' and transforms the other-ed into a participant-subject of a totalised, *commensurable* order of governmentality, that is, of *this* World. The distinction between colonisation and conquest/subjugation can therefore be simply stated thus: the colonial order asserts an institutional norm-alisation of subjugation; colonisation manifests an experiential-phenomenological subjection of Beingness. The difference is critical.

In the context of global coloniality in the *colonial* phase, prior that is to the resettlement of the 'declaration of independence', we see that colonialism and colonisation were commonly understood and spoken of mutually. Crucially, we see this in the phenomenological accounts of much *anti-colo-nial* writings of the time; this is the (non-)being that Fanon spoke of as the 'Negro',[14] that Memmi described as the 'colonised',[15] that Biko referred to as the 'Black Man'.[16] These describe the ontology and phenomenology of the 'colonised', of the conditions of *being-colonised*, of being made-subject to that universe of names and meanings as inscribed, a beingness made *non-Being* by the colonial philosophies of the time. Indeed, this phenomenology of trans-mogrification, and the resultant anguished realisation of *being-colonised*, is clearest in Fanon's *Black Skin, White Masks*; Fanon, we understand, is the 'negro', *made* into Non-Being without authenticity by the simple call of the child, and this is the core of his *colonised* rage.[17] On this there might be little disagreement. But a more pertinent point need be made. The power of that

---

13 On the complex workings of colonialism/colonisation both with respect the 'coloniser' and the 'colonised' in the context of India, see Ashis Nandy, *The Intimate Enemy: loss and recovery of self under colonialism* (Oxford: Oxford University Press, 1983).

14 Frantz Fanon, *Black Skins, White Masks* (London: Pluto, 1986).

15 Albert Memmi, *The Colonizer and the Colonized* (London: Souvenir Press, 1974).

16 Steve Biko, *I Write What I Like* (London: Bowerdean Press, 1978) 28-320.

17 There is obviously incessant debate on what Fanon said and meant on all of this; for a flavour see Lewis R. Gordon, *What Fanon said: a philosophical introduction to his life and thought* (New York: Fordham University Press, 2015); David Macey, *Frantz Fanon: a biography* (London: Verso Books, 2012 (2nd edition)); David Macey, *Frantz Fanon: a life* (London: Granta, 2000); Anthony C. Allesandrini (ed), *Frantz Fanon: critical perspectives* (London: Routledge, 1999).

call that so affected Fanon, of that utterance of the name 'Black' directed towards him, lies precisely in that it is heard by a Black-ed, *colonised*-Fanon; it is to this 'subject' made (non)being that the words are meaningful, it is in the *World* that claims the (non)Beingness of the *colonised*-Fanon that Fanon, as a (non)subject finds meaningful, that this call, in and of itself, is meaningful. This is indeed the situation of the *colonised*. *Few* emerge from this anguished initial contemplation of the colonised-condition to then articulate an *anti-colonial* repudiation, to recover from colonised-Beingness an imagination and praxis that rupture the asserted, inflicted (b)orders of enclosure; Fanon's subsequent work *The Wretched of the Earth* may be understood as thus, and this is his genius and enduring potency. Others – take Albert Memmi as an example – were less able so to do.[18]

My point is this: we concede too much to colonial philosophies that seek to norm-alise the World when we conflate the fact of *'colonial' subjugation* with the situation of *colonisation*. This is what we do when we assume that all peoples subjugated under 'colonial' governmentality are spoken-for in their generalised entirety by the phenomenological accounts of articulate 'colonised' commentators.

Such commentaries might indeed resonate profoundly with 'our' own experiences of rage, of dispossession, of being 'lesser' within environments of norm-ality in which we remain other-ed as we aspire towards commensurable recognition. It is true that we, many of us, who read Fanon, Memmi, Biko, for example, understand them, are familiar with their descriptions and rage; ours may indeed be a shared experience and understanding, of *being-colonised* in our present. This is an important, even if disconcerting, realisation requiring a pause. What if we, in recognition of our beignness-as-colonised, understand those that we take as the most illustrious and celebrated writers, thinkers, and leaders of the past and present of 'post/decolonial' thought, might indeed have been and are, as most of us still remain, the ones utterly *colonised*? Perhaps we mistake such particular anguished articulations as reflective of *the* general condition of beingness under-(post-)'colonialism'. Perhaps we mistake the experience of the *colonised* as true and generalizable expressions of the entirety of the *conquered/subjugated*.[19] As such with *our* 'post-colonial' preoccupations with phenomenologies of colonised-beingness we in turn reify the colonised

---

18 Memmi provides a sustained lament on the inabilities of the presumed 'decolonised', as 'new citizen' and as 'immigrant', to take up the challenges of the 'post-colonial' reality; see Albert Memmi (trans. Robert Nononno), *Decolonization and the Decolonized* (Minneapolis: University of Minnesota Press, 2006).

19 This is, in my reading, an important lesson that Ashis Nandy teaches us; see *The Intimate Enemy*.

condition – of *subjection*, of being made-subject – and assign it totalising force, forgetting that *non-colonised*, even if *conquered*, cosmologies of Being-(other- wise) persist co-evally;[20] the experiences of beingness here less anguished by realisations of a being-negated, their rage more centred around their experi- ences of material and social dispossession and subjugation. Coloniality, as the perpetuation of structures and regimes of differentiated (b)ordering, in this respect, is little challenged by the reification of colonisation as a philosophical category; indeed, the assumption of 'colonisation' under colonialism, and of 'decolonisation' as a passing into the 'post-colonial', provide amenable alibis for the perpetuation of continuing *(post)colonial conquests*, now cleansed of the *colonial* taint. This is the 'persistent past in the present' that (post)colonial philosophies continue to regulate and enforce through new forms of rational- isations, this the continuing work of *colonisation*, the work of the norm-alisa- tion of coloniality, which is to say, of the *Reason* of *licence* and the exigencies of *containment/a(ban)donment*.

A Return to Anti-Colonial Reason

We begin by acknowledging the 'post-colonial' actuality. We ignore neither the 'post-colonial' state nor the 'International' order as actualities of (b) ordering. Their oppressive regimes of cruelty are all too real. For this reason, they must absolutely remain open to scrutiny and judgement as contingent inventions of *anti-colonial* imaginations and aspirations. From this point of departure, my argument is as follows.

With respect to the 'post-colonial' settlement, a return to anti-colonial Reason means that the 'post-colonial' state and the 'International' order, as institutional manifestations born out of struggle grounded in the material- ities of subjugation, have no *a priori* claim to philosophical and 'political'

----

20 As an example, we note that Amilcar Cabral fully relied on this resilience of the people to remain uncolonized in elaborating his arguments on the role of 'culture' in the struggle for liberation. As Cabral observed:

> The colonial experience of imperialist domination in Africa shows that (with the exception of genocide, racial segregation and apartheid) the only purportedly positive solution found by the colonial power to break the cultural resistance of the colonized peoples has been *assimilation*. But the total failure of the policy of progressive assimila- tion of the native populations is patent proof of the falseness of this theory, as well as the capacity of the dominated peoples to resist attempts to destroy or degrade their cultural legacy. (emphasis in original)

Amilcar Cabral, *Resistance and Decolonisation* trans. Dan Wood (London: Rowman & Littlefield, 2016), 163. See also, Nandy, *The Intimate Enemy*. If anything, it would appear that this process of colonised assimilation has had much more success after colonialism, in the 'post-colonial' enforcement of global coloniality.

legitimacy or interminability.[21] As such, a reassertion of the anti-colonial present entails a necessary re-evaluation of the materialities of subjugation, and the structures and rationalisations of (b)ordering within the resettled 'post-colonial' contexts of the social relations of contemporary global coloniality. This includes, fundamentally, an interrogation of the very onto-epistemological categories of 'political-legal' norm-ality itself – state, sovereignty, territory, rights, citizenship etc. But not just as an interrogation of abstract concepts but fully as manifest material actualities. The 'post-colonial' state, attached with its 'sovereign' juridical assumption within an idealised 'International' order of 'sovereign equality', has far too long served as a front and an alibi, has far too long been given liberty to perpetuate the emplaced and embodied cruelties that we appear to assume as *normality* – (un)violence, I call it.[22] To fetishise the state-nationalist form of an historical anti-colonial praxis is therefore to ossify hope and imagination and, perversely, to fully enable and facilitate the reconfigurations of global coloniality, now enforced through the institutional structures and discursive registers of the 'post-colonial', 'International' order.

Note the observation of Neil Lazarus and Priyamvada Gopal:

> The central task enjoined upon scholars working in the field of post-colonial studies ... we would say, is to work towards the production of a new 'history of the present' – a new reading, above all of the twentieth century, liberated from the dead weight either of the Cold War or of a compensatory 'Third Worldism'.[23]

I agree. I suggest however that the anti-colonial intellectual task requires more than a reaffirmation of some original liberated 'national' spirit as imagined by Lazarus and Gopal. It requires rather a recovery of the unceasing *Reason* of anti-colonial struggle which not only repudiates capitalism as a global systemic order but extends beyond a closure of categories, to interrogate the 'post-colonial' configuration of the 'national-state' itself as a situation of on-going anti-colonial encounters. It requires, in other words, an interrogation fundamentally, and constantly, of colonial-modern norm-ality, including the assumed *materialist* tenets of 'progressive' colonial-modern categories.[24]

---

21 This reclaiming of an authority to judgement is especially critical in countering the many claims of the Postcolony to unbridled 'nationalist' Rights to 'obedience' and of those of the 'metropolitan' state to 'nationalist' Rights to 'exclusion'; see Chapter 4, below.

22 See Chapter 6 for an elaboration of this argument.

23 Priyamvada Gopal and Neil Lazarus, 'Editorial', *New Formations,* 59, 2006, 7-9.

24 Lazarus is scathing of the tendency he sees in 'postcolonial' theorists to 'disavow decolonisation':

Fundamental to my argument is a clear understanding of the philosophical significance of *methodological post-colonialism,* as discussed in Chapter 1. It is precisely this manoeuvre that has erased the anti-colonial as situation and praxes. We correct this philosophical erasure here.

While it has come to be considered that the emergence into 'political-be-ingness' through the ascription of 'sovereignty' constitutes the ruptural signif-icance of anti-colonial struggle, a deeper condition inheres as fundamental to an anti-colonial imagination. Mbembe alludes to something similar:

> If decolonization was an event at all, it's essential philosophical meaning lies in an *active will to community* ...This will to community is another name for what could be called the *will to life*. Its goal was to realize a shared project: to stand up on one's own and to create a heritage.[25]

Mbembe speaks of this aspiration as something past. I mean something more than a rationalisation of an 'event', more than merely a memory in "our blasé age, characterized by cynicism and frivolity".[26] The error has indeed been to fixate on the 'event', as we have seen, to associate the 'declaration of inde-pendence' as the significant *moment* of 'decolonisation'.[27] I affirm instead a

---

> In much of the work currently issuing from within this field [of postcolonial studies], the massive nationalist mobilizations of the decolonizing years are thoroughly disavowed. ...Even the remarkable achievement of political independence is viewed less as an ineradicable, if inev-itably limited, advance than as a strengthening and confirmation of "Western" hegemony.
>
> In the face of such cynical and anti-political representations – which concede nothing, incidentally to the ultra-leftist discourse of 1970s Third-Worldism – it is important to try and keep alive the memory of the "revolutionary heroism" that was everywhere in evidence in the struggle for national liberation.

Neil Lazarus, *Nationalism and Cultural Practice in the Postcolonial World* (Cambridge: Cambridge University Press, 1999), 120 (note and reference omitted). For Lazarus, much of the 'post-colonial' criticism against the failures of 'decolonisation' undermines the actualities of historical achievement, and more importantly, disables the grounds on which contemporary struggles against capitalism and imperialism may be articulated and enacted. Lazarus argues instead for a reclaiming of 'nationalism' of a "socialist, nationalitarian, liberationist, internationalist" standpoint imbued again with the 'revo-lutionary heroism' of the past. Although I agree with his anti-imperialist stance and understand his intention to maintain the significance of the 'post-colonial' state for this purpose, I regard this as an idealisation and reification of the 'state' form, of an historical organisational imagination that is little reflected in its contemporary operation. In this sense, Lazarus's appeal for a 'socialist, nationalitarian, liberationist, internationalist' recovery reads equally vague and little different to Ramon Grosfuguel's preference for a 'radical universal decolonial anti-capitalist diversality project'; see above Introduction, above.

25 Achille Mbembe, *Out of the Dark Night: Essays on Decolonisation* (New York: Colombia University Press, 2021), 2-3 (emphases in original).

26 *Ibid.,* 3

27 Clearly, this is not to suggest that decolonisation is completed by the event. Mbembe's entire project can be understood as exploring the full depth of the problematic of decolonisation as he sees it. My point is less concerned with the entanglements of 'decolonisation' but with the assumption of the

fundamental *Reason*, that is *anti-colonial*. This is more than a particular 'philosophical interpretation', it is philosophy itself. Anti-colonial *Reason* grounds an understanding of solidarity in struggle whereby the weakest, most marginalised, most vulnerable, most wretched of the 'community', to the highest situation of consideration for judgement. Put differently, it is the 'social' condition of the most vulnerable that is the basis of any subsequent claim to 'post-colonial' authority, not as a matter of abstract political-legal theory, but as a matter of social actuality, a praxes of material and relational situatedness.

The implication of the praxeology of being-anti-colonial is, therefore, profound; there is no other single premise that could otherwise defend a 'universal' assertion that domination by one over another, that subjugation of one by another, for whatever reason, is invalid. Other than by this foundational 'principle of Humanity',[28] there is no inherent *Reason* whereby the 'national elite' of a 'colonial' territory may not be duly humiliated, despised, exploited, by the 'colonial Master' any more than their abject impoverished masses might subsequently be so inflicted by them, no *Reason* founding a purported 'right' of 'self-determination' that attaches to 'post-colonial sovereignty' such that authorises absolute *Right* over 'post-colonial *subjects*'. Simply stated, without the social prioritisation of the *damned* in the situatedness of a community of solidarity and struggle, there is no cogent or coherent justification for a 'post-colonial' situation in philosophy.

Understood thus, it is not some metaphysical 'political' ideal of a 'post-colonial' state-in-the-International that founds the claim to 'sovereign equality' but the actual, *wordly,* 'social' insistence of human regard for the beingness of the weakest, most impoverished and most vulnerable that originates the idea of a 'universal' *Humanity*. Without such an ascription of the priority to the social condition of suffering, no worth can be attached to an abstract, decontextualized 'political' configuration, be it of the reified *Human* of *Humanity* or the fetishised '*state-in-the-Inter/National*'. It is uniquely this insistence of substantive 'social' priority to be accorded to the 'lowest of the low' that

---

'new' implied in the 'post-colonial' settlement that thereby purportedly terminates the anti-colonial situation. That we are so confounded by the intractability of giving full effect to 'decolonisation' is, in my view, itself an effect of the 'post-colonial' deceit.

28 I borrow this term from Ted Honderich, *Terrorism for Humanity: Inquiries in Political Philosophy* (London: Pluto Press, 2003). Also, *Humanity, Terrorism, Terrorist War: Palestine, 9/11, Iraq, 7/7 ...*, (London: Continuum, 2006). Honderich's formulation of this principle may be understood as designed to assert a 'right' to 'inclusion' into the *World*. I adopt it instead more for rhetorical purposes, to suggest that if anything at all, this 'principle' remains alive in the praxes of the anti-colonial *frontline* as an affirmation of *desubjectification*, that is to be otherwise than 'subjected' by the (b)orderings of (post)colonial Totality.

marks out *anti-colonial* praxes as radically departing from the assumptions (and assertions) of abstract 'subjectivity' of colonial-modern political-legal philosophy. As such, 'taking suffering seriously', as Upendra Baxi implores,[29] is not a matter of appeal for attention, it is not even an assertion for 'justice'. It is simply a matter of categorical definition; to ignore the suffering of the most deprived, or worse, to inflict it upon them, is to nullify the anti-colonial credentials of any 'post-colonial' claim. Bearing this often neglected *Reason* of the anti-colonial in mind, we see that whatever the assertions of (post-)colonial philosophies regarding the settlements reached in framing the 'declaration of independence', and the categories of (b)ordering and (un)belonging that are thereby 'constituted', such claims to 'representative' regulatory authority are precarious, open to interrogation and judgement, vulnerable to repudiation. No 'post-colonial' settlement that renders 'the global poor' a *meaningful* condition of subject-beingness therefore, can prevail. Simply, *anti-colonial Reason* cannot be subsumed by any assertion of 'post-colonial' finality.

We are thus able to situate more concretely what Michael Neocosmos calls the 'national-liberation struggle mode' of anti-colonial praxes in its historical context[30] minus its subsequent ossification to serve as the stuff of commemoration in museum displays and extravagant 'national day' theatrics. Quite simply, it is better understood as a particular imagination and historical assertion of desubjectification, relevant to its time as an instance of repudiation and affirmation. There is no reification in this view of the 'post-colonial' state so constituted; historical context and contingency matter. Particular philosophies of collective re-affirmation – of 'nation' and 'nationalism' – significant as they were (and remain to be) within the public spaces of 'post-colonial' posturings and diplomacy, these did (and do) not quite encapsulate the whole, or even main, story of anti-colonial aspirations and struggle as effected by the 'politics of the people'.[31] For all the attention and focus on the 'post-colonial' as a 'political-becoming', the priority of the social condition remains; Basil Davidson provides an important reminder:

> Down the line of agitation and organization, among the mass of
> rural and urban supporters of the anti-colonial movements, there

---

29 Upendra Baxi, *Taking Suffering Seriously: Social Action Litigation in the Supreme Court of India*, Third World Legal Studies 4, 1985, 107-132.

30 See Michael Neocosmos, *Thinking Freedom in Africa: Toward a Theory of Emancipatory Politics* (Johannesburg: Wits University Press, 2016), 124-30.

31 I borrow this expression from Ranajit Guha, *Dominance Without Hegemony: History and Power in Colonial India* (London: Harvard University Press, 1997) x.

was small sign of any developing loyalty or attachment to this or that colony-turned-nation. What the multitudes wanted, by all the evidence, was not a flag for the people or an anthem for the people, nearly so much as they wanted bread for the people, and health and schools for the people, while caring precious little, as these same multitudes would overwhelmingly prove in the years ahead, about winning frontiers for the people. The jubilant crowds celebrating independence were not inspired by a "national consciousness" that demanded the nation," ... They were inspired by the hope of more and better food and shelter.[32]

The material contexts of hope and struggle therefore are the very definitional core of any claim to 'post-colonial' authority. This being so, imaginations of refusal to abide by the inflicted norm-alities of 'post-colonial' domination/ subjugation are not subject to the authority of any attempted assertion of closure and finality. None of this downplays, as Davidson himself put it, the "tremendous central gain of anti-colonial independence".[33] On the contrary by affirming the continuing significance of this underlying 'inspiration' of and for struggle against the *Reason* of coloniality, we breathe a living spirit back into the enclosures of the so-called 'post-colonial' present to provoke within the now norm-alised institutional 'comprador' re-settlements of (post)colonial arrangements the reverberations still of anti-colonial judge-ments and dreamings. The 'anti-colonial' in any given situation understood thus is, by spirit and imagination, a living articulation and manifestation of and for beingness-otherwise than *made-subject*, such affirmations of being-ness do not cease in time, even as they may lie dormant in circumstances. And this, we find, is indeed the other actuality of the present.

Let me restate the argument. The (post)colonial World, asserted as 'post-colonial', is a totality *(b)ordered* and enforced through the philosophies and technologies of global coloniality. Indeed, the norm-alisation of Colo-nial-Modern (b)orders through the universal rationalisation of the 'post-co-lonial' situation is precisely the fulfilment of the onto-epistemological and material processes of *colonisation*. Against this totalising force remains the persistent presence of *anti-colonial Reason*. As a situation and praxes what this means is the repudiation of the assertion and attempted norm-alisation

---

32 Basil Davidson, *The Black Man's Burden: Africa and the Curse of the Nation-State* (London: James Currey, 1992) 185.
33 *Ibid.*, 196.

of (post)colonial (b)orders. Asserted instead are worlds of *frontlines,* that is to
say, worlds fully to be reclaimed, renamed, remade, otherwise.

On (B)orders as the Norm-alisation of Coloniality

We know this: this *World,* as we know it, as we assume it to be, is made by
(b)orders, discursive and physical, matters of philosophy and of technology.
In *this* World are the 'global poor' (persistent) *subjects.* Their enduring fate is
not simply the consequence of intransigence by philosophers of the 'Global
North' to recognise and effect the claims of 'global justice', but fully the
actualities of the norm-alised (b)ordering of this *World.* All talk of politics
and law and its philosophies, of 'development' and 'security' and 'rights'
and its associated theories, all of these are, at their core, talk of (b)orders and
(b)ordering. And it is precisely the effects of 'colonisation' that a particular
regime of words and meanings, a particular architecture of (un)violence, a
particular imagination of possible futures of a *World* of obscene wealth and
utter abjection, has come to be understood as sensible, even if inhumane,
meaningful, even if perverse. That we understand this *World* as norm-ality is
fully the result of the enforcement of the assumption and assertion of (post)
colonial (b)orders and (b)orderings.[34]

Now, given such actualities, it is not as if there have not been sustained
interrogations of 'borders' as technologies of *World*-making.[35] We know that
(b)orders are elusive, they appear here, there, then somewhere else. Critical
theorists have anguished over this problem, seeking to get a handle on the
border, and on the elusive theory-practice of 'sovereignty' as a (b)ordering category of law and politics. They have understood that the *border* is more than
merely a 'line in the sand', revealing clearly the racialised, biopolitical violence
of global (b)ordering. They ponder over the implications of the shifting nature
of borders under regimes of contemporary global surveillance and enforcement
now pervasive under the ever-expanding conditions of the 'war on terror'.
Their insights are rich. And yet, they miss the underlying point.

For all the critical contemplation of the coloniality, and imperialism, of
borders as a discourse and technology of bio/necropolitical separation and

---

34 As we will see, this, a point I repeat throughout this work.
35 See, for example, Saskia Sassen, 'Bordering Capabilities Versus Borders: Implications for National
    Borders', *Michigan Journal of International Law* 30, 2009, 567-97; Nick Vaughn-Williams, *Border
    Politics: The Limits of Sovereign Power* (Edinburgh: Edinburgh University Press, 2009); Harsha Walia,
    Undoing Border Imperialism (Oakland: AK Press, 2013), and *Border & Rule: Global Migration,
    Capitalism, and the Rise of Racist Nationalism* (Chicago: Haymarket Books, 2021); Nadine El-Enany,
    (B)ordering Britain: Law, Race and Empire (Manchester: Manchester University Press, 2020).

differentiation, we remain entranced, it seems, by its claim to 'worldliness'.[36] Even as the operation of (b)orders has been much considered, the essential idea of *border,* as a philosophical sensibility, as a regime of meaning-fulness upon the World, remains largely uninterrogated, simply assumed.[37] This we see at work even in recent 'decolonial' efforts to directly open to question the presumed normality and finality of *borders* through the pedagogy and episte-mology of 'border thinking'. Walter Mignolo and Madina Tlostanova:

> [border thinking is] the epistemology of the exteriority; that is, of the outside created from the inside. ... Border thinking brings to the foreground different kinds of theoretical actors and principles of knowledge that displace European modernity (which articulated the very concept of theory in the social sciences and the humanities) and empower those who have been epistemically disempowered by the theo- and ego-politics of knowledge.[38]

In this description we see that the 'border', as an onto-epistemological category, is retained as the point of reference from which 'exteriority' is sought to be retrieved and brought to the 'foreground'. 'Border thinking' thinks from the 'border' as point of departure, critically so, yes, but in the situation of the 'border' nevertheless. This is already to concede everything, in that it fundamentally accedes to the assumptions of coloniality that renders (b)orders meaningful.

The 'border', we recall, is a categorical inscription upon worlds, the result of colonial assertions of material appropriation and discursive impo-sition. It makes sense as a consequence of imposed namings and negations,

---

36 See Achille Mbembe:

> In fact, everything leads back to borders – these dead spaces of non-connection which deny the very idea of a shared humanity ... But perhaps, to be completely exact, we should not speak of borders but of "borderization". What, then, is this "borderiza-tion," if not the process by which world powers permanently transform certain spaces into impassable paces for certain classes of populations?; *Necropolitics* (Durham: Duke University Press, 2019) 99.

While Mbembe points directly to the ubiquitous absurdity and violence of 'borderization', the idea of the 'border' remains intact, inhumane, yet intact. In the attempt to bring to attention, the effects of 'borderisation' – in Mbembe's usage the effecting of borders as spatial demarcations – what is lost is an opening to question of the very assertion of 'borders' itself as a philosophical manoeuvre of bordering that inheres in the assumption of coloniality-normality.

37 El-Enany's recent examination of the imperial origins and continuities of British (b)ordering and her argument for an anti-colonial response to contemporary 'colonial space' is a notable exception to this general rule; see *(B)Ordering Britain.*

38 Walter D. Mignolo and Madina V. Tlostanova, 'Theorizing from the Borders: Shifting the Geo- and Body-Politics of Knowledge' *European Journal of Social Theory* 9(2), 2006, 205-21, 206-7.

of demarcations, differentiations, permissions and prohibitions that follow from this original assertion of 'author-ity', of the *Right* to *name* the situation. Given this assumption of predominance, 'border thinking', even as it intends to rupture the assertion of totality that seeks to define 'exteriority', is to already think as 'subject-ed', already to succumb to the *World* made by the colonial imagination. 'Border thinking' might therefore enable the negotiation of epistemological variances of 'alterity' to the categories of the normal – from the 'exteriority' as Mignolo and Tlostanova put it – but it remains subject and subordinate; the many examples of 'indigenous rights' claims, its 'successes' and 'failures', being examples of the various *re-settlements* of the hierarchical relationship between '(b)orders' and 'border thinking' in this regard.[39] Notwithstanding Mignolo's 'decolonial' intention to 'de-link' – to change not simply the 'conversation' but its 'terms'[40] – the 'border' remains the 'sovereign' location and situation which demands *a priori* recognition, defining therefore the terms upon which any conversation is deemed comprehensible, permissible, remaining secure as both a material marker upon the World and preeminent discursive category with which to speak the *World*. I understand something fundamentally different than 'border-thinking' when I speak of an 'anti-colonial' situation. Against the assumption of the priority and primacy of '(b)ordered' namings and meanings, and the assertion of a fundamental commensurability of *subjected*-beingness, the reclaiming of *frontlines* radically repudiates any claim of the *border* as essentially 'meaning-ful'. If the *Idea* of the *border* aims to settle the question of coloniality, it is the intention of the *frontline* precisely to open it right up.

I will return to a fuller elaboration shortly. First, we de-reify the 'border' as a category relevant to 'political-legal' philosophy.

(B)orders, whatever they might be, be they ones that demarcate ('national/international') territoriality, or those that define regimes of regulation (of ascribed differentiations), are simply temporal inventions that assert a settlement, of time, place, and peoples within a social, political-legal imagination. To name and claim a '(b)order' is in effect to demarcate History, to

---

39 For a scathing critique of the 'politics of recognition' in this regard, see Glen Coulthard, *Red Skin, White Masks: Rejecting the Colonial Politics of Recognition* (Minneapolis: University of Minnesota Press, 2014). In contrast to the mediated appeals of 'indigenous rights' as articulated for State-sovereign dispensation, the recoveries and rememberings of incommensurable cosmologies offer a very different knowing of worlds; see the rich collection of essays in Lynn Stephen and Shannon Speed (eds.) *Indigenous Women and Violence: Feminist Activist Research in Heightened States of Injustice* (Tucson: University of Arizona Press, 2021.

40 See Walter D. Mignolo, 'Delinking: The Rhetoric of Modernity, the Logic of Coloniality and the Grammar of Decoloniality', *Cultural Studies* 21(2-3), 2007, 449-514.

settle the infinite possibilities of the future within a fixed meaning of the past-present. The *border*, thus understood, operates as a technology of norm-alisation that renders meaningful the 'orders' thereby created and enforced, that render commensurable the inscriptions and ascriptions of 'subjection/subjectivities' thereby norm-alised. The 'worldliness' of borders is key to its operation. By wordliness I mean the apparent assumption of the meaningfulness of the *Idea* – the border – in our understanding and sensibility of the *World*, of our very imagination of *this* World. When the *border* is spoken of, when it is critiqued, when its 'injustices' are denounced, it is not the veracity, or the contingency of the *Idea* that is at issue, simply the particular (re)distribution of inscriptions of *names* and ascriptions of *meanings*, or put differently, a particular resettlement of (b)ordered 'subject-beingness', that is opened up for renegotiation. The *border* as such, in this situation, is understood as sensible and meaningful, in and of itself, no matter the many depravities thereby inflicted upon those deemed unwanted. With the assertion and the (violent) enforcement of the *Idea* of *borders* as a worldly category, therefore, is the colonial-modern *World* 'made' and norm-alised. Out of the original, colonising and imperial philosophy of *frontiers* – that assumption of a worldscape of *Nothingness* beyond the *Self* open to 'discovery' and 'conquest' – is the assertion and normalisation of the Idea of (b)orders entrenched in philosophies of rationalisation and technologies of 'govern-ment'.[41] Thus is the *World* and its markers asserted as ubiquitous, its inscriptions of (Non) Being made sensible, its absurdities of differentiated 'life' made meaningful, its *Reason* rendered 'natural'. This is coloniality resettled in the 'post-colonial' arrangement; this, the work of (post)colonial philosophy to do. There is different work, long neglected in the delusion of the 'post-colonial', now to be done.

On Frontlines as Situations of Encounter

An *anti-colonial* praxis begins with a repudiation of the assumptions and the enforced norm-alisation of (post)colonial (b)orders the result of insurgent thinking-being that persists in struggle. We describe here, in simple terms, an *encounter*: the frontline is the anti-colonial location of encounter, a 'ground' – both of 'name' and matter – reclaimed from the (post)colonial assertion of (b)orders. The frontline, in other words, is the assertion of a location of thought against the assumption and infliction of (b)ordered subjection. The

---

41 See for example Henk van Houtmum and Rodrigo Bueno Lacy, *Frontiers https://henkvanhoutum.nl/wp-content/uploads/2017/03/Frontiers.pdf* (last accessed, 20 April 2021)

point is critical: what is assumed as the *norm-ality* of the *World* is simply an *assertion* of a philosophical totality, enforced thereby by the manifold technologies of normalised violence upon those subjected with the ultimate intention of *colonisation*. It is precisely this assertion of a (b)ordered Totality – of 'making-subject' to and within a totality of names and meanings, words and imagination – that is opened up, made visible, and repudiated, by the anti-colonial insistence of encounter, of the *frontline*. Therefore, with this assertion, of a claiming back of beingness as such, all 'names' and meaning that are sought to be imposed as (b)orders of the *World* lose their assumed worldliness and become clear as little more than a contingent philosophoscape and architecture of a particular imagination and desire, parochial and fragile. Obviously, it is this fragility of the *World*, this utter lack of solidity of the names and meanings that purportedly make *this* World, that must at all costs be hidden from view. And so it is, the hard work of (post)colonial philosophy to police and regulate, to *norm-alise*, the ontological categories and epistemological frames of knowing the *World*. All this effort notwithstanding, the *anti-colonial* presence of *frontlines* remains a persistent actuality. (B)orders, in other words, are less fixed in their colonising effect than we, (critical) 'political-legal' thinkers/practitioners, might assume them to be.

If *border thinking* seeks to bring to attention *exteriority* as a location and origination of thought, to reinsert *alterity* as an actuality of beingness in the situation of the 'border', the assertion of *frontlines* breaks open the assumption of the *border* entirely. In this situation we confront an incommensurable encounter, not *exteriority* within a (b)ordered totality, not alterity to a presumed norm-ality, but an open situation in which the very assumptions of 'totality' and 'norm-ality' are repudiated. It is necessary to stress that we are not simply dealing with a play of words here – *borders/frontlines*; although the difference might initially appear as an argument over terminological abstractions, the consequences of the categorical difference I assert are radically significant. On the one hand, we address the meaningfulness of (assumed) *borders* as the norm-alisation of violent *orders* even as we oppose them, and against that, on the other, we speak of the praxes of struggles that repudiate the very foundational claim of asserted (b)orders to totalisation. Indeed, our words determine the lens through which we view, see, and understand the actualities we encounter. In their difference lies the claim to the *World* itself.

What I describe as frontlines, therefore, is not a new invention for philosophy, nor is it in any way a description of *extraordinariness*.[42] Resistance to subjection and onto-epistemological closure, that is to say, to *being-made-subject* by (post)colonial (b)ordering, is a pervasive presence that ruptures the assertions of totality that inhere in dominant political-legal re-presentations of (un)belonging. 'Frontline' struggles in this sense have never ceased and will never do. Indeed, they are the everyday struggles that resist attempts at subjugation now enforced under all manner of 'post-colonial' guises and reasons. When understood in this light, *frontlines* mark out situations of incommensurable encounters of struggle and regeneration wherein beingness in its materiality is reclaimed from (post)colonial settlements. From the very origins of namings which rationalised and enforced the racialised trans-Atlantic slave trade and subsequent colonial subjugations have such refusals to be contained within assigned names and enforced wretched-beingness been entirely co-eval; the 'maroon thinking' of rebellious slaves in their liberated territories being the very early assertions of being-otherwise from the inscriptions of inflicted universal commensurability.[43] Examples of assertions of refusal, past and present, abound and we frequently invoke them in our critiques of the *World*. How we understand them, interpret them, invoke them, however, are matters of philosophical positioning, of literally being on one side or the other of the colonial divide, of being on one side or the other of the '(b)order/frontline'.[44] It is this point

---

42 For a discussion on the preoccupation of the 'extraordinary' in critical 'Eurocentric' thought, see Jayan Nayar, 'Some Thoughts on the "(Extra)Ordinary": Philosophy, Coloniality, and Being Otherwise', *Alternatives: Global, Local, Political* 42(1), 2017, 3-25.

43 See Catherine Walsh, '"Other" Knowledges, "Other" Critiques: Reflections on the Politics and Practices of Philosophy and Decoloniality in the "Other" America', *Transmodernity: Journal of Peripheral Cultural Production of the Luso-Hispanic World* 1(3), 2012, 11-27.

44 Taking historical examples, so we might understand Frederick Douglass' repudiation of the call to liberty attached to the US celebrations of the 4th of July; Mohandas Gandhi's proclamation of *Swaraj* that denies the British claims to legitimate subjection; Bhimrao Ambedkar's repudiation of the Hindu 'caste' system and its rationalisation of socio-religious hierarchies; Steve Biko's affirmation of "Black Consciousness" as a reclaiming of thought and being from White denials and subordination; Amilcar Cabral's call to 'cultural resistance' as a means of mass mobilisation against colonial 'cultural occupation'; Paolo Freire's intent of "conscientisation" as a pedagogy of refusal to abide by the namings and emplacements of extant regimes of oppression; Gloria Anzaldua's rebellious courage of being "mestiza" in the "borderlands"; all as articulations of being-ness that refuse the inscriptions of prescribed names and emplacements within the norm-alised (b)orders of subjection and subjugation. See Frederick Douglass's, 'The Meaning of July Fourth for the Negro', *History is a Weapon*, available at <http://www.historyisaweapon.com/defcon1/douglassjuly4.html> (last accessed 26 September 2020); Mohandas K. Gandhi *Hind Swaraj* (Ahmedabad: Navajivan Pub. House, 1938), available at <http://www.mkgandhi.org/ebks/hind_swaraj.pdf> (last accessed 20 August 2020); B.R. Ambedkar, *Annihilation of Caste: The Annotated Critical Edition* (London: Verso, 2016); Steve Biko, *I Write What I Like; A Selection of His Writings* (London: Bowerdean Press, 1978); Amilcar Cabral, 'The Role of Culture in the Struggle for Independence' in Amilcar Cabral, *Resistance and Decolonisation*, 159-179; Paolo Freire *Pedagogy of the Oppressed* (London: Penguin, 1974); Gloria Anzaldua, *Borderlands/La Frontera: The New Mestiza* (San Francisco: Aunt Lute Books, 1987).

specifically that I stress here. While we are inundated with the many instances and affirmations of beingness in *frontlines*, it appears we have rather less dignified them with philosophical import. This is our failure.

Frontlines persist, ever as contemporary contexts of *anti-colonial* praxes in (post)colonial presents, even if we are beguiled to not recognise their pervasiveness. So long as we are enthralled by the distractions of (b)orders derived from the norm-alising categories of (post)colonial philosophies, even as we protest their workings in the *World*, we continue to reinforce the coloniality of the 'post-colonial' settlement and its assertion of the *Right* and *author-ity* of 'just' violence as norm-ality, as totality. By doing so, we in effect affirm both the work of (post)colonial philanderers who have made *this* World of violence though their actions, and the work of (post)colonial philosophers who in turn have rationalised this *World* through their Words. More significantly, unforgivably, we negate the actualities of frontlines everywhere present.[45] This, ultimately, is a betrayal of thought.

So, this is what it means to return the anti-colonial situation to philosophy. From the vantage point of (b)orders, there is an inside and outside. From its discursive *universe,* there is an 'us' and 'them, 'legality' and 'illegality', 'security' and 'terror'; the terminology is familiar. From the vantage points of the *frontline*, however, we see the *World* – *this* World – differently, where both meaning and sense evaporate. We see that the magnificent constellation of names and philosophical categories mentioned above, and the complex architecture of rules and institutions that together seek to govern the actualities and possibilities of human beingness, all bear little actual meaning to the lives subjected to deprivation and subjugation in the everyday normalities of this *World*, bar in its brutal enforcement. We understand that for all the grandeur of proclamation and the sophistication of philosophical erudition attached to these Ideas of Humanity, these are little but edifices constructed out of shadows and ghosts, real only through their repetition, true only through their deceit, yet for all that, utterly material in the cruelty and violence they inflict upon those subjected to their predation. This *World* of the present in its entirety we see clearly as a *(post)colonial* artefact, necessarily, as Ariella

---

45 As examples of the global pervasiveness of varied contexts of resistance despite the increasing levels of political violence meted out for the 'security' of 'business-as-usual' the world over; see generally, Amory Starr, Luis Fernandez and Christian Scholl, *Shutting Down the Streets: Political Violence and Social Control in the Global Era* (New York: New York University Press, 2011); Kate Khatib, Margaret Killjoy and Mike McGuire, *We Are Many: Reflections on Movement Strategy from Occupation to Liberation* (Chico, Calif: AK Press, 2013); Boaventura Monjane (Ed.), *We Rise for Our Land: Land Struggles and Repression in Southern Africa* (Quebec: Daraja Press, 2021)

Aïsha Azoulay invites us to do, to be 'unlearnt'.[46] Precisely the *World*, therefore, is in question.

Against the assumption and incessant violent assertions of *(b)orders* – as a norm-alised totality of settled inscriptions of names, ascriptions of meanings, and the affixing of architectures of demarcation, differentiation, and separation – always latent, persistent, are the refusals and disruptions of imaginations that name (b)orders seditiously as *frontlines*. And this is an incontrovertible truth: every border, wherever they might be erected and enforced, remains co-constitutively a *frontline*.[47] It can never be otherwise in the actual worlds of human-beingness, whatever the totalising desires of the rulers, and plunderers of the world. If *(b)orders* assert a settlement of the many worlds whose names and meanings are denied and sought to be erased to make the *World* as a Totality, *frontlines* call to remember, disrupt, refute, reconfigure worlds, otherwise than *colonised*. It is this reality that underpins the *anti-colonial* as a philosophical situation.

Therefore, On Praxis

As I assert it, the *anti-colonial* situation is entirely intended as a situation of experience; it is, simply, a restatement of a lived philosophy. I am not here concerned with a play on words even as the choice of words are essential to my understanding and argument. *(B)orders* and *frontlines*, these I have suggested as the fundamental incommensurability of assertions in claiming presence in the *World*/worlds. Situation and praxis, I have used these in conjunction to put forward the significance of what I mean by returning the *anti-coloni*al to philosophy. By these words I intend to communicate a way of being-in-the-world. *Praxis*, therefore, in conjunction with the assertion of a *situation*; together they point to the convergence of philosophy and life, as if any separation was ever truthfully possible.

My usage of praxis is quite uncomplicated; it is rooted in the pasts and presents of anti-colonial struggle and experience. Praxis, as anti-colonial beingness, is not so much burdened by the apparent difficulties of returning the 'practical' to philosophy, a problem that appears to have afflicted *European* ruminations on the question.[48] A different understanding of praxis

---

46 Ariella Aïsha Azoulay, *Potential History: Unlearning Imperialism* (London: Verso, 2019).

47 It is interesting that practitioners of (b)ordering are fully conversant with and attentive to frontline thinking. We see much reference to borders as frontlines in the discourse on 'security', 'migration', 'terror' etc. where indeed the protection of (b)orders are proactively and 'pre-emptively/preventively' undertaken as frontline operations against global threats! For a discussion, see José Pedro Zúquete, 'The new frontlines of right-wing nationalism, *Journal of Political Ideologies*, 20(1), 2015, 69-85.

48 From Marx, then to Gramsci and onwards, the idea of praxis has generated a thread in post-'European

persists. In this the 'practical' is always present as a vibrant collective space of thought-action regardless of whether philosophers of the 'European Enlightenment', and later, of 'post-colonial' governmentality, understood it or were willing to accord it recognition. This is praxis as an actuality of living thought, of thinking-being confronted by the impositions and possibilities of the *World* as experienced.[49] And precisely this actuality of anti-colonial beingness is that which (post)colonial philosophy cannot abide, the 'practical' as a location and instance of philosophy is precisely negated by the languages of the (b)orders which essentially has to be maintained as abstractions, pristine, even sanctified, as constructions of idealised, reified totalities of imagination.[50] From an anti-colonial perspective, from perspectives for which (b)orders are entirely 'practical' in their violence and subjugating oppres-

---

Enlightenment' critical thinking to return the realm of the 'practical' to philosophical contemplations. This is an interesting, internal, discussion, a familial sociological argument one might say, that seeks to achieve two outcomes as I see it: first, to make philosophy relevant to the material world as a contemplation of the dialectical relationship between 'thought' and 'action' in social change, and secondly, relatedly, to transfer the philosophical situation from the realm of the ideal – a location and space reserved for the privileges of 'sovereign' power – to that of the mundane, the locations and situations of struggle, of resistance, of transformation. For a discussion of this tradition of thinking the 'practical', see Eva von Redecker (trans. Lucy Duggan), *Praxis and Revolution* (Columbia University Press, 2021)

49 I adopt here a view which is inspired by Paolo Freire, even if I do not quite adopt it in terms of any presumed understanding of 'liberation': "Liberation is a praxis: the action and reflection of men and women upon their world in order to transform it."; Freire, *Pedagogy of the Oppressed*, 60. For my purposes, it is praxis rather than liberation that is of anti-colonial consequence, the question of 'liberation' perhaps an imagination too heavily invested in 'post-Enlightenment' mythologies. In any case, the emphasis for Freire, remained 'pedagogy' as praxiological.

50 On this, Partha Chatterjee's excellent evocation of the 'politics of the governed' can be understood as an important correction; *The Politics of the Governed: Reflections on Popular Politics in Most of the World* (New York: Columbia University Press, 2004). Chatterjee's innovation is in correcting the 'empty homogenous time-space' of politics as it is assumed to be in its conventional restrictive understanding with the multi-layered and textured description of 'heterogenous time'. In this way, is the apparent dichotomy between the abstracted 'citizen' that is the subject of political-beingness' and the actualities of diverse and intractable 'populations' left mostly outside of the scope of conventional political reckoning bridged, both the effects of 'government' and of the very real presence of such 'populations' as political 'subjects/agents/actors returned to clearer visibility. This is of obvious importance. However, Chatterjee's insights remain in the frame of (b)orders, the intention to correct what is properly understood as 'political society' and 'democracy'; while presence and vitality is understood and recognised, even celebrated, what is retained is an analysis that assumes the norm-ality of the structures and discourses of 'government' from which, against which, the politics of the governed becomes meaningful. The following succinctly explains Chatterjee's intention:

> What I have tried to show is that alongside the abstract promise of popular sovereignty, people in most of the world are devising new ways in which they can choose how they should be governed. Many of the forms of political society I have described would not, I suspect, meet with Aristotle's approval, because they would appear to him to allow popular leaders to take precedence over the law. But we might, I think, be able to persuade him that in this way the people are learning, and forcing their governors to learn, how they might prefer to be governed. That, the wise Greek might agree, is a good ethical justification for democracy. (77-78)

Mine is a different argument.

siveness, there is no such difficulty, reifications of idealised 'philosophies' of the pristine less enchanting it their allure. Seen thus,(b)orders are essentially fragile, and praxis as the condition of beingness in frontlines, essentially resilient. Always so. Never mind 'theory's' difficulties of incorporation of the 'inexistent'. Never mind, philosophy's discomfort with the recalcitrant. The fact of the *World* is that the *subjected-subjugated* do speak, do judge, do act, indeed, they do 'think'.[51]

A clear and unambiguous statement, take it as an assertion, of the following *principles of praxes* that lie at the crux of what it means to return the anti-colonial to lived philosophy, is appropriate here. We might regard these indeed as the *attitude* of what it means to be *anti-colonial-in-encounter*:

- *Judgement*: the assumption of the presence/power to judge the enforced *norm-alities* of the *World* and to name as violation that which is otherwise proclaimed as normalcy.
- *Authorship*: the assumption of the presence/power to author normative and regulatory philosophoscapes of sociality and to define the structures and nature of social relationship conducive to life.
- *Control*: the assumption of the presence/power to control the processes of decision-making and judgement in relation to the matters which affect the conditions of social beingness.
- *Action*: the assumption of presence/power to effect the 'regulation', 'implementation', and enforcement. of alternative visions of social relationships.

There is nothing surprising here, nothing particularly 'radical' in the affirmation of this actuality; all incidences of 'resistance' simply manifestations of some aspect of these principles of thinking-being in the World. Who dares argue otherwise?

Let me be clear. These principles – of judgement, authorship, control, action – are not 'theorisations' of perceived 'practice'. Neither are they accounts of 'agency', of the capacities that might be discerned for 'subaltern' thought/action in the grips of hegemonic/dominant constraints of the 'political'. They do not, in other words, serve as theoretical postulates which seek to insert the *governed* into the sphere of the *political*. All of these presuppose

---

51 See Hamid Dabashi, *Can Non-Europeans Think...* It is necessary to point to the absurdity of this indulgence, by way of indignation to the constant affront of 'European' philosophers, in addressing the question "Can Non-Europeans Think?" Hamid Dabashi and Walter Mignolo do a fine job in eviscerating Slavoj Zizek (and Santiago Zabala, who's initial ruminations prompted Dabashi's reaction) in this work; this is not the point. The point is that the ignorance and arrogance of Zizek is even deemed worthy of attention such that a response was felt necessary.

the givenness of (b)ordered totalities into which insertions are imagined. The anti-colonial as praxis in my account of *frontlines* begins from an altogether different point of departure. As such, these principles of praxes are advanced as an assertion, properly a claim against the World made by those, entirely present, encountering the *World* as an actuality of enforced subjection/subjugation. They are, therefore, assertions that arise in situations and locations of thinking-being which repudiate the regimes of inscriptions derived from (post)colonial *Reason*; indeed they assert a reclaiming of *worlds* both as a matter of philosophy and material reality. In judgements regarding the actualities of the World, through authorship of the meanings and materialities of located beingness, by assuming control of the many implications of thinking-being in encounters against *colonisation*, in effecting the actions of *lived-life* in space and time, whatever they might be, 'violent' or not, we see in all such actualities of 'resistance' and 'regeneration' what it means to encounter the enforced (b)orders of (post)colonial subjection. Simply put, in these principles are found and expressed the foundations of, and extrapolations from, the (extra)ordinary affirmations of the original "*No!*" that are worldwide persistent, followed – and this is less considered in 'critical theory' – by so many persistent recoveries of being-'other-wise'.[52] We might usefully recall Freire here:

> Human existence cannot be silent, nor can it be nourished by false words, but only by true words, with which men and women transform the world. To exist, humanly, is to *name* the world, to change it. Once named, the world in its turn reappears to the namers as a problem and requires of them a new naming. Human beings are not built in silence, but in word, in work, in action-reflection.[53]

And yet, silence is precisely the assumption and enforcement of (post)colonial philosophy which begins and ends with the silencing of lived lives-as-such as it ever exalts the (lifeless) Being(-Becoming) of Life-in-subjection. This is philosophy as containment, as domestication, the taming of life into the false words of (post)colonial categories – of the 'political' and the 'legal' – that are indeed the false words that *build* the *colonised-subject*.

---

52 Catherine Walsh's describes this as 'pedagogical action', of importance is its persistence, its ubiquity, its refusal to be disappeared, perpetually in movement, 'asking' while 'walking; Catherine Walsh, 'Decolonial pedagogies walking asking. Notes to Paolo Friere from AbyaYala' *International Journal of Lifelong Education*, 34(1), 2015, 9-21, at 11-12

53 Freire, *Pedagogy of the Oppressed*, 69, (reference omitted. Emphasis in original)

So, this the point, the moment, the situation of philosophical significance. Against the fixations and closures of a philosophy of *(b)orders*, the praxis of *frontlines* as a matter of lived philosophy, as a vital expression and manifestation of beingness-in-the-World, this I understand as entirely untameable, the actuality of human-beingness un-*colonised*. This is simply to state, to bring to attention, what is, always so, even as it might appear otherwise. It is by reason of these 'principles' of praxes that 'resistance' comes to be, that struggle is manifest, that *colonisation* remains ever incomplete, even as (post) colonial conquests are ever sought to be realised.[54] This indeed is a matter of living, of the everydays of (un)heroic presence, the judgements, authorship, control and action of communities of struggle against the attempted norm-alisations of coloniality These realities of *being-anti-colonial* are everywhere present, open to view and to understanding. All it requires is that *we*, interpreters of the *World*, repudiate the manifold invisibilisations and silencings that is the work of both the philosophies, and the violent technologies, of (post)colonial (b)orderings. This is my intention.

In the chapters that follow, in Part Two, I address some of the assumed closures of thought, of imagination, that purportedly define the *World*. These are, I argue, foundational, the essential categories – false words – that remain categorically entrenched. I do not cover issues of complaint as such, on 'development' or 'human rights', of 'migration' or 'climate injustice', of 'humanitarian interventions' or 'land grabs', on the numerous issues that have indeed been, rightly, repeated causes for complaint. What follows instead are examinations of the foundational categories of the (post)colonial *making* of the *World* as we assume it to be, as norm-alised, as *normal*. Precisely this repudiation of 'false words' and the assertion of new 'namings' are the tasks involved if we mean to return the *anti-colonial*, as situation and praxis, to philosophy.

---

54 We return to these points in our discussion on the Postcolony in Chapter 4.

PART TWO

Much of critical work from the 'Global South' has sought to engage with the philoso-phers of (post)coloniality as if such corrections to their racism, their imperialism, etc, would shed light upon their errors and thereby rectify the 'injustices' of this World. My intention is different.

I begin with the argument that what we regard as the norm-ality of the World is enitrely a (post)colonial worldscape originally constructed out of particular regimes of names and meanings imposed upon conquered/subjugated populations, then norm-al-ised, as a commensurable totality through the 'post-colonial' settlement. This move to construct a 'state-territorial' architecture of global (b)ordering was significant. It was not, however, terminal. I assert this fundamental point: the anti-colonial as a philo-sophical situation cannot, is not, terminated by any prescription of a 'post-colonial' settlement. Put differently, the World remains subject to anti-colonial judgement.

The work of anti-colonial philosophy is to ask the questions that de-normalise the colonial assertion even as it does not promise ready answers to questions of the future. When viewed from this vantage point the philosophical significance of recasting the assertion of the (post)colonial border as a question of an anti-colonial frontline is clear. The anti-colonial frontline – a question opened up by an assertion of encounter – marks a refusal to be-colonised, that is, to be-subject; it is an enactment of de-naming the (b)order, of refusing totalising orders of subject-beingness and emplacements. The anti-colonial frontline, therefore, is a praxiological space of desubjectification. It is disruptive in intent and rebellious in imagination. The de-naming of (b)orders through the enunciations of the frontlines is that philosophical move which enables us to pries open the closures of 'post-colonial' settlements – in all of their many and varied material and discursive manifestation – to continuing interrogations which reassert the priority, still, of anti-colonial Reason.

Let us be clear as we proceed. Philosophers of domination, of (post)colonial norm-ality, may object to any such presumptuousness to repudiate their claims to World-making. Quite simply, this is of no concern; ours is the work to think notwith-standing such demands for 'civil-ised' compliance. This is the intention of the chapters that follow.

Enough with generalities. We begin. False words. Essential frontlines.

3

On Black(-ed) Lives (and White) Matter

'Splendour in squalor', let us keep this description close to attention, the desperate impoverishment of the many and the vulgar enrichment of the few.[1] This is the *World* we know, a world in which the pathology of greed and cruelty is normalised, regulated and enforced not as a particular or parochial imagination but as an assertion of universality. All this the legacy, the artefact, of a worldscape, borne out of a philosophoscape that we know as Coloniality-Modernity.

This chapter takes on, as a matter of a *frontline,* the most basic foundation of this totalising philosophoscape. I am interested here in the issue of a *World* 'racialised', 'coloured-in', as it were. When we speak today of 'White' in the World, of 'Black' and 'Coloured' in the World, of all that is literally skin-deep, what is at issue is the implicit background, and frame, within which the entire architecture of meaning of what we now regard as fundamental 'political-legal' categories is constructed and maintained. This is what is fundamentally involved, what is fundamentally at stake: the very 'racialised' foundations of (post)colonial (b)orders.

'Black Lives' Matter?

We are familiar with outrage: "Black lives matter", we say, "please don't shoot", "I can't breathe", as we protest the collective trans-generational 'knee' on the incalculable lives of so-called 'people of colour'. This we do upon instances

---

1 See Ngũgĩ wa Thiong'o, *Secure the Base: Making Africa Visible in the Globe* (London: Seagull Books, 2016); *Jason Hickel, The Divide: A Brief Guide to Global Inequality and its Solutions* (London: Windmill Books, 2017).

of outrage, yet another after another, against 'Black' lives. And so, we recite names, too many names, too frequently recited.

There are other numbers too, of course, of 'Black-ed' lives, less conspicuous in their disposability. These are seldom with name, a global account of excess of sorts: x die of starvation daily; y children are malnourished; z have inadequate shelter/access to clean water/sanitation...the litany of numbers in columns that spell out destitution, abjection, wretchedness, *normality*, as a mass condition of global (in)humanity! We are so used to this bureaucratic accounting of wretchedness, so accustomed to begin our analyses, diagnoses, prescriptions therefrom, to record our dismay and disgust at these *routine* perversions, these cruelties, these insufferable realities, as we protest again, appeal for action again, demand rectification again, seemingly unceasingly, to account for these instances of violence and systemic normalities of inhumanity.[2] And this is the point: *normality*. Or more accurately, as I have repeatedly stated, *norm-ality*.

'Black' live matter? The situation is this. It is 500 years and more of an onto-epistemology of insatiable appropriation and subjugation that is the legacy calling for change. This is a big order. But magnitude aside, something more profound is at stake. The question is: what will account for a radical overturning of this 'system of reality' as James Baldwin called it so many years ago,[3] a system entrenched, normalised, and legislated for, founded as it was on the undisputable fact of oppression and racialised differentiation. Amongst critical circles, we have come to call this system of reality 'Global Whiteness', we identify the normativity of 'Whiteness-as-property' projected upon a global scale.[4] It will take more than 'reform'.[5] More than a few repeated acknowledgements. More than a few statues toppled or taken down. More than a few 'coloured', 'minority', installations in high offices, more than marches organised and fists shown, and knees taken. More than some progressive passing of legislation, even. All of this is no doubt valuable, but none quite go to the core of the problem.

No, the truth of it is that 'Black' lives don't matter. They cannot. Not in this *World*. It is important that we recognise that this is categorically so, to

---

2 See Chapter 6 for an elaboration of what I term 'routine un/violence'.

3 James Baldwin, 'James Baldwin debates William F Buckley 1965', *aeon*, 8 August 2019, available at <https://aeon.co/videos/the-legendary-debate-that-laid-down-us-political-lines-on-race-justice-and-history> (last accessed 18 February 2022).

4 Cheryl I. Harris 'Whiteness as Property', *Harvard Law Review* 106(8), 1993, 1710-789.

5 For a concise and self-critical comment on the past and present of the struggle against White supremacy in the United States, see Glen Ford, 'Protest and Power', *Black Agenda Report*, 2 July 2020, available at <https://www.blackagendareport.com/protest-and-power?fbclid=IwAR1bIPmbbcCBs0t_IQroT-sIppK_C65W0-gUhN63fpyaygDtpLBroERm5Mjo> (last accessed 9 July 2020).

understand the weight of this truth however unpalatable it might first appear. *Black*-ed lives don't matter.

A System of Reality and a Problem for Thought

We agree that the prevailing system of the World – Baldwin's system of reality – is that of global 'White'-ness.[6] This said, consider the question: can we imagine and realise a 'Black'-beingness that is not categorically co-constituted by an ontology of *being-Black-ed*?

Let me begin by saying that I view all 'disturbances' effected by the protests regenerated by the disregard for 'Black'-ed lives as entirely within the realms of utter reasonableness; indeed, it has all been too reasonable – this is a point we will return to. The assumptions and normalities of 'Whiteness' within the metropolitan centres of chattel slavery and racialised colonialism deserve every bit of disruption coming to them, every revelation of the *underside* of complacent and normalised Whiteness, pressed against the faces of those resisting such unruly emergences into 'polite' public spaces, is both necessary and worthwhile as expressions of historical rage. Having said this, what we have witnessed thus far is little in the larger scheme of things; worse, they risk the danger of distraction and deflection, entirely insufficient to substantively address the problem of *White-ness* as a conditioning structure of global coloniality. Something fundamentally different is required, both philosophically to understand fully the situation of the present, and materially to then encounter and engage the *World* of enforced *White*-ness. But before I proceed to outline what I mean by this, it is essential that we first address a prior, fundamentally erroneous, assumption.

On Life, as Such, and Lives as Such

I want here to dispose of a prevailing and undoubtedly appealing belief: that *life*, as such, matters, and from this, that *lives* as such matter. This is the critical error through which the cunning of metaphysical 'European' – let me call it that – 'White'-ness operates at its most devious.[7] I realise that I here

---

6 I consider the usual naming that is adopted – 'Whiteness' – problematic, as it does not quite capture the full implication of 'White' itself being an invented ontological category, nor does it indicate the full relationality of 'White/un-White-making' that founds the Colonial-Modern *World*. I prefer therefore to make clearer these significant points through the more specific assignation of 'White'-ness. I adopt the term 'Whiteness' when I refer to those occasions and situations when this ontology is simply asserted or assumed. On a different note, I fully realise that many would not agree to this assertion, nor understand what is meant by global White-ness as a prevailing system, but I am here not speaking to them, their intransigence is of no concern to me. The implications of global 'White'-ness, however, are matters of significance.

7 For a fuller discussion of the cunning of 'Europe' as a *World*-making category, see below, Chapter 4.

make a claim that in every respect might appear regressive, but it needs to be stated bluntly. I say this not as an indictment, but simply as an actuality: *life, as such, does not matter.*

We are taught, very firmly so, to hold on to this belief that life matters. We are taught that this, as an ideal at the very least, is what defines 'Humanity', a 'post-Enlightenment' bequeath upon 'civilisation'. Even if remaining yet an unrealised ideal, we are taught to believe, are seemingly inclined so to do, that this remains *the* ideal. We might regard it even a sacred principle, notwithstanding all the empirical evidence that points otherwise, to be championed still, cherished, striven for, the goal to be attained, to demand: '(All) Lives Matter'.

This is a familiar refrain to us of course. It is often stated as a response to the rage expressed when once again it is proved that ('Black-ed') lives are ever dispensable. And we understand it clearly as a deflection. But still we are disarmed. Who could disagree after all? So, we too repeat: "Yes, all lives matter" and for this reason, we insist, "Black' lives *also must* matter!" This, after all, is the core of the argument. And so affirming, in apparent agreement about the sanctity of life, as such, both sides stare from across the battle lines, separated by an incommensurable divide. All lives purportedly matter when lives abundantly do not. We might regard this an unsettling conundrum. Yet, it is not quite as perplexing as it might seem.

So long as we believe this, so long as we abide by the falsehood that lives count for something other than its instrumental value in registers of profit and loss, we are enslaved by this deception that, one day, 'Black' lives (too) may matter. In its apparently unarguable appeal lies its vulgar cruelty which inflicts the truth of 'Humanity' as it is in its full actuality: life, as such, *does not* matter. It never has, not in the reckoning of a *World* constructed and norm-alised as *White-d matter*. Indeed, 'Whiteness' – the invention of White/un-White' – is precisely, and specifically, the negation of any such possibility. And given this is the case, *Black-ed* lives, Black being *the* category of disposability in the face of White-ness, are fully the lives that matter not. To be put simply, to be a life Black-ed is to be disposable matter.

It is useful at this juncture to remind ourselves of the history of normalised terror inflicted in the name of (*White-European*) civilisation. More than the facts of it, what is more instructive is the utter lack of timidity, by the philosopher-apologists of conquests and plunder, in the assertions and enforcement of a self-proclaimed 'right to (righteous) violence' as it were – as a right of universal 'natural justice' no less –in originally naming and making the *World*.[8] This was the original philosophical foundations of *this* World: the assumption of the *Right* to name and claim the 'discovered' un-White-d ('Black-ed') peoples so encountered as racialised property, as commodity, indeed as raw *matter* for 'White' *World*-making. As Charles Mills teaches us, this indeed is the fundamental tenet of the 'Racial Contract', that material actuality that underpinned all that metaphysical nonsense of the so-called 'social contract'.[9]

All this we know. The point worth repeating is simply this: our very understanding of *this* World obtains from the foundational principle that, by virtue of an (universal) *Idea* of Life as purportedly sublime and pure, mundane life as such – in the worlds of lives in their mundane multitudes – matters not one jot. Such has been the defining feature of (*White-European*) 'civilisation'. And it remains entirely so, now in many 'post-colonial' and 'multi-cultural' variations, entrenched, normalised, *whitewashed*. Not a matter of oversight or neglect. It is, to borrow from Christina Sharpe in her description of 'antiblackness', both 'normative' and 'necessary': "it is the ground we walk on".[10] And as Kathryn Yusoff meticulously demonstrates, the 'ground' itself, as 'geology', is racialised, matter-in-Whiteness, matter of and for Whiteness.[11] So, we see the coherent threads that connect 'Colonial-Modern' pasts to 'post-colonial' presents as a series of *afterlives*:[12] of slavery, (neo)colonialism, property, simply of 'ecocide' and 'genocide' inflicted together in the pursuit of the appropriation of matter in the name of *White*-Spirit. When all is said and done, this then is the underlying *Reason* of global coloniality: the norm-alised disposability of 'life/matter' in the appropriation and subjugation of 'matter/property'. All else is the theatrics of rationalisation, colonial/racial/patriarchal philosophy in the service of racialised capitalism as the prevailing 'system of reality' of our (post)Colonial-Modern age.

In making this point, let me stress that it is not simply the fact of violence that is at issue here.[13] There is nothing exceptional about violence from a

8 For a concise but telling account of the many rationalisations of 'White' might and Right, see Bernard M. Magubane, *Race and the Construction of the Dispensable Other* (Pretoria: University of South Africa Press, 2007). It is even more telling that even in the face of what might be regarded as embarrassment, there is still little actual timidity amongst contemporary historians of Empire in recounting the violence of the past. That rationalisation of such 'excesses' is still acceptable polite discourse, subject to rational contestations and if need be self-critical admonishment for 'errors' and 'misjudgements', perhaps, is itself telling of a certain normalisation of inter-generational cruelty. We will return to this normality of (non)violence later in our discussion.

9 Charles W. Mills, *The Racial Contract* (Ithaca: Cornell University Press, 1997).

10 Christina Sharpe, *In the Wake: On Blackness and Being* (Durham: Duke University Press, 2016), 7.

11 Kathryn Yusoff, *A Billion Black Anthropocenes or None* (Minneapolis: University of Minnesota Press, 2018).

12 See Saidiya Hartman, *Lose Your Mother: A Journey Along the Atlantic Slave Route* (New York: Farrar, Straus and Giroux, 2007).

13 We will return for a fuller discussion of these issues in Chapter 6.

historical point of view; empires have risen and fallen each with their own particular style and disposition towards human cruelty. What is of importance is that the violence of contemporary Colonial-Modern times is predicated on the unambiguous and insistent claim to universalism in the regard of Humanity. This is quite a novelty. We are witness now to a unique rationalisation of normalised terror, no longer through the discursive registers of violence, but now cleansed, spoken of, understood as, argued over, as matters of 'regulation', 'enforcement', 'policing', 'security', all in the service of the preservation of universal 'Life'.[14] In the operation of global coloniality, therefore, one thing we see is consistent; ever accompanying the cruelties of *norm-ality* are the promise of 'liberation', of 'freedom', of 'human rights' for all, rolled-out for inculcation into the despairing imagination of those inflicted by *White*-violence, for those abandoned to immiseration, fully as the opiate for the weak.

The audacity of this deceit is grotesque. It is best to state is starkly. To this day, for all its sanctimonious grandeur, and for all the serious and anguished deliberations conducted in the august settings of 'global summits', there is not one artefact of so-called universal 'Human Rights' or one assertion of the sanctity of 'life' that has prevented, or prevents, the capriciousness of death-making or the lasciviousness of life-taking that are the everyday normalities of the regulated 'civilisation' of global predatory capitalism. Ever greater the grand gestures and proclamations that all lives matter as an abstract value, ever normalised our World where embodied lives, as experiential and material, are utterly defiled, walled-in or out, separated, cast-out, disposed of. So, it is that we hear pontifications on the universal truths of non-violence and the supreme value of 'life' while a normality of systemic destitution in the face of obscene enrichment is maintained, indifferent to, if not derisory of, the abjection of desperate human struggles for safety and refuge. This, as the *normal* way of the *World*. Even as we might protest its most extreme instances of violence and perversion, we remain abiding by its enforced 'legality of perversion', as Enrique Dussel called it.[15] This is, I repeat, the way of the World. How else might we account for the 'right' that is asserted to enforce the inviolability of 'national borders' against the 'migrant

14 Such is the norm-alisation of the utter disregard for 'life', as such, that we have as ubiquitous the racialised governmentality of 'algorithmic' surveillance, where 'human' subjectivities are reconfigured through 'data constructions for the determination of 'threats', quite rightly the 'subject' for elimination by globally mobile and 'surgically' effective 'killer robots'; see John Emery, 'Killer Robots, Algorithmic Warfare and Techno-Ethics', 2018, at <https://blog.castac.org/2018/03/killer-robots/> (accessed 30 November 2022)

15 See Enrique Dussel, (trans. Aquilina Martinez and Christine Morokovsky) *Philosophy of Liberation* (Eugene: Wipf and Stock, 2003).

hordes'? Or the apparent mundane ordinariness of industrial killing and incarceration in the name of public order and global peace? Or of the wantonness of the destruction of human and planetary life-system in the guise of civilisational 'progress', all as normal and persistent, fully the everyday business of *this* World. All this as we repeat the mantra: "All lives matter", "Black Lives (Must) Matter', "Dalit Lives Matter", and now, "Palestinian Lives Matter etc, etc, etc!

A cruel deceit. To abide by this promise that life, as such, matters is to be utterly disoriented. It is to disbelieve what we blatantly see all around us, and what we fully know in our gut to be the actualities of the World. As evident as this is to us, we appear not to take this lesson seriously. Perhaps it is too painful a realisation. It is easier, more convenient, to perpetuate this deceit.

So, this is the true nature of the problem we confront. The philosophers of *White*-ness, and more so the practitioners who (re)make the *World* in its manifold images, are little moved by impassioned calls for the sanctity of life. The hard facts are such that the fundamental core belief and enduring practice of *this* World as we know it is that no life, simply as life as such, matters when it comes up against the concerns of *White-d* matter. To say that Black-ed lives matter in this context is, quite simply, to speak a non-sense.

On Radical Blackness?

It is true that the problem for life, understood consciously as such, has always been to contemplate its place in the World. The problem for Black-ed life is compounded in that it is precisely this contemplation that was forcibly denied to those inscribed, originally and definitionally so. This we know. It was an invention of *White*-ness that co-constitutively ascribed encountered 'Other'-lives as Black-ed/un-White-d, 'coloured', as *matter* to mould, use and dispense, to educate, chastise, civilise, celebrate or denigrate, always as objects whose beingness being reflections, or more precisely shadows, of 'Whiteness' in the *World*, meaningful only in that *White*-ness gives original meaning to the 'alterity' that is 'Black/coloured' lives. It is of course equally true to say that 'Whiteness' itself is only meaningful in this mutual relationship of 'alterity', but in in saying this, we acknowledge that we are discussing a question of power. I will say more on this below. Here, we consider the implications of Black-ness as an inscribed category of *subjection*.

We have long studied the problem of the 'Negro',[16] the 'coloured' and the

---

16 The list is long: E.W.B Du Bois, Marcus Garvey, C.L.R. James, Frantz Fanon, James Baldwin, Malcolm X, Angela Davis, Audrey Lorde, Walter Rodney, Steve Biko, Sylvia Wynter, Cedric Robinson, Achille Mbembe, Saidiya Hartman, Kehinde Andrews, etc. I intend no priority of importance or influence in those I have included and the many not mentioned. Suffice to repeat, we are not

'Black-ed', as, to borrow from Nahum Chandler, a 'problem for thought'.[17] The combined lesson we have learnt is that the moment we are 'made-coloured' in whatever way, by the stroke of a philosopher's pen, or an utterance or perception of assignation (we recall Fanon's moment of clarity upon the child's call, "Mama, see the Negro"[18]), or the judgement of a 'police' officer in the many 'reasonable' conduct of lethal 'enforcement', in that moment we are entirely configured, transmogrified, into a precarious beingness-under-*Whiteness* as a *matter* in/to the *World*. It is after-all the particular way in which the shadow of 'European' *White*-ness falls upon us that determines that particular shade of colour that has been emblazoned upon our bodies and beingness; we are 'known' by these names, named by imperialism as 'History', and thus made-appear – out of an original dis-appearance – into the *World*. How we understand our-selves and our relationships thereby arising, both as a matter of personal perception and of institutional and structural locatedness, therefore, are not simply the result of 'unequal' treatment in the present, not simply a matter of 'prejudice'[19] to be rectified by a recognition of an 'injustice' and a response of recognition, of respect, even reparation. If it were, perhaps some kind of 'human' conversion might solve the problem, perhaps through 'education', training, 'sensitisation', 'allyship', whatever it may be. But human relations, even as they are institutionally structured, are not the heart of the problem. The heart of the problem rather is a matter of *matter*,[20] that is to say, of the *World* made, of the meaning of the World, as a *World*, purportedly defined not from a particular point of view, partisan and parochial, but as insistently universal, absolute, final, and total.

This is what *White*-ness as 'property' means in its totality; it is fully a claim to the *World* – as a totality of meaning and imagination – within which all

in any way impoverished with regard to the knowledge on Blackness.

17 Nahum Chandler, *X: The Problem of the Negro as a Problem for Thought* (New York: Fordham University Press, 2013).

18 Frantz Fanon, *Black Skin, White Masks* (London: Pluto, 1986). And for a similar realisation, some time before Fanon, with an unequivocal response, see Achmed Abdullah, "Seen Through Mohammedan Spectacles", The Forum October 1914, 484-97, available at <https://www.unz.com/print/Forum-1914oct-00484/> (last accessed, 15 July 2020).

19 See Eduardo Bonilla-Silva, 'More than Prejudice: Restatement, Reflections, and New Directions in Critical Race Theory', *Sociology of Race and Ethnicity* 1(1), 2015, 73–87.

20 Mbembe provides a powerful descriptor of the 'Black Man' in this sense as "the name par excellence of the slave: *man-of-metal, man-merchandise, man-of-money.*"; Achille Mbembe (trans. Laurent Dubois), *Critique of Black Reason* (Durham: Duke University Press, 2017), 47 (emphases in original) While it is true that other ascriptions of colour in the grand scheme of imperial global naming has less of an earthy root, the fact nevertheless remains that every naming currently comprehensible as universal markers of difference derive from the material relations enforced by imperial-colonial assumptions of the right-to-name.

else is named, (b)ordered and emplaced, and judged. In this way are 'Black-ed'
and 'coloured' lives lives originally tainted, definitionally so, categorically such
as containing meaning only within the propertied schema of the White-claim;
Coloured-in lives – White, Black Red or any other – originate therefore as a
relationships to matter. But all this we know. And all this we repeatedly recount
in our excavations and denunciations of racialised, colonial pasts, in our doing
of 'wake work', as Christina Sharpe calls it, and in our continuing revelations
of *afterlives* – of slavery, property, racialised capitalism etc. All this we know.

And because we know this, because we have recovered and regenerated
a way of thinking Beingness out of past negations, we commit a critical
mistake: we think that *we* have changed, that we *are* changed. Because we have
recovered this memory, this voice to articulate our re-membering, this sight of
re-viewing, it is tempting to think *we* have come out of the shadows, no longer
defined and enslaved by the ontological fate assigned us by the philosophers
of *White*-ness, now as 'subjects' liberated from the coloniser's dehumanisa-
tion and negation. *We* have claimed our name so to speak: no longer nigger,
nor Negro, nor coloured, but 'Black', 'people of colour' some say, in any case,
now thought and named by our-selves as radical Beingness liberated from
White-ontological ownership.[21] From a beingness-negated as *Non-Being*,
dispossessed of language, memory, kinship, land, fully made nothing to
be-made-slave, the struggle to be-in-the-World defines the onto-epistemology
of Black liberation as a political imagination and praxis. The long legacy of
taking on this 'problem for thought' is precisely what Cedric J. Robinson
famously described as the 'Black radical tradition',[22] a legacy built on centuries of struggle and refusal to abide by the *Nothingness* inflicted upon by the
Master/coloniser: *Negritude,* Black power, Black is Beautiful, these the assertions of a *Self* reclaimed. The result, as Achille Mbembe put it, the 'Black
consciousness of Blackness'.[23] We might understand all these efforts as ones
to resolve the problem for thought that inheres in Coloniality-Modernity,
engendered as it was by the dislocations of the trans-Atlantic regimes of
enslavement and the colonial orders of World-making thus originated. As a
recent and important example of this tradition, we hear the powerful call of
'Back to Black' by Kehinde Andrews.[24]

---

21 As examples, see Molefi Asante, *Afrocentricity* (Trenton: Africa World Press, 1988) and Lewis R. Gordon,
   Existentia Africana: Understanding Africana Existential Thought (London: Routledge, 2000).
22 Cedric J. Robinson, *Black Marxism: the making of the black radical tradition* (London: Zed, 1983).
23 Mbembe, *Critique of Black Reason*, 30.
24 Kehinde Andrews, *Back to Black: retelling Black radicalism for the 21st century* (London: Zed Books,
   2018). See also, George J. Sefa Dei '"Black Like Me": Reframing Blackness for Decolonial Politics',

Blackness is understood by Andrews as a break, both philosophical and material, that brings into the *World* a new *Being*, a 'Self' reclaimed from 'White' negation, transcending the limits of state-nationalism to articulate and manifest a transnational imagination arising from a consciousness that 'Black is a country'. [25] There is no idealistic imagination here for a 'colour-blind' integration into 'White' society:

> Blackness was never created by Whiteness; it is a rejection of it. I am not racialised into Blackness; I am Black. My Blackness is a declaration of self and resistance, not a position of victimhood and oppression. [26]

> Blackness is the rejection of the [social death] of the Negro and therefore the cure to the disease of racism. Blackness is the opposite of social death; it is the rejection of the condition imposed by the West. Not in the sense of being proud, or finding moments in cultural resistance, but in proclaiming an uncompromising commitment to the Black revolution. Ruminating on how social death still frames Black life is not the Black radical project. Calling into being the methodologies, strategies and politics for overturning the political system and building the Black nation is the work that needs to be done. [27]

This is powerful stuff. Powerful, and yet, the assertions overreach. The call to Black resorted to by Andrews (and others), has a rich historical legacy, no doubt. But invocations of a collective beingness, born out of a particular experience, are undoubtedly also of their time. Being so, the difficult question to be confronted is the extent to which, and in what specific ways, 'Black' remains a coherent and meaningful assertion of beingness-in-the-World in the face of the material problem of 'global Whiteness' in the contemporary.

It is imperative that we understand the situation as it is. Especially in these moments when we might be tempted to think that our demands may seem to be on the political ascendency. Leaving aside a minority of naysayers – foolishly loud and obnoxious as they may be – philosophers and enforcers of

---

Educational Studies 54(2), 2018, 117-142; and Cheryl I. Harris 'Whiteness as Property', *Harvard Law Review* 106(8), 1993, 1710-1791.

25 Andrews, *Back to Black*, 67-100.

26 Andrews, *Back to Black*, 201. This recalls also the appeal by bell hooks for 'loving blackness' as a praxis of political resistance; bell hooks, *Black Looks: Race and Representation* (Boston: South End Press, 1992).

27 Andrews, *Back to Black*, 245.

White-ness are manifestly keen to accede to the claim and assertion that 'Black Lives' matter, that is, to be precise, to the *assertion* that 'Black' (as opposed to *Black-ed)* lives matter. We see this in the media response, in the rush to corporate endorsements, in the through-the-ceiling sales of 'Black' literature (mostly published and sold by *White*-capital it must be said), in the quick move by public authorities to revisit the 'problem of the problematic patrimony of streets and buildings and towns. There is a global rush, a collective tripping over one another, to join in the clamour that 'Black Lives Matter'. For one simple reason: that while the impassioned movement for 'Black lives' might impinge upon some hitherto assumed privileges and moral comforts of (some) 'White-folk' and their 'cultural' and identarian sensibilities, 'Whiteness' itself, as norm-ality, remains entrenched, safe, indeed reinforced as the framework for redress. While the Black Lives 'movement' gains prominence, no change is envisaged in the materiality of global *White*-ness, in the brutality inflicted upon *Black-ed* lives under the persisting 'racial contract' of the *World* made thus. We return to this distinction between Black as an assertion of name, and Black-ed as an infliction of beingness. What is at issue here is the question of power and the power of invocations.

Andrews' impassioned appeal for a return to radical Blackness is revealing of an underlying problem. We have invested everything, it would seem, on the apparent appropriation, and the invocation, of the name, 'Black'. There is indeed power in the invocation of names. So much is obvious. But names as such do not exist unchanged in an environment. Even as they carry the weight of memories, of past meanings and mythologies of articulatory origins, they remain dynamic social invocations, their power generated by the social conditions within which they are renamed and claimed. These are not stagnant, nor are they *essential* in that they do not pertain to some unchanging quality – be it biological or social – derived in and of itself. A name invoked does not come into an uninhabited World. It is to assert a relationality, to assert a locatedness and a meaning within the World, as an encounter with the World. This then is what is at stake when names are invoked, this encounter of names, invoked with purpose and in purpose to claim a position in philosophy, 'history' and most importantly, in relation to the matter of the World.

What, therefore, do we (think we) mean when we invoke Blackness today? Blackness is a country, Andrews insists. Indeed this is to call on the long and rich tradition of radical thinking that imagined a solidarity of resistance, antiracist, anti-'White', anti-imperial, anti-colonial. This is useful for rhetorical purposes, powerful when chanted, when employed as slogans for solidarity, no doubt. But what does it mean, actually mean, in significant material terms that impinge upon the conditions of life today, of a global capitalism in the contemporary 'post-colonial' context? In the actual domains of economics, politics, even social and psychological affiliation and support, what does it mean this purported unity of identification and belonging supposedly grounded on Black-African diasporic beingness? In this 'White' World, where is this 'country', named 'Black', to be found? What are its contours and its characteristics?

In previous times, perhaps meanings were clearer, the apparent front-lines more easily marked. Then, White meant 'White-folk', the 'European' architects and agents of colonial/imperial designs. Against this, 'Black' signified either an encompassing political assignation, or a consciousness of racialised resistance along with the other varieties of Worldly 'colouration', in either case, a beingness that was, by definition, anti-colonial, anti-imperial. Simple as that. Things are less Manichean now it would seem, more nuanced, complicated, let us say.

How close are the radical, anti-colonial Black affirmations of Marcus Garvey, Franz Fanon, Malcolm X, Steven Biko, Sylvia Wynter, Walter Rodney, to the current evocations of Blackness? What affinities the politics of 'living' of Amilcar Cabral, Thomas Sankara, and others like them to the 'post-colonial' actualities of contemporary 'Black' polities? The solidarity of 'Blackness' is little seen in the conduct of the business of *this* World, this is clear; indeed, it is the hard truth that alien 'White' capital is more the Schmittian 'friend', and the abject 'Black' citizenry, the 'seditious' Schmittian 'enemy' in these 'post-colonial' times.[28] What connection the radical naming 'Black' to the global facts of dispensable, disregarded, despised, *Black-ed* lives the world over, scattered as they are across actually (b)ordered countries of 'Black-folk'? What of the malleable new subjectivities of the 'transnational White' emerging out of variously 'coloured' skins, 'Black' included?[29] What are the actual figurations of the global 'colour line' under the complex regulatory registers of 'global law', and the multiple 'assemblages' of differentiated global

---

28 For a discussion of the misplaced fixation of many a critical thinker with Carl Schmitt's positions on 'sovereignty' and the notion of the 'political', see Jayan Nayar, 'On the elusive subject of sovereignty', *Alternatives: global, local, political* 39(2), 2014, 124-147.

29 See Michelle Christian, 'A Global Critical Race and Racism Framework: Racial Entanglements and Deep and Malleable Whiteness', *Sociology of Race and Ethnicity* 5(2), 2019, 169 –185; Sedef Arat-Koc, 'A Transnational Whiteness? New Middle Classes, Globalism and Non-European 'Whiteness'', in Nicky Falkof and Oliver Cashman-Browd (eds.), *On Whiteness* (Oxford: Inter-Disciplinary Press, 2012) 59-68.

geographies of enrichment and impoverishment, acquisition and dispossession where such 'multicultural global Whiteness' operate and profit?[30] Under these conditions, and in these situations of global coloniality, while we march to the chants of 'Black Lives Matter', what connects the contexts of anti-colonial 'Black' thinking of the past to that of contemporary assertions of 'Back to Black'? The purpose of posing these questions is that they point to the necessity of connecting the invocation of names as identity/consciousness-of-beingness with the materiality of beingness as such. This connection between name and matter is critical. And it has largely been neglected.

So, let us consider the question again: does the call to 'Black'-ness remain the same now, in meaning and context and import, as it did in those past iterations? It seems to me that we rather assume it does. Because we claim the same name, repeat the same call, articulate the same assertion, we think we invoke the same power. But a whole bunch of distance separates the present from the past. Once, Blackness, and Black power – 'political Blackness' as it was powerfully invoked by Ambalavaner Sivanandan – were invocations of an imagined possibility otherwise to global 'Whiteness' as a material, imperial force.[31] This was *Black*-ness intimately tied to the actualities of global struggle, as a beingness born out of a transnational, 'Tricontinental', solidarity of anti-colonial imagination, not as mere assertions of a 'racial identity', but as a manifestation of a being-otherwise in lived experiments of 'liberation'.[32] The 'anti-colonial' context is fundamental to an understanding of *Black*-ness in this sense. No longer so, it seems to me.

The words may be the same, but its meanings and implications have much changed. 'Black', in the contemporary context of global *White*-ness, however we might wish it to be, however we might assert it to be, calls into being neither a transnational actuality of beingness nor a generalised affirma-

30 See generally, Andreas Fischer-Lescano and Gunther Teubner, 'Regime-Collisions: The Vain Search for Legal Unity in the Fragmentation of Global Law', Michigan Journal of International Law 25(4), 2004, 999-1046; Catá Backer, (2012). The Structural Characteristics of Global Law for the 21st Century: Fracture, Fluidity, Permeability, and Polycentricity', *Tilburg Law Review* 17(2), 2012, 177-199; Saskia Sassen, *Territory, Authority, Rights: From Medieval to Global Assemblages* (Princeton: Princeton University Press, 2006).

31 Ambalavaner Sivanandan, *A Different Hunger: Writings on Black Resistance* (London: Pluto Press, 1982); *Catching History on the Wing: Race, Culture and Globalisation* (London: Pluto Press, 2008). It is of note that Andrews strongly opposes the notion of political Blackness, considering it even 'dangerous' as it is seen to undermine the power of 'African Diasporic Blackness' as a core concept of Black resurgence; see Kehinde Andrews, 'The problem of political blackness: lessons from the Black Supplementary School Movement', *Ethnic and Racial Studies* 39(11), 2016, 2060-2078.

32 For a recent retracing of the Tricontinental imagination and tradition, and its contemporary salience, see Anne Garland Mahler, *From the Tricontinental to the Global South: Race, Radicalism, and Transnational Solidarity* (Durham: Duke University Press, 2018).

tion of consciousness.[33] Time and place and context matter, and with that so too the import of assignations, of names assumed and invoked. And herein lies the problem. For too long, understandably so it might be added, the quest for thought and being has been to overcome the all-consuming negation of 'Black-ed'-beingness, to find a place in the World through the question: 'who are we' in the face of colonising *White*-ness? In this quest to find ontological meaning apart from the Master, much has been recovered in the form of *wake-work*. *We* might have claimed for ourselves a name and place in the World-made-out-of-Whiteness. However, as we have done so, the *White*-Master himself has remained steadfast, even as he has appeared contrite, receding as he has to the background in such conversations even if not in the actual affairs of *this* World. And from the shadows, he is quite content – most of the time – to allow us to think that we are making our little dent upon the *World* by measure of the volume of our clamour. He need do little else. For, in terms of material consequence, of *World*-changing transformation, we do little through our invocation of 'Blackness'.

For all of the stridency of our call, notwithstanding Andrews' assertion, 'Blackness' today remains a shadow of *White*-ness, its meaning and experience intimately corresponding to the *World* as a *White-d* artefact. The *Negro*, as Mbembe, is correct to identify, is ever-present in the figure of the *Black*.[34] There is little evidence of it being otherwise. We see here in operation Sivanandan's distinction between two forms of 'racism': the racism that discriminates and the racism that kills.[35] Notwithstanding our grander claims, it is clear that our resort to the invocation of the name 'Black', our assertion that 'Black Lives' matter – even as it pertains to the killing of *Black-ed* lives – is in actuality an appeal against discrimination. All we are saying, truly, is "please don't kill us". We call out individual names for the remembering of lives brutally cut down, individual names that is for the condemnations of guilt and the call to account, but little else than that; the system that kills as a matter of global norm-ality remains untouched, fully intact. Yes, we claim more. A 'Black History' month. A plaque here and a statue there. A curriculum revised – we grandly call this 'decolonised' – to reinsert *Black*(-ed) pasts

---

33 See for example, Godfrey Mwakikagile (3rd ed), *Relations between Africans and African Americans: Misconceptions, Myths and Realities* (Dar es Salaam: New Africa Press, 2007); Harry Garuba, 'Race in Africa: Four Epigraphs and a Commentary', *PMLA* 123(5), 2008, 1640-1648, available at <https://www.jstor.org/stable/25501967?seq=1> (last accessed 30 July 2020).
34 Achille Mbembe, *Necropolitics* (Durham: Duke University Press, 2019), 7, 163, 178
35 See Kwesi Owusu, 'The struggle for a radical Black political culture: an interview with A. Sivanandan', *Race & Class* 58(1), 2016, 6-16, 14.

and beings into (*White*-d) Humanity. All this in *White*-universities, built and maintained with *White*-capital, fully invested in the extractive system of 'profit' from the exploitation of (distant) *Black-ed* brothers and sisters.

I put it harshly, perhaps unkindly. Only to make us take a hard look at ourselves. Notwithstanding our claims to Blackness as radical Beingness – and we are not shy in making this claim – we have neither thought, nor lived, our way out of the norm-ality of *White*-ness as the system of reality that kills. Whatever our enraged intent, whatever the very real struggles of grounded activists and community organisers who invoke it, the call to 'Black' today is quite of a different register of power and implication from that of its histor-ical origins in liberation praxis.[36] This is not to erase nor undermine the very present pain, and hope, of the call, nor of the suffering that infuses its name in struggle; 'loving Blackness', as bell hooks invoked it,[37] is a necessary and signif-icant articulation and realisation of respite, healing and resistance against the assumption of 'White' norm-ality and its negations. But for all this, and what-ever our intention, there is no escaping the realisation. From an anti-colonial, anti-imperial assertion of a radical other-*Beingness* against *White*-ness, while periodic episodes of collective rage might highlight *Black*-ness as defiant being-ness against structural violence, what we witness instead as the everyday invoca-tion of the call is 'Blackness' domesticated into *White*-matter, as 'identity' (at its best, as a political recovery of healing, at its worst, as fashion, as commodity) with place in the *White*-World, celebrated (occasionally) when its articulation is deemed to abide by the general rules of polite society, but always precarious to (*White*) judgement and punishment when deemed to have transgressed. Simply, the Master oversees us still. The aspirations of hooks, and Andrews, notwithstanding, it is to *Him*, still as Master, that we vent our rage and claim our resistance and demand/appeal for 'recognition'. And He – that Big He, as structural *White*-ness – knows this. So, He provides us a place at the table in the proverbial Big House, inviting us to come in, to be 'recognised', perhaps even

36 I do not mean by this that the demand that 'Black Lives Matter' is without any significance whatever. I do not intend to diminish the subjective affirmation that the call to Blackness might engender as a consciousness of resistance and dignity. In its terms, confined predominantly to the contexts and discursive traditions of Euro-American 'civil rights' preoccupations, it is capable of instigating certain outcomes of redress; the call to Blackness may be understood as an assigned cultural assertion seeking rent and profit within a register of 'citizenship' – we might call it an epistemology of 'justice' – from the prevailing 'system' of Whiteness as Master onto-epistemology.

37 bell hooks, *Black Looks: Race and Representation* (Boston: South End Press, 1992). See also in this context Prentis Hemphill, 'Healing Justice is How We Can Sustain Black Lives', *Huffington Post*, 7 February 2017, available at <https://www.huffpost.com/entry/healing-justice_b_5899e8ade4b-0c1284f282ffe> (last accessed, 5 August 2020).

feted, as 'Black'.[38] And we accept. We have seldom done anything other than accept, never mind Fanon, Malcolm X, Steve Biko. They are long gone now.

This is the heart of the problem. We remain, us 'Black-ed', utterly *colonised*. To revise and extend a Fanonian insight, as *Black Skin, Black Masks, proudly so, perhaps, but White-d Matter still*.

I don't make these observations lightly. I wish I believed differently but I simply cannot find any evidence for an opposite view.

For the colonised, the conquered who are then *made-unmade* through negation in thought, there is always the burden to think through and overcome the enforced emptiness of a *(Non)Being-in-the-World*. The hope, that out of this 'emergence', this 'becoming', we might stake our claim to the *World*, *this* World. This being so, it is imperative always to remember that the struggle for thought and being is never conducted in the abstract, they are material and embodied and for this fact, they must remain paramount in any consideration of a philosophical argument. It is important that we understand the generational efforts to think-*Black* out of enforced *White*-ness in these terms. But as we recognise this historical and material groundings of thought, the question how we think out of the coloniser's regimes of wording/making the *World* is a critical matter for reflection and judgement. In this, it is not always the case that familiar categories of resistance, once envisaged as encapsulating a powerful consciousness of radical (potential) liberation, remains as such, potent still to overcome the Master's meaning-making. What I am suggesting is that whether we like it or not it is necessary to consider the assumptions and material implications of a call to 'Blackness'. The problem for thought remains.

Look, 'White-Folk'?

We have conceded too much to the enforced norm-ality of *White*-ness. Indeed, we have allowed it to entrench itself as a 'racial' category, as 'Whiteness', normalised as such, made a matter of phenotypical colouration rather than a structural relationality that pertains to the matter of the *World*. This needs to be attended to.

For too long, we have been distracted by an attempt to critically understand the 'soul of the perverted beingness of 'White-folk'. We have rather

---

38 To be fair to Andrews, he is one of the few contemporary thinkers who is explicit in his recognition of our complicity as we occupy positions of middle-class comfort in the academic at the heart of Euro-American capitalism. Such candid self-criticism is refreshing, and rare. But it does not however explain why 'we' who occupy such positions think it a contradiction worth enduring for the sake of some self-perceived importance of voice and influence that this location might offer us in the larger struggle against White, imperial-capitalism. Why us? Is this not still so much self-assuaging?

assumed, in this critical endeavour, that such a creature as this exists,[39] whose soul it is necessary to fathom, even save perhaps. I argue for a different approach where it is the very assumption, and assertion of 'White'-ness attached to a 'folk', as a folk, itself that is the fundamental *frontline* for praxes. What we need to understand are the implications of the making 'White'-folk. The difference between the assumption of 'White'-folk and the ascription of 'White-folk' is of fundamental significance.

'White'-ness, as a global system of reality, is more than what might appear as the petty sensibilities of those we have come to identify as 'White-folk'; a great deal more than the limited aspects of 'cultural' life, their privileges and dispensations, the trials and tribulations and sensitivities and fragilities attached to what we commonly understand as 'White'-folk is involved in the structural actualities of global *White*-ness. But this is the cunning; *White*-ness is dependent, as a central pillar of its architecture, on precisely such affectations of 'White-d'-folk as an invented 'caste' in the racialised *World*,[40] and it certainly cannot survive without their agency as a mobilised and militant force when 'White' is invoked as a call to arms to protect the *World*. To get to the heart of *White*-d-ness, it is necessary therefore to see through the many distractions of 'White-skin' while at the same time understanding the force of its invocation. It is our fundamental error to have insufficiently attended to this problem, not out of ignorance clearly – for we have known of the invention of 'White'-folk for a long while now – but because we appear to have inculcated ourselves into its apparent norm-alisation.[41] We have so long considered the question "how to think/make Black?", we have insufficiently

---

39 As an example of this assumption, see David Gillborn, 'We need to Talk about White People', Multi-cultural Perspectives 21(2), 2019, 97-101, 97-98:

> It is useful to start by reminding ourselves that "Whiteness" and "White people" are different things. In general terms, "Whiteness" refers to a system of beliefs, practices, and assumptions that constantly center the interests of White people, especially White elites. People who identify and/or are identified by others as "White" may act in the interests of Whiteness, but it is not automatic nor inevitable. White-identified people can challenge Whiteness, just as people of color can sometimes become vocal advocates for Whiteness."

40 See Isabel Wilkerson, *Caste: The Lies that Divide Us* (London: Allen Lane, 2020).

41 We have no shortage of literature on this the invention of Whiteness and its effects. For few exemplary works see; W.E.B. Du Bois, 'The Soul of White Folk' in W.E.B. Du Bois, *Writings* (New York: Library of America, 1987), 923-38, 927, available at <https://loa-shared.s3.amazonaws.com/static/pdf/Du_Bois_White_Folk.pdf> (last accessed 28 June 2022); Theodore W. Allen, *The Invention of the White Race: Volume 1, Racial Oppression and Social Control*, (London: Verso Books, 1994, 2012); and *The Invention of the White Race: Volume 2, The Origin of Racial Oppression in Anglo-America*, (London: Verso Books, 1997, 2012); David Roediger, *The Wages of Whiteness: Race and the Making of the American Working Class* (London: Version, 1991, 1999); Nell Irvin Painter, *The History of White People*, (New York: W.W. Norton & Co., 2010); Nicky Falkof and Oliver Cashman-Browd (eds.), *On Whiteness* (Oxford: Inter-Disciplinary Press, 2012). See also Mbembe's description of the 'fantasy of Whiteness'; Mbembe, *Critique of Black Reason*, 43-45.

attended to the fundamental question. "how to unthink/unmake *White*?". And we have paid the price for it.

Recall how we are constantly charged that we engage in a contradiction, a hypocrisy even, that what we do by emphasising 'Blackness' – as attached to a group of people 'raced' as Black – in order to purportedly repudiate the normality of racialisation and the violence of racism is exactly to perpetuate racial thinking. How frequently we have been called up on this by the advocates of a 'colour-blind' anti-racism, proponents of some ahistorical, astructural, amaterial 'post-racial' 'class' politics.[42] Yes, we are able to explain away this contradiction, we have many forceful arguments to stress the continuation of racialised beingness as a fact of differentiation, of structural inequalities and violence enforced in the *World*, but there remains, uncomfortably, a kernel of truth in this objection. Simply, we cannot escape the perpetuation of 'race-thinking' in the way in which we have claimed 'Blackness'; indeed, much of our 'successes' rely precisely on such thinking, inevitably so: take 'Black History', 'Black Music' as examples. We rationalise and justify this, of course. However, there remains a problem we cannot overcome. By ignoring the category of 'White' fundamentally as a matter of philosophy, in accepting 'White'-ness as an assumed 'racialised'/ethnic actuality attached to a 'folk', we reinforce the effectiveness of its technologies of (b)ordering the *World*.

'White'-ness, we know, is an invention. And it has historically, and through many a permutation, operated to make-'White' a 'folk'. Importantly, and it is quite the work of magic, the power of *White*-ness as it attaches to an assigned, invented 'White-d'-folk is precisely that it does not require justification; it simply operates as a normality.[43] *White*-d-folk are 'White'; this apparently has come to be understood as a given. Nothing more than that need be said. Nothing more is expected to be said. We, the 'un-White', have apparently accepted it to be so. We know of course that this is a meaningless ascription as such, the 'Whiteness' of 'White'-folk. But knowing this is one thing. Thinking through the implications of its invention, ascription, and invocation, is quite another task. It is quite a feat of *colonisation* that this underlying invention of Colonial-Modern ontology has escaped the 'liberation' of 'decolonisation'.

---

42 In the UK context, a prime 'think-tank' for such a self-claimed post-racial, anti-establishment, working-class libertarian politics is *Spiked Online,* with Brendan O'Neill as its charismatic ideologue/mouthpiece at the helm; see <https://www.spiked-online.com> last accessed 18 February 2022.

43 "Whiteness is not a culture", Noel Ignatiev, famously pointed out; Noel Ignatiev and John Garvey (eds), *Race Traitor* (New York: Routledge, 1996).

How ubiquitous still this idea that there exists a category within Humanity, disparate, without a shared language, culture, ethics, religion, history, memory, none of this, and yet somehow still ascribed, meaningfully it seems, as 'White', self-recognised as such with little incredulity. Immense critical resources now are expended in the study of this peculiarity under the broad ambit of 'Critical White Studies'.[44] All this attention to understand a collective that requires no explanation in and of itself, no thought before its invocation. The collective merely is: 'White-folk'. All this effort inadvertently continues to *make-White* as a social reality. Absurd. And most telling of this absurdity is that we are now concerned to talk seriously of the apparent trauma experienced by 'White-folk'; 'White rage', 'White backlash', 'White fragility' all being conditions, it appears, for serious discussion in the wake of the threat to their assumed (privileged) place in the *World*. In all of this apparent critical interrogation of an invented and structural 'Whiteness', 'White', as such, remains, affirmed, strengthened. Notwithstanding our best efforts to bring notice to the 'injustices' of 'White nationalism/supremacy', and despite the efforts of 'race traitors' such as Noel Ignatiev, David Roediger, Vincent Jungkunz and more like them,[45] 'White' persists as a 'race' in the *World* of 'racialised' folk wherein 'White-folk' walk this *World* still, now strengthened it would appear with a (un)self-conscious 'racial identity' in their own right.[46] They might well be less than cohesive as a folk, this is true, and yet, they appear now unconsciously, even inadvertently, more than ever before possessing of a shared 'soul'; even as ally to 'Black'-ed-folk, even as they might be explicit in their rejection of 'privilege', it is seldom that 'White-folk' question their purported *fact* of 'White'-ness. This, it would seem, is the current situation: there are the 'White-folk' of 'White Supremacy', racist, despicable, incorrigible, then there are those who are just, simply, 'White', suffering varying degrees of 'White-guilt', whole-hearted in their desire to 'decolonise', eager to be 'ally' to 'Black' folk, materially and structurally privileged, perhaps, but spiritually innocent – just folk that are, as a matter of fact, 'White'.

It is necessary to look again.

44 See, generally, Richard Delgado and Jean Stefancic (eds.), *Critical White Studies: Looking Behind the Mirror* (Philadelphia: Temple University Press, 1997); Zeus Leonardo, 'The Souls of White Folk: Critical pedagogy, whiteness studies, and globalization discourse', *Race, Ethnicity and Education* 5(1), 2010

45 See for example, Ignatiev and Garvey (eds) *Race Traitor*; David Roediger, *Towards the Abolition of Whiteness: Essays on Race, Politics and Working Class History* (London: Verso, 1994); Vincent Jungkunz, 'Dismantling Whiteness: Silent Yielding and the Potentiality of Political Suicide', *Contemporary Political Theory* 10, 2011, 3-20.

46 See for example, Ashley Jardina, *White Identity Politics* (Cambridge: Cambridge University Press, 2019); Eric Kaufmann, *White Shift: Populism, Immigration, and the Future of White Majorities* (New York: Abrams Press, 2019).

Whiteness-as-Fragility

I have called it absurd, this notion of 'White fragility'. This is not to say however that I think the idea of 'fragility' as attached to 'White'-ness is not of significance. Quite the opposite: it reveals an important point. I am not interested here to discuss the 'self-help', 'workshopping' type of ideas contained in Robin DiAngelo's best-selling book; I am not concerned to salvage the souls of 'White-folk' as I consider this ascription a nonsense.[47] I am interested in the implications of the notion of 'fragility' itself. My argument is that, rather than a condition 'suffered' by 'White-folk' in the present, the assertion of *White*-ness, in it very origination, is by definition an ascription of fragility in the *World*. To understand this is to see that it is precisely the foundational assumption of 'fragility' that points to the necessary anti-colonial point of departure.

"White Man, Think again" implored Anthony Jacob, writing in 1965 in the face of a perceived threat to the 'Anglo-Saxon' race in South Africa, as well as in the wider world, by the insidious advance of the lesser races devoid of 'civilisation', decrying the 'egalitarian fallacy' that permits such a fate to portend.[48] "The Jungle grows back" Robert Kagan observed in similar warning in a contemporary, 'post-racial' invocation of this same imaginary to assert the dangers faced by liberal 'America', in a hostile world, should 'leadership' be relinquished.[49] While it might be the case that we are familiar with the former-type, 'White-nationalist', points of view being dismissed as 'extremist', it is notable that the latter view remains fully respectable and, indeed, is shared by many as wise. They are however little different – I will return more fully to this point later in this discussion. For now, in essence, what both assume and assert is the civilisational righteousness of 'White'-ness and action in response to any assertion of a claim to the *World* by those deemed lesser. Both, in other words, are prescriptions for action to protect a fragile and sacred *Right* against ever-present danger. Indeed, this is

47 For a recent and well-intentioned attempt to assist 'White'-folk in their struggle to fight 'racism', see Emma Dabiri, *What White People Can Do Next: From Allyship to Coalition* (London: Penguin, 2021). Conversely, for an expression of exasperation that such work is required, see Reni Eddo-Lodge, *Why I'm No Longer Talking to White People About Race* (London: Bloomsbury Publishing, 2018).

48 Anthony Jacob, *White Man Think Again!* (London: Ostara Publications, 1965, 2017). Jacob was in no way an original thinker in this regard. Very similar arguments of fragility and threat had long before been articulated; for example, Madison Grant, *The Passing of the Great Race: Or the Racial Basis of European History* (New York: Charles Scribner's Sons, 1916); and Lothrop Stoddard, *The Rising Tide of Colour Against White World-Supremacy* (New York: Charles Scribner's Sons, 1923).

49 Robert Kagan, *The Jungle Grows Back: America and Our Hostile World* (New York: Alfred A. Knopf, 2018). Samuel Huntington's worldviews of 'civilisational clashes' might be similarly understood; *The Clash of Cilizations and the Remaking of World Order* (New York: Simon & Schuster, 2011).

'White-backlash'! 'Backlash', in response to perceptions of fragility, we see, is the essential operating mode of a politics that seeks to entrench the structures of *White*-ness and its *Reason* of appropriation and dispossession.[50]

When attached to a 'folk', 'Whiteness' is invoked precisely as fantasy, as the imaginary of a beingness of sacred fragility pitted against the profane worlds of bestial occupation.[51] In this fantasy 'Whiteness' is forever precious in possibility yet ever precarious and requiring of nurture and protection from the forces of depravity. 'White'-ness in this sense has always been 'fragile', always over-determined by the threat of 'invasion' and miscegenation. And given its original assertion as a fragility against all that is impure and hard in the *World*, 'backlash' against the forces of backwardness, if not of evil itself, is precisely and fully its inescapable calling. *White*-ness has no meaning otherwise. Against darkness, in confronting evil, the invocation of the norm-ality of 'White'-ness is a call to a return to that imagination of fragile possibility, against all odds, in defence of Humanity. How often, and in how many different ways, we see the operation of this politics in the global normalities of racialised everydays. 'White'-ness as exalted status, and as endangered precarity; the so-called 'White working-class' now the torchbearers of this new, vulnerable, 'identity' and politics; in their name, and in reinforcing their sensibilities and expectations of "public deference" and the benefits of "public and psychological wage" as Du Bois put it, does 'White'-ness find its most fertile contemporary flourishing.[52] This, if nothing else, when all else appears lost, 'White-d-folk' can cling on to, their place in the *World* meaningful still as *Not*-Black/Brown/Red/Yellow or whatever the denigrated lesser hue of racialised human-beingness might be perceived as threat on the given occasion. It doesn't matter for, as Harris notes, "[o]nly whites possessed whiteness", this the most "exclusive form of property."[53] Being-'White', meaningless as it is, and even if it is no longer an absolute

50 A succinct history of backlash politics in the US is provided by Lawrence Glickman, 'How White Backlash Controls American Progress', *The Atlantic*, 21 May 2020, <https://www.theatlantic.com/ideas/archive/2020/05/white-backlash-nothing-new/611914/> (last accessed August 8, 2020)

51 Two aspects of global whiteness – as an ascription of 'caste' – come together in this fantasy. One, in which transnational, non-ethnic/racial assumptions of Whiteness retain the same logics of status, of precious fragility, and second, in which apparent Whiteness finds congruence with other casteist rationalities of domination; see Isabel Wilkerson, *Caste*. Also, Sedef Arat-Koç, 'A Transnational Whiteness? New Middle Classes, Globalism and Non-European 'Whiteness', 59-68.

52 See W.E.B. Du Bois, *Black Reconstruction in America 1860-1880*, (New York: The Free Press, 1998), 700. Also, Paul Gilroy, *There Ain't No Black in the Union Jack* (London: Routledge, 1987); David R. Roediger, *How Race Survived US History* (London: Verso, 2008); Robbie Shilliam, *Race and the Undeserving Poor* (Newcastle-upon-Tyne: Agenda Publishing, 2018); Jardina, *White Identity Politics;* David Gillborn, The White working class, racism and respectability: victims, degenerates and inter-est-convergence. *British Journal of Educational Studies*, 58(1), 3–25

53 Harris, 'Whiteness as Property', 1724.

determinant of privilege, is all that matters therefore. In fact, it is all the more prized in these times for that fact, invoked as an identity of threatened and righteous norm-ality, of a remnant, an imagined purity of Spirit, a superiority that is never seen or understood as enforced privilege, of course.[54] And the worst of this manifestation, the violent affirmation of masculine 'race-fragility', a victimhood that intimately connects racial purity with misogynistic entitlement.[55]

So, what are we to make of this essential fragility? I believe much of the critical response to *White*-ness, as a problem in the *World*, has not been able to quite come to grasp with this issue. We have mistakenly understood it as a problem of 'racism'. Two approaches dominate: one, to repeat the argument regarding the perpetuations of 'structural racism' and the necessary 'redistribution' of resources and opportunities; and second, the denunciation of the extremist racism of 'White-supremacy'. Neither of these put to question the mundane *norm-ality* of *White*-ness. Both, I suggest, are duped by the fragility of 'White'-ness.

Du Bois long ago wrote:

> Here is a civilization that has boasted much. Neither Roman nor Arab, Greek nor Egyptian, Persian nor Mongol ever took himself and his own perfectness with such disconcerting seriousness as the modern white man. We whose shame, humiliation, and deep insult his aggrandizement so often involved were never deceived. ... We have curled our lips in something like contempt as we have witnessed glib apology and weary explanation. Nothing of the sort deceived us. A nation's religion is its life, and as such white Christianity is a miserable failure.[56]

54 The point is well-made by Hua Hsu:

> Away from these predominantly liberal arenas, however, white identity has found a more potent form of salience. For poor and working-class whites, skin color no longer feels like an implicit guarantor of privilege. There is a sense that others, thanks to affirmative action or lax immigration policies, have nudged ahead of them on the ladder of social ascent. Their whiteness is, in fact, the very reason they suspect that they are under siege. Marginalized by a black President, as they imagine, and alienated by urbane élites of every hue, they have begun to understand themselves in terms of identity politics. It almost doesn't matter whether their suspicions are true in a strictly material sense. The accident of white skin still brings with it economic and social advantages, but resentment is a powerful engine, particularly when the view from below feels unprecedented.

Hua Hsu, 'White Plight', *The New Yorker*, 25 July 2016, available at <https://www.newyorker.com/magazine/2016/07/25/the-new-meaning-of-whiteness> (last accessed 21 July 2020).

55 For a discussion of this violent expression of this resentment, of the intimate connections between 'White' nationalist/supremacist convictions and the misogynistic 'victimhood' of incel or 'involuntary celibacy', see Chris Wilson, 'Nostalgia, Entitlement and Victimhood: The Synergy of White Genocide and Misogyny', *Terrorism and Political Violence*, 2020, available at <https://doi.org/10.1080/095465 53.2020.1839428> last accessed 15 July 2021.

56 Du Bois, 'The Soul of White Folk', 927.

It seems we have become deceived, our lips less curled now, our contempt seemingly tempered, even as we remain enraged. We have made the error to focus on the apparent 'extremism' of particular manifestations or assertions of 'White'-ness, of the structural conditions, behaviours, artefacts, that these generate. We have made the error, that is, to focus on the racism of 'White-ness', and not on the proper *matter* of *White*-ness as 'racially' rationalised. To understand the problem as one of racism, be it structural or relational, is to render invisible and norm-alised the underlying materiality, the *matter*, of the onto-epistemology of *White*-ness as a *World*-making category. It is, to put it differently, to enable 'Whiteness', as a deflection of *White*-ness, an escape into innocence. We see this clearly in operation in the ways in which the fragility of 'White'-ness has established itself on equal footing, it must be noted, in serious discussions on 'racism'. As we contemplate the real dangers, of life and death that is, faced by Black-ed folk, sensitivity to the fragile sensibilities of the 'innocent majority' – of non-racist 'White'-folk – is now imperative. There can be no insinuation that 'anti-racist' action could ever possibly be 'anti-White'; this would automatically disqualify any such claim as itself 'extremist' and 'racist'. And 'extremism' is precisely what should be avoided in this register of 'justice'. When all is said and done, in the very contempla-tion of the protection of 'Black-ed' lives, 'White-ness', we see, must still be protected. Thus, has *extremism* come to be the publicly disavowed discursive alibi for the mundane materiality of *norm-ality*. But it is not the extremism of *White*-ness that kills.

White-ness in a Black-ed World

So, we see, 'White-d folk' are originally a manufactured people moulded out of the contingent contexts of time, place and 'economic' exigency, their perverted souls – their 'psychosis' as Andrews called it – precisely the malleable meaninglessness that gives greatest force and venom to the arbiters and agents of the cruelties of global coloniality.[57] It is our mistake to have misjudged the potency of meaninglessness attached to any 'cultural' invoca-tion of 'Whiteness' as such. A different *Reason* is at work. This is *White*-ness in the *World*.

We who proclaimed ourselves proudly 'Black' (or otherwise 'coloured'), after a brief attempt to come to terms with the difficult implications of 'decol-

---

57 This 'backlash' of 'European' White-folk must be understood against the backdrop of the rising of what might be regarded as the new demographic of 'transnational Whites'. This is an important devel-opment. What we are witnessing is the beginning of a new epoch in which Whiteness no longer is dependent on 'White-folk' as understood thus far under colonial-modern registers of classification.

onisation', continue to abide by a *World* made in the imagination of *White* norm-ality. Recall the heady days of imagined liberation out of 'Whiteness', of a Fanonian "new history of Man" and all that,[58] all this we so readily repeat in our scholarship on Blackness. But seldom do we reflect upon what we have actually fulfilled, or not as is rather more to the point, in furtherance of this imagination, this aspiration, now as we stand, still, observing the fate of Black-ed lives in this (*White-*)*World*.

Keeanga-Yamahtta Taylor, in reviewing the history of struggles for liberation in the United States, understood this:

> The struggle for Black liberation requires going beyond the standard narrative that Black people have come a long way but have a long way to go – which, of course, says nothing at all about where it is that we are actually trying to get to. It requires understanding the origins and nature of Black oppression and racism more generally. More importantly, it requires a strategy, some sense of how we get from the current situation to the future.[59]

This is absolutely right. She continues:

> Perhaps at its most basic level, Black liberation implies a world where Black people can live in peace, without the constant threat of the social, economic, and political woes of a society that places almost no value on the vast majority of Black lives. It would mean living in a world where Black lives matter. While it is true that when Black people get free, everyone gets free, Black people in America cannot "get free" alone. In that sense, Black liberation is bound up with the project of human liberation and social transformation.[60]

Here, the error. This falls back into the trap of seeing the problem of 'Blackness' as something distinct from the matter of the *World*, as if 'Black' liberation is a matter within *this* World, capable of correction such that 'Black' lives can matter in the *World* made-by-*White*-ness. What does it mean for 'Black people to get free'? Indeed, it is a question of human liberation and social transformation, and this is the crux of it, the problem which requires "some

---

58 Frantz Fanon, (trans. Constance Farrington), *The Wretched of the Earth* (London: Penguin Books, 1967 (2001 reprint)), 254.
59 Keeanga-Yamahtta Taylor, *From #BlackLivesMatter to Black Liberation* (Chicago: Haymarket Books, 2016), 194.
60 *Ibid.*

sense of how we get from the current situation to the future."[61] My disagreement is in the assumption that the problem of 'liberation' is one defined by
the differentiations of 'race' and the operations of 'racism'. In such a view it is
possible to understand 'liberation' as a condition where 'Black lives matter',
as if this is a possibility within a *World* where the problem is understood as
one where 'White' and 'Black' remain merely matters skin-deep. This is to
misunderstand the problem, to regard 'racism' as existing separately from the
materiality of the fundamental categories of *White-d*-ness and *Black-ed*-ness,
distinct from the fundamental onto-epistemological (b)ordering of making-
White and making-*Black-ed* as a matter of the *World*-made. A different
'strategy' *is* necessary. We need to understand the workings of 'White'-ness in
a *Black-ed* World. This is to see clearly 'White'-ness as an invented beingness
of fragile innocence, set by Nature (and God for good measure) the task of
overseeing the Black-ed matter of the *World*.[62] This more than a problem
of 'structural racism', more than a matter of the redistribution of resources,
more than the question of *equality*.

We are dealing here with the matter of the *World* (b)ordered as imagined and enforced through five centuries of philosophical norm-alisation and
militaristic totalisation, fully the connection between *White*-ness and coloniality. And our response cannot be anything less than a renewed anti-colonial praxis. I am not suggesting here that thought as such will transform *this*
World, perhaps the problems of *White*-ness can never be resolved.[63] This is
beside the point. I am arguing that it is necessary, if we wish to make such grand
claims of ourselves, if we have the audacity to claim 'decolonisation' and 'decolonial' thinking, to assert being-radical and a radical-beingness, then we must
have the temerity to *think* – not just to repeat old analyses – but to actually
think through the problem as it is currently in the *World*. This is the burden
of the *anti-colonial* after all, to transform the (b)orders of coloniality – both
philosophical and material – into *frontlines*, so as to be no longer named and
emplaced as such within the imagination of colonial-thought and the regimes
of colonial rule. *White*-ness remains precisely this, a fragile (b)order-frontline
for anti-colonial repudiation. This we have insufficiently addressed. It is not our
job to placate 'White-folk', to assuage them of our non-threatening intentions.
Instead, we need to understand that the essential fragility of *White*-ness, even

---

61 *Ibid.*
62 Jacob waxes lyrical on this point in a lengthy chapter titled, 'Black and White' in *White Man, Think
     Again!*
63 This appears to be the assessment for the foreseeable future for Jardina; see *White Identity Politics.*

as it is entrenched through the sentimental fragility of folk ascribing to being-*White-in-the-World*, must exactly be that which we fully reveal and forcefully assert as an uncompromising matter of philosophical praxis.

'White'-ness as an invention, we recall, is a sociogenic totality that gave/gives meaning to 'race' as a structure of the *World*. In this connection, it is precisely sociogenesis that is ever in effect. That is to say, 'Whiteness' is reinvented and comes into reinvigorated force as a formation of beingness and identity on every occasion that articulations of 'coloured/Black-ed-beingness' are asserted. Put differently, if *White*-ness in the past was the onto-epistemological referent which (b)ordered and regulated 'racialised/coloured' beingness, the cunning of it is that today 'Whiteness' just *is*. As *we* claim our 'Blackness', so is the 'soul' of *White*-ness reinserted into rejuvenated 'White-d-folk' as a constant reinvention. Not necessarily consciously, for no such burden of awareness is required. The 'White'-ness of 'White-folk' is a latent power, dormant as the norm-ality of the *World*, yet ever available for invocation especially when it is called upon as an identitarian and civilisational affirmation in response to perceived existential threats. And the point of significance is this: 'White'-ness, is indeed invoked, and when done so, its intention is precisely to assert *Right* in the *World*, *Right* to the *World*, consciously, 'righteously', to terrify *us*, to put *us* back in our allotted places, either as 'subject', if we are fortunate, or as disposable matter, if we are not.

In this way, we must understand *White*-ness as precisely the original and (fragile) authorial claim to (sacred) *supremacy*, to the norm-ality of *Right*, to make and acquire the *World*, and towards this (righteous) end, with impunity, to kill. There is no other reason for its invention or its invocation. It is as Anthony Jacob put it:

> This is the only possible destiny of the White Christian race: to rule the world! Anything short of this would be a negation of the destiny for which we alone are shaped, and would unquestionably result in our obliteration. Racially we would be a failure, and would pay the price for failure.[64]

The assertion of *White*-ness – that is to say, the asserted presumption of a *beingness-in-the-World* essentialised as 'White'-ness – is *supremacy*. This is, quite simply, the underlying *Reason* of *White* as a category in and of the *World*,

---

64 Jacob, *White Man, Think Again!*, 450.

the underlying *Reason*, that is, of the norm-ality of coloniality.[65] Nothing but this. We have long known this, long identified its actual workings, but have simply ignored the full significance of the evidence.

Our conclusion is plain. There is no escaping the truth that *White*-ness is utterly incorrigible; no salvation or rescue, is possible. There is no negotiating with *White*-ness. There is no equal existence between folk made-'White' and folk Made-'Black(-ed)'. What I am arguing is not any insertion of 'Blackness' (or 'Brownness', or any other 'people-of-coloured'-ness) into the *World*, but the total dismantling of this pervasive structuring *Reason* of *Right*, of supremacy, that has come to be invisibilised, norm-al-ised, as 'White'. As a system of reality, *White* either rules, as a *Right* to the *World*, or it must be destroyed. There is no other possibility. And so might the 'folk', be they ones inflicted by its hatred, or ensnared by its apparent ubiquity, have their 'souls' set free. And thus, the anti-colonial imperative. *White*-ness, that is, the *Idea* and practice of 'White' as racial-category and subjective aspiration, must be repudiated unequivocally. Indeed, borrowing from the lexicon of those fragile and petrified 'White supremacists' – and it is truly laughable that they regard themselves so – it is precisely 'White'-Re-placement that is necessary. Nothing else will suffice to transform the *World* as a philosophical situation.

'White' Replacement as Anti-Colonial Praxis

It is time the un-'White' of the *World* cease this pandering to 'White' fragility.

The great 'White' fear is that the historic civilisation born out of 'Europe' – the one and only true civilisation that has mattered – will be swept away if left unchecked by the 'rising tide of colour', as Lothrop Stoddard put it in 1923.[66] For Stoddart:

> Here is the truth of the matter: The white world to-day stands at the crossroads of life and death. It stands where the Greek world stood at the close of the Peloponnesian War. A fever has racked the white frame and undermined its constitution. The unsound therapeutics of its diplomatic practitioners retard convalescence and endanger

---

65 This was, of course, the significant insight of Anibal Quijano that has since defined the 'decolonial' theoretical movement; see Anibal Quijano, 'Coloniality of Power and Eurocentrism in Latin America', *International Sociology*, 15(2), 2000, 215-32. What I stress – and this is something quite ignored in the decolonial literature with their emphasis on the 'epistemological' – is that this original effect of 'race' and racialisation is also fundamentally grounded in the materiality of social relations.

66 Lothrop Stoddard, *The Rising Tide of Color against White World-Supremacy* (London: Chapman Hall, 1922).

real recovery. Worst of all, the instinct of race – solidarity has partially atrophied.[67]

Central to this existential anxiety is the observed facts of declining 'White' birth-rates in the face of the perceived indiscriminate procreation of the lesser 'coloured races', and the impending tides of immigration and miscegenation that are viewed as threatening the 'inner dikes' of European borders; this the ultimate portend of doom:

> The inner dikes (the areas of white settlement), however, are a very different matter. Peopled as they are wholly or largely by whites, they have become parts of the race-heritage, which should be defended to the last extremity no matter if the costs involved are greater than their mere economic value would warrant. They are the true bulwarks of the race, the patrimony of future generations who have a right to demand of us that they shall be born white in a white man's land. Ill will it fare, if ever our race should close its ears to this most elemental call of the blood. Then, indeed, would be manifest the writing on the wall.[68]

Today, the same anxieties regarding racial extermination and the demand for countervailing action to remain pure, and supreme are articulated and repeated by the notions of 'White Genocide', and 'The Great Replacement'.[69] A host of philosophers, intent on protecting the imperilled 'White' race, repeat the same essential message and warning.[70] However, it would appear times have changed; these current proponents of an explicit assertion of global 'Whiteness' are widely condemned within 'mainstream' political circles as an extremist fringe. This is the 'anti-racist' normality, or so it would seem: we are all of 'racial equality' now, at least in so far as polite speech is

---

67 *Ibid*, 196.
68 *Ibid*, 226.
69 It is interesting, and telling, that the literature that proclaims in the most grandiose terms the supremacy of 'Whiteness' is precisely that which exposes 'White'-ness as a most tenuous and fragile identity, utterly susceptible to erasure. For a discussion of the origins and trajectories of these terms/slogans, see Kevan A. Feshami, 'Fear of White Genocide: Tracing the History of a Myth from Germany to Charlottesville', *Lapham's Quarterly*, 6 September 2017, available at <http://www.laphamsquarterly.org/roundtable/fear-white-genocide> last accessed 30 July 2021; and 'David Lane', *Southern Poverty Law Center*, available at <https://www.splcenter.org/fighting-hate/extremist-files/individual/david-lane> (accessed 2 August 2021).
70 The most concise and infamous of such statements now rendered as essential slogans of the alt-Right, White-supremacist movements are David Lane's '14 Words', and Bob Whitaker's 'The Mantra'; see Feshami, 'Fear of White Genocide', and Ryan Lenz, 'Following the White Rabbit', *Southern Poverty Law Quarterly*, 21 August 2013, available at <https://www.splcenter.org/fighting-hate/intelligence-report/2013/following-white-rabbit> last accessed 2 August 2022.

concerned. I am not interested here to argue against these views, to counter their logics or their fears. Quite the opposite. For the un-'White', it has been precisely the supreme mistake to assume this posture of arguing against these assertions of 'White'-ness and to regard them as somehow other than their essential meaning. My concern is exactly the opposite, to provoke a *frontline* repudiation of the underlying categories that 'make' this *World*. With this in mind, we clarify the implications of the deflection of *White*-ness that is served by the purported extremism of 'White-Supremacy'.

The basic understanding of those who fear the demise of 'Whiteness' are the following:

- There is, as a matter of biological fact, a White 'race', originating in the northern regions of 'Europe';
- The White-race are responsible for the origination of the one true worthy civilisation to benefit the World;
- 'White'-ness is, by biological fact and civilisational evidence, superior to all other lesser 'races' of the World;
- There is an intentional global threat to the perpetuation of White-supremacy the result of the rising tide of lesser races/nations resulting from their uncontrolled reproductive rates and incessant immigration into White-lands.
- The protection of 'White'-ness requires a concerted transnational White-solidarity to repulse the threat of 'replacement'.

These then might be regarded as the basic principles that define *White-Right* and *White-anxiety/fragility*. I suggest we grant them these convictions fully. If it is their intention to subscribe to this view, leave them be. We need not concern ourselves with attempts to convert them or to convince them that we mean not to threaten their peace of mind as *White*-folk. Our concern instead is to re-make the *World*.

I want to make one thing clear at this juncture. What I speak of is not some resort to 'extremism' in the sense that I am provoking a 'race-war' or instigating violence against 'White-folk'. My discussion on violence will come in a later chapter. For now, my attention is concentrated, as a matter of anti-colonial repudiation, on the elimination of a philosophical-'racial' category. In this sense, I do indeed intend to instigate for the elimination of ' *White*'-folk. This is not a 'racial' matter, not simply a case of 'race'-relations or relations of 'races' in the international field.[71] It is rather a matter of the norm-ality of

---

71 See the collection of essays in Alexander Anievas, Nivi Manchandra and Robbie Shilliam, *Race and Racism in International Relations: Confronting the Global Colour Line* (London: Routledge, 2015).

the *World* itself. What is of importance is that the so-called 'color-line' foundationally defines the violent and differentiated lines of (post)colonial regulation. Let me illustrate my meaning by reference to two statements that might initially appear as originating from quite separate philosophical orientations: The first, Anthony Jacob:

> [W]e must reject any vague belief in the inevitability of progress ... We have to strive for what we want; and in order to strive steadfastly we need to have in front of us, not a progressive vision, but a fixed and unalterable one. Thus, if we speak of progress we have to mean that we are changing the world to suit our vision of what we want it to be, and not that we are changing our vision to suit the world. ...
>
> With regard to this vision we would, I am sure, desire to see a fair and verdant world of the future in which our golden progeny might safely and happily dwell...[I]t can never come about unless we pursue a policy of outright White World Supremacy. White Supremacy is synonymous with White Survival; for if it is not to be White Supremacy it will be Non-White Supremacy (specifically Yellow Supremacy), with all its unthinkable consequences... we must reduce every other race and sub-race to servitude or dependance; at the very least to a position where effective resistance tour domination will be impossible.[72]

This we today read as beyond the pale, the unacceptable, racist, extremist view of a deranged 'White-supremacist'. The second, Robert Kagan:

> We have witnessed amazing progress in the past seven decades... Yet this progress was not the culmination of anything... It has been the product of a unique set of circumstances contingent on a particular set of historical outcomes... What we liberals call progress has been made possible by the protection afforded liberalism within the geographical and geopolitical space created by American power. This was not the inevitable unfolding of some Universal History. On the contrary, the creation of the liberal order has been an act of defiance against both history and human nature.
>
> People today ask what threatens the present, but that is the wrong question. ...The question is not what will bring down the liberal order but what can possibly hold it up? If the liberal order is like a garden, artificial and forever threatened by the forces of nature,

---

72 Jacob, *White Man, Think Again!*, 446.

preserving it requires a persistent, unending struggle against the
vines and weeds that are constantly working to undermine it from
within and overwhelm it from without.

Today there are signs all around us that the jungle is growing back.
... Where thirty years ago the dreams of Enlightenment thinkers going
back three centuries seemed to be on the cusp of fulfillment, today a
Counter-Enlightenment of surprising potency stirs in Moscow, Buda-
pest, Beijing, Tehran, and Cairo, in parts of Western Europe, and even
in the nation that saved liberalism seventy-five years ago.[73]

The contrast could not appear to be greater, between the racial self-centred-
ness inherent in Jacob's appeal and the global responsibility that motivates
Kagan's concerns. But they both speak of an anxiety, of a concern with a
perceived passing of an 'order' by the growing threats of encroachment, and
of the need for resolute and steadfast commitment to preserve the status quo
– the 'garden' of virtue and progress against the 'jungle' of vice and depreda-
tions. No doubt Kagan presents a more sophisticated and subtle description
of the urgent situation, but the implications are little distinguishable. We
see here an assertion of *Right*, couched in terms of a burdensome *responsibility*, but of *Right* nevertheless. If in Jacob, it plain to see the supremist
underpinnings of the claim to make and preserve the World as a Right of
'White'-ness, in Kagan, the crude marker of 'White'-ness is replaced by the
burden of 'American' exceptionalism as the sole protector of the progressive,
precarious, 'liberal' order. Kagan's concern is to emphasise the necessity to
hold firm to this responsibility, to maintain the difficult burden to 'intervene'
in the *World* in order that 'Order' is protected from the invasions of the
Jungle. In this, weakness of resolve must be countered:

Americans, it is fair to say, have not enjoyed power too much. These
days they would prefer to wield it less. Yet the struggle for power in
the international system is eternal, and so is the struggle over beliefs
and ideals. If it is not our system of security and our beliefs shaping
the world order, it will be someone else's. If we do not preserve the
liberal order, it will be replaced by another kind of order, or more
likely by disorder and chaos of the kind we saw in the twentieth
century. That is what the world "as it is" looks like. ...and would lead
to in the future if not continually shaped, managed, and resisted.[74]

---

73 Kagan, *The Jungle Grows Back*, 8-10.
74 *Ibid*, 162.

I have given considerable space here to Kagan because it is this type of philosophical positioning, mainstream in that it informs the discourse and actions of international 'policy-makers', that is largely unattended to by most 'radical' thinkers. The *World*, plainly, is less determined by our 'epistemological' excursions, and incursions, in 'decoloniality' than it is by the rather simple and unashamed assertions of norm-alised power. There is no equivocation in this position put forward by Kagan, no pandering to the high values of a global order predicated on anything other than the acquisition and preservation of power for material interests. This is what is euphemistically referred to as the 'liberal' order, that same order that presides over 'splendour in squalor'. The *World* as *matter* informs this understanding of norm-ality, prescribes this philosophy of (b)ordering. In pursuit of this intent, the racial 'extremism' of past and present 'White'-supremist views are conveniently eschewed, no longer the explicit schema of differentiation. 'Race', we see, is replaced by a more abstract register of 'value', a new code for *Right* premised now on an apparent *Reason* of 'liberal' capitalist materiality, fully retaining within it the underlying assumptions and assertions of the Colonial-Modern legacy of *White*-Right.

To repeat the point, the misdirection of 'White-supremacy' as extremism is to provide an alibi to the pervasive norm-ality of *White*-ness which in turn structures the 'racialised' *World*. Indeed, this is to truly disarm the anti-colonial response. Let us not be deceived. I regard 'White' fear of 'replacement', of 'racial' demise, as revealing the unfiltered truth of *White*-ness as an indefensible and precarious infliction, and in turn, of the fact that *White*-ness can only be maintained through the non-negotiable assertion of supremacy and racialised subjugation of all others. The explicit nature of this foundational philosophical frame of global coloniality is precisely what is obscured by the liberal norm-alisation of 'Whiteness' as nothing more than a racial category, one amongst many, of the 'Whiteness' of a folk who are amenable to peaceful coexistence with folk of other (invented) colourations. This is the actual conspiracy that maintains the (b)orders of *this* Colonial-Modern World. As I see it, we need to make fully visible the operation of *White*-ness and to expose fully the truth behind 'White' fear and fragility. The anti-colonial position is clear. Those who might regard themselves *White-in-the-World*, who might insist on this assumption and assertion of original and normative *supremacy* as *Right*, it is right that they heed the warnings of their predecessors. It is precisely the replacement of global *White*-ness that is intended. In this statement, there are also significant implications on the *un-White*.

The question is this: to what extent do we, the *un-White* of the *World*, stand ready to challenge the assertion of *White* norm-ality? To what extent, notwithstanding all the protestations and the 'radical' theorisations of 'Blackness', are we able to reclaim the matter of *White*-matter, to counter the confident assertion of philosophers such as Robert Kagan that the truth of the *World* is indeed that of 'White/'American' supremacy? This *matter* that I speak of includes the very territories of the 'coloured lands' of the so-called 'post-colonial' global order. Where in this (post)colonial *World* is the evidence of radical Blackness – of Black being a 'country', to recall Kehinde Andrews – in the actual countries established under the (post)colonial settlements of 'decolonisation'? A system of reality, James Baldwin called it, this is a reality born out of the philosophies of coloniality, of *White*-ness and its 'post-racial' revisions. To what extent are we willing to cease our complaint and begin instead a praxis of '*White*-Replacement'?

Let me suggest a beginning. Baldwin was correct, in 'On Being White... And Other Lies', to call out as lies the fateful consequences of the 'moral choice' that was *White*-ness.[75] "[B]ecause they think they are white", Baldwin repeated, because they think they are White, they – White-folk – "have brought humanity to the edge of oblivion."[76] But he missed something in this analysis, or at least he did not develop the observation; he did not see that the 'lies' went deeper, that the lies of *White*-ness were themselves based on prior Lies constructed out of generations of philosophical investment informed by the *Reason* of coloniality, that is to say, of the desire to name and claim the *World*. These Lies therefore form the implicit foundations of *White*-ness as a normative system of reality, deeply ingrained such that they operate almost as a universal 'common-sense'. And we have long permitted these Lies to pass. We were enraged, true, but we allowed it to endure, this *World* built on 'White Lies', by accepting the Lies that make *White*-ness and its (b)ordered *World* of matter, imaginable, even in all its violence and perversity, meaningful.

On the ground of these Lies then are the claims and norm-alities of *White*-ness rooted, and by these Lies are the 'souls' of 'White-d'-folk, as 'White-folk', sustained. If we are serious about the matter, then it is necessary that we move beyond the periodic appeal for 'Black Lives' to have a place in this *World*. Instead, we need make visible the Lies that sustain *White*-ness in

---

75 James Baldwin, 'On Being White... And Other Lies (1984)' in David Roediger (ed.), *Black on White: Black Writers on What It Means to Be White* (New York: Schoken Books, 1998), 177-180.
76 *Ibid*, p. 180

the *World* and affirm explicitly the anti-colonial position we hold, to revoke the authority of (post)colonial (b)orders and to claim them instead fully as legitimate frontlines of anti-colonial praxis. In such an assertion of sedition against the norm-alities of the present, we must not be shy to also affirm the inevitable implication of 'decolonisation': 'White lives', that is to say the assertion of beingness by those who knowing the facts remain insistent on claiming the ascription of supremacy that is *White*-ness in the *World*, is precisely the condition of beingness that "loyalty to Humanity", for the sake of *all* Life, requires obliteration "by all means necessary".

4

On 'Europe' and the 'Postcolony'

As we have seen, when we speak of *White*-ness as a *World*-making category, as a system of reality', it is more than the problem of 'racism' that is at issue, more than a deliberation of (in)justice that is called for. At issue is the norm-al-isation of categories, as a global regime of commensurability, that define the *World* as a totality and prescribe the ontologies of differentiated *subjection* within it, the work of *(b)orders* to enforce. Nothing less than the entirety of the *World* as a (post)colonial artefact is, in fact, at stake.

I have previously explained the implications of 'methodological post-colonialism', that is, of the philosophical manoeuvre that entrenched, as a *Worldscape*, a global totality of commensurability. This requires elabora-tion. What is left to be done is, first, to reveal the undergirding categories which provide the foundations on which the re-settlement of (post)colo-niality under the 'post-colonial settlement' is affected; indeed, it is the effect of these ontological manoeuvres that give meaning to the very notion of the 'post-colonial' as an asserted political-legal reality in the present. And from this, secondly, to repudiate these (post)colonial assertions of *(b)orders* as fully *frontlines* of anti-colonial praxes. Indeed, here we attend to 'false words', to foundational *White-Lies*.

In what follows I elaborate on the two categories through which the outrageous and the absurd is made ubiquitous: *Europe* and *Postcolony*. In their intimacy and correspondence, they entrench a philosophoscape of coloniality, founded and premised on domination and subjugation and on which a norm-ality of territorialised differentiated subjection continues to be maintained, now cleansed of its *colonial* taint.[1] To be clear, I don't mean by

---

1 I adopt the term 'intimacy' not its affective sense to describe the relations, the connections, between

Europe and *Postcolony* geographical entities or political units. I don't examine them as particular 'places' in the *World*, to investigate their specific cruelties and contradictions, their betrayals or possibilities. This is not to diminish the very real violence that the (b)ordering of 'places' of subjection continuously inflicts. But I am focussed rather on how the reification of these categories perpetuates structures and systems of differentiated subjection that norm-alises such perverse actualities of (b)ordering into and within such 'places'. As such, the meanings that have attached to them as 'place', and the associa-tions thereby following regarding their bearing upon questions of subjection, of *inclusions* and *exclusions*, are precisely the norm-alised consequences that I mean to open up to view. I speak of *Europe* and *Postcolony*, therefore, as (post) colonial philosophical constructs that, as *World*-making categories, norm-alise the regulation and management of coloniality in the 'post-colonial' present. To state it differently, I speak of them fully as *(b)orders-frontlines*.

On *Name*-ing and *Place*-ing the *World*

At the heart of the (post)colonial problem is our apparent incapacity to see beyond this structure of the *World* as anything other than as a reification, as seen and thought through the conceptual categories of the (b)ordered geography of 'territories' and 'subjects' now deemed 'post-colonial'. Let us remind ourselves of the basic 'structure' of the 'post-colonial' *World*scape as commonly understood:

- The territorial geography of the earth is demarcated by assigned names attaching to delimited spatial units variously categorised, the primary categorical unit of normative significance being the named territorial ('post-colonial') 'State' as an authoritative jurisdictional sphere of order recognised, as one within a totality of States, through the consensual affir-mation of 'International Law'.[2] Thus is the state assigned temporal and spatial authority in the constructed totality of the *World* as a systemic ideational whole. The origins of this systemic regime of territorial/

'subjects' – a common preoccupation amongst contemporary critical theorists – but to describe 1) connections derived from categorical assumptions; and 2) structural and material relatedness. In this respect, both Ashis Nandy's, *Intimate Enemy: Loss and Recovery of Self Under Colonialism* (Oxford: Oxford University Press, 1983), and Lisa Lowe's, *The Intimacies of Four Continents* (Durham: Duke University Press, 2015) serve as relevant inspirations. My concern is to demonstrate intimacy and correspondence as the structural foundation of the *World* as an artefact both of a Colonial-Modern philosophoscape and (post)colonial Worldscape. Matters of affect, no doubt, flow from the experienced effects of the philosophoscapes and worldscapes in operation.

2 See Sundhya Pahuja, 'Laws of Encounter: A Jurisdictional Account of International Law', *London Review of International Law* 1(1), 2013, 63-98.

jurisdictional (b)ordering, we are invited to accept, are the vagaries of many 'accidents of history' sanctified retrospectively via the declarative political-legal technology of the 'declaration of independence'.

- With the spatial segregation of the *World* thus affixed upon the imagination, so assigned are the human inhabitants of territory with corresponding 'citizenship-names' that inscribe upon bodies the norm-alised and prescribed spatial possibilities, and crucially, limits, of their being-in-the-*World*, as political-legal *subject*. To be-subject is thus, first and foremost, to be *contained-in-territory*, with *inscribed Name* in *assigned Place*. Any deviation from this assignation of subjection, any transgression of territorial-emplacement, is (differentiatedly assumed to be) *prima facie* 'irregular', a breach of (b)orders as it were, unless by virtue of the possession of appropriate *exemptions*.
- The order of the *World* is thereby fixed by the borders of inscribed names and meanings. And by this order are the regulation of social relations prescribed by the organisational and institutional dictates of the global order thus agreed upon and norm-alised as a consequence of the 'post-colonial' global settlement. *To-Be-in-the-World* is thus to be defined by the territorial and relational possibilities and limits so availing, the result of the purportedly 'negotiated' settlements prescribed by the politico-juridical processes instantiated by the 'post-colonial', 'International' system of global regulation.

Simply put, what this describes is the 'universal' onto-epistemological and institutional structure of 'Sovereignty-Citizenship' that purportedly encapsulates the meanings and implications of jurisdictional place and subject-names, these the fundamental categories of (b)ordering on which the entirety of Colonial-Modern 'political-legal' philosophy is built. What is appealing in this structuring of normative *Beingness-in-the-World* is the asserted objective universality of these categorical inscriptions. In this scheme, 'sovereign equality' defines the ontological quality of states recognised as a juridical, even if not empirical, fact. The beingness of all 'Humans' – as an abstract category of subjection – is similarly recognised through the inscription of 'citizenship' as 'subject-beingness' under the jurisdiction of 'sovereign' care and control by law, unless *exceptionally* exempted by law. So goes the 'theory' of 'international' law/politics, now rendered 'post-colonial'.

And so, we have the situation of the present: a global (post)colonial totality of enforced and regulated (b)ordered *subject-beingness-in-territory*, accounted for, and emplaced, duty-bound so *to-Be*, respectively in our assigned, (b)ordered jurisdictional 'places'. Thus, with name, from place, are the socialities of all Human-Beingness recognised and regulated, the 'Modern' imagination completed as a result of the arduous journey of universal Humanity culminating in the 'post-colonial' settlement of a global regulatory totality of political-legal (b)ordering. This is the work of Law to (b)order, to enforce. 'Name' and 'Place': the foundations of the *World* as a commensurable totality of meaning.[3]

But none of this is convincing, of course. We have long known this formation of the *World* to be precisely the norm-alisation of coloniality, of Du Bois' 'Global Colour Line', imagined and violently drawn upon the soils of the Earth by the marker that is 'White'-ness. A useful recent re-statement of this actuality is Harsha Walia's analysis of 'border imperialism':

> Border imperialism ...disrupts the myth of Western benevolence toward migrants. In fact, it wholly flips the script on borders ... Border imperialism depicts the processes by which the violence and precarities of displacement and migration are *structurally* created as well as maintained.
>
> Border imperialism encapsulates four overlapping and concurrent structurings: first, the mass displacement of impoverished and colonized communities resulting from asymmetrical relations of global power, and the simultaneous securitization of the border against those migrants whom capitalism and empire have displaced; second, the criminalization of migration with severe punishment and discipline of those deemed "alien" or "illegal"; third, the entrenchment of a racialized hierarchy of citizenship by arbitrating who legitimately constitutes the nation-sate; and fourth, the state-mediated exploitation of migrant labor, akin to conditions of slavery and servitude, by capitalist interests. While borders are understood as lines demarcating territory, an analysis of border imperialism interrogates the modes and networks of governance that determine how bodies will be included within the nation-state, and how territory will be controlled within and in conjunction with the dictates of global empire and transnational capitalism.[4]

---

3 Vasuki Nessiah provides an excellent tracing of the colonial-legal histories and implications of this matter in 'Placing International Law: White Spaces on a Map', *Leiden Journal of International Law* 16, 2003, 1-35.
4 *Ibid*, 5-6 (emphasis in original).

The description is accurate. It clearly reveals the work of 'borders', as a technology of (b)ordering,[5] in norm-alising the many ways in which differentiated-'subjects' are regulated as a global totality, the precarity of 'subject-beingness' – or 'citizenship' if you prefer the reified terminology – precisely the operation of a global 'management of populations'.[6] There is abundant literature on all of the various issues Walia raises in this useful summary – on the plight of 'migrants' and the conditions of global migration, on the politics and cruelties that attach to the regime of 'refuge', on the workings of predatory capitalism and its many operations of extraction and displacement, on the increasing tendencies of securitisation and surveillance of 'suspect' populations on whatever grounds deemed offensive to corporate-state interests, on the racialised discourses and regulatory normalities of (un)belonging etc. – and it is not my intention to repeat the analysis and critiques here.[7] My interest here is not on the substance of the complaints. My interest is rather how we understand, as a matter of/for philosophy, the situation of (post) colonial *(b)orders* given the understanding that we have of this actuality.

Allow me what might appear an indulgence.

I was named, upon birth, in a *Register of Births* in *Malaysia*.[8] The result of my parents' subject-identities, my subject-beingness was further qualified by a 'racial/ethnic' inscription of meaning – this being an important marker of subject-ed identity in Malaysia – as Indian, and by a further genitalic ascription: Male. This is Me-as-subject as originally authored by *Malaysian Law*, itself a 'jurisdictional' regime subject to and (b)ordered by *International Law*. Thus, philosophically speaking, am I (re)cognisable as a *subject* in/of *Law* in the *World*. And on my death, I will be equally inscribed by Law – as

5 Achille Mbembe speaks of 'borderization' in this context; see *Necropolitics* trans. Steven Corcoran (Durham: Duke University Press, 2019), 99. I return to the implications of this regulatory work below.
6 Barry Hindess, 'Citizenship in the International Management of Populations' *American Behavioral Scientist* 43(9), 2000, 1486-1497.
7 See Harsha Walia, *Border & Rule: Global Migration, Capitalism, and the Rise of Racist Nationalism* (Chicago: Haymarket Books, 2021) This recent update by Walia, in my view, is less innovative in that it repeats the usual accounts of injustice with little analytical insight to add to the earlier analysis of border imperialism. The discussion on the various 'nationalist' backlashes, notwithstanding the many arguments raised in Walia's book, and in others like it, should be a cause to pause, to reflect on the realisation that 'justice-talk' impresses little. A more fundamental 'philosophy', more than the empirical realities of (in)justice of 'borders', is at work; this is my concern to elaborate.
8 And it should be added that the particular naming conventions within the Malaysian jurisdictional register has caused all manner of inconveniences in its departure from the Euro-Christian conventions of naming, assumed as universal norm-ality, as applied, for example, in the United Kingdom. And so, we (aspiring and aspirational) global(ised) subjects bend over backwards to conform, to modify our *Names* to suit the convenience of commensurability to a 'standard of civilisation', of sorts, still very much in operation for the 'subject' of the *postcolony* to abide by in the metropole.

deceased – to be made no-longer Being, no longer present and representable as a subject(ed)-body in the bounded body-politic, *ceasing* that is to Be-subject within a Colonial-Modern cosmology of beingness. But philosophical issues of *subjectivity* aside, more significant is the consequence that with such inscriptions and ascriptions of name and meaning am I materially *made-subject* to the prescriptions of 'Political-Legal' jurisdiction, so determined as commensurable notwithstanding civilisational traditions or cosmologies, enforceable in all of the *World* as such, meaningful as the marker of global subjection as such. And between the two containing events of birth and death – my becoming-subject, and my eventual ceasing to Be-subject – a whole range of further qualifications (in both senses of the term, enabling and disabling) operate as my actual (rather than philosophical) beingness is regulated through the manifold (b) orders of the *World*. And thus, I am enabled beingness as an emplaced *subject*, subject-ed, (b)ordered, inscribed by the names and meanings that have come to define the register of *Humanity* – through the enforced processes of (post) colonial *civil-isation* – as a universalised, globalised construct, made commensurable, cognizable and enforceable the *World* over. Malaysian (Indian), male, (precariously) UK-resident, 'son' of a heterosexual atomic family organisation of socio-economic-cultural (re)production, (ex)husband and father within the same, 'university graduate', 'employee', 'tax-payer', possessor of a 'credit-rating', targeted consumer, there is here a whole bunch of meaning derived from Colonial-Modern 'History' (and from the countless immiserations that have gone into their norm-alisation across times and places);[9] all of these names, and the implication and implicatedness that follow from them, meaningful only in that they are all technologies of commensurability to make-*Be* in this 'post-colonial' *World* as *colonised-being-ness* in *this* (post)colonial World.

What an astounding feat of *World*-making this, this totality of commensurability that we assume as given, as meaningful, a system of names and meanings norm-alised precisely for the purpose of enforcing, through subjection, differentiated subject-beingness in and across juridical 'State'-territories. In my current locatedness, *I-am-subject*, as 'citizen', of a juridical 'State' space/ place in the *World*, permitted, precariously to 'remain', within the juridical space of another – the 'United Kingdom' – the result of my successful *qualifications* and inscription into the relevant registers of subjection within a global *World*scape of *Names* and *Places*. But all of this is contingent, of course, on

---

9 Achille Mbembe's notions of 'entanglement' and 'time of entanglement' are relevant in this connection; see Mbembe, *On the Postcolony* (Berkeley: University of California Press, 2001) 14-17.

being a 'good subject',[10] with right-ful/less name in ascribed place performing sanctioned *duties*; this precisely is the condition of 'subjectivity' in/as containment, the operation of a global system of commensurable *Name-ing* and *Place-ing* of 'populations'. A different subjectivity, that of abjection and abandonment, is the fate of those who do not, or cannot, abide by this regime of inscribed meaning, those who are disobedient by transgressing the (b)orders of Name and Place. While much effort is made to speak of these 'experiences' of 'subjects' through the purported universal rationality of 'Rights', the simple truth of the matter is that the rationality of global (b)ordering has little to do with concern for the vulnerabilities of disposable 'subjects'.[11] We say this is *unjust*. We expose it to be the operation of 'border imperialism'. Norm-ality, nevertheless.

So, what is the point of this autobiographical confession? It is obvious from my description that in every *meaningful* way, my beingness in the *World*, in the manner described,[12] is wholly, inscribed by the categories of (post)coloniality that originates this philosophoscape of Colonial-Modern *subjectivity-subjection*. And by this subjection am I, as a walking-talking-abiding subject-beingness of this (post)colonial *World* properly, right-fully/lessly, emplaced, contained, with possibilities of licence – should 'I' be so fortunate – and/or ever susceptible to abandonment, should I be less so. This is so much (b)ordering-work in operation. None of it unfamiliar to us. We hardly give it a second thought this magnificent invention.

How is it that we have arrived at this impressive global system of subjection? To understand it as norm-ality, even if abhorrently so? How is

10 Let me just add this final thought. The fact is that for all intents and purposes, that is, for all that is relevant to the managers and enforcers of (post)colonial (b)ordering, I have indeed been a 'good subject', notwithstanding whatever critical posturing I might have presented within the spaces of so-called 'academic freedom' afforded me, or even in the streets in more 'activist' modes of expression, I have abided by my inscribed names and places, and reported my-'subject-self' duly so to be accounted for. I suspect many of you reading this might also have done just so. And here is the simple, and necessarily uncomfortable truth: for us (post)colonial 'subjects' who have been permitted, by appropriate processes of 'qualifications', presence at the Master's house, and perhaps even to partake at his table, for those of us who have been granted opportunities of privilege by 'virtue' of abiding by our *subjection* under the philosophoscape authored by the imagination of 'White'-ness, and the *Worldscape* thereby enforced, there is a lot at stake in preserving this norm-ality, this (post)colonial 'system of reality'. This clearly gives rise to grave implications when any imagination of a worlds otherwise is to be contemplated. We will return to this later.
11 I elaborate on this argument in Jayan Nayar, 'The Non-Perplexity of Human Rights', *Theory & Event* 22(2), 2019, 267-302.
12 This is to acknowledge that this cosmology of 'Self' is not the only means of locating the 'person' in the world, but this is what I have inherited, and it is, in my case, the only way in which my beingness in the world is open to my understanding. This, simply put, is the proof of *colonization*, proof of *my-being-colonised*.

it that we can look upon this *World* thus made commensurable, see clearly all its absurdities, its cruelties, the utter banality of the cruelties of its absurdities, and still remain blinded by a philosophoscape that appears impervious to revelation, remaining ever obscure in its fundamental operations? There is, obviously, a backstory in operation.

The *World* as Intimate Correspondence of Belonging-Separation

All that we are here speaking of, as 'political-legal' fact, is the legacy of a continuous line of thought that originates with a *World* 'discovered' and given meaning by the authorial *I* of Colonial-Modern philosophy – the *ego conquiro* – who claimed all worlds as fully *White-matter* through the vocabulary and semantics of *discovery* and *civilisation*. We know this. And with the continuities of subjugation and domination still intact, so was it resettled, the remnants of *ruination* now redeemed as 'post-colonial' juridical fact.[13] We know this also. Indeed, we have accurately mapped the cruelties of the *World* time and time again. But these efforts remain inadequate. We remain, notwithstanding our 'post/decolonial' assertions, enchanted by *this* World. Our interrogations and explications, for all their value in describing the 'post-colonial' present, do little to explain the underlying operation of the *World*, not simply as a system of regulation as such, but as a system of reality. Here we arrive at the heart of the matter.

Much of our analysis and prognosis assumes that fundamentally, and howsoever distributed, the problems of the 'World' pertain to questions of 'inclusion' and 'exclusion', that is to say, of the determinants of 'belonging', on the one hand, and 'separation', on the other.[14] Thus is the *World*, as we

---

13 See Ann Laura Stoler, *Duress: Imperial Durabilities in Our Times* (Durham: Durham University Press, 2016).

14 For an interesting attempt to redefine the premise of inclusion and exclusion in political-legal conceptions of 'citizenship', see Ayalet Shachar, *The Birthright Lottery: Citizenship and Global Inequality* (Cambridge: Harvard University Press, 2009). Shachar is concerned with the inequities that derive from regimes of 'citizenship' based on the birthright tenets of *jus soli* and *jus sanguinis*, that is, on an onto-epistemology of political-legal (b)ordering premised on the claim to 'soil' or 'blood'. In attempting to correct 'inequalities' of 'inclusion' and 'exclusion', Shachar adopts a view of 'citizenship' that retains an idealistic understanding of the ascription of *subjection*, of the situation of *being-(made)-subject*. Shachar is concerned with the question of 'rights', the assumption being that whatever the dispute, of concern is the distribution of that which pertains to the 'rights' of the 'citizen' – to the public 'inheritance' – as part of an overall calculation of 'justice'. We note that in this view, the (b)ordering regime itself, of the so-called 'inheritance', remains assumed, it is simply the distribution of rights as a measure of justice – the correct/appropriate distribution of *belonging* and *separation* – and the rationalities of their assignation, that are in contention. What is at issue, in other words, is a concern with 'subjectivity', with the 'political' possibilities of *becoming-being-subject* within the regime of global bordering. A different view would be one which sees the *Reason* of *subjection*, understood through a non-idealist perspective, to be at the very core of the inscription of (un)belonging. Understood thus, the *History* of (Colonial-Modern) (b)ordering has been precisely one that from time

have been civilised to know it, constructed as a totality of ascriptions that
we familiarly understand as the mapped territoriality of *Names* and *Places*,
markers, that is, of belonging *and* separation. No doubt, it has been the
matter of great struggles, this story of Name and Place. But this was already a
struggle limited by a particular prescription of imagination. And more than
this, the investiture of Name and Place performed a potent philosophical
function of re-(b)ordering. Recalling our discussion in Chapter 1, key to the
entrenchment of (post)colonial situation was the (purported) rupture of the
'colonial' totality that is marked by the ontological event of the 'declaration
of independence', the event, that is, that invests Name and Place unto the
World as imagination and matter. From the 'colonial' to the 'post-colonial',
this is the categorical shift we take as given, the consequent philosophoscape
and *World*scape now resettled, re(b)ordered, redeemed, *after* 'colonialism'.[15]
To repeat from Chapter 1:

- the 'colonial' and the 'post-colonial' are marked as distinct temporalities,
  and ontologies, of global (b)ordering;
- the 'National' and the 'International' are demarcated as distinct, and categorically opposed, territorialised 'political' rationalities of regulatory and
  enforcement regimes/structures/technologies of global (b)ordering.
- the 'citizen' is inscribed as a new and universal subject-being under 'post-colonial' *sovereignty*, a beingness purportedly liberated in philosophy from
  colonial subjection, and materially from colonial subjugation-subjection.

We have seen this settlement come to full fruition as a grand deceit, the territorial marking of the *World*, and its emplaced inscriptions of 'belonging' and
'separation', fully a technology of (b)ordering (post)coloniality. But more
than the ascription of territorial belonging *and* separation is at play in the
'post-colonial' deceit. What we understand as the operation of coloniality, of
'border imperialism' in Walia's terms, is revealing of a fundamental construction of social beingness and locatedness. Rather than *(b)ordering* being a
question of the distribution of the wages of belonging *and* separation, of
calculations of the distinct distributive accounts of each as indeed separate

---

to time adaptively recounts the distribution of appropriations-inheritance; aside from the 'sovereign'
Rights of *licence*, it is not 'birthright' but *birth-duties* of subjection-containment that are primary. This
pertains to the duty to *be-subject*, fully to be available, at the minimum, to 'labour' (or not as the case
may be) for the benefit of the 'common-wealth', extending to the duty to be available for death in the
'defence' of the 'sovereign'. This is what I have described as the fundamental *Reason* of coloniality in
its operations of *containment* as an integral part of the global totality of (b)ordering.

15 See Vivienne Jabri, *The Postcolonial Subject.: Claiming Politics/Governing Others in Late* Modernity
(Abingdon: Routledge, 2013).

and separating, it is better understood as a mediation of ontologies, that is to say, of the correspondence of categories founded on the intimacies of what is properly understood as *belonging-separation*.[16]

Negotiations of belonging *and* separation presupposes the existence of distinct ontological entities in relational tension. Belonging-separation, on the other hand, is co-eval in that it pertains to each of the categories innately, and as such, is constantly remediated, simultaneously defining the onto-epistemology of any given situation of ascribed beingness: the belonging-separation of the conqueror and the conquered; the coloniser and the colonised; the settlor and the native; the colony and the metropole. In all of these purportedly Manichean situations, of the seemingly utter duality of beingness, a co-evalness and simultaneity of belonging-separation operate as a dangerous and discomforting intimacy that defines each of these ascriptions (and following from this, the inscriptions) of *subjection* as a coherent and commensurable totality.[17] The philosophical work of *Name-ing* and *Place-ing* is key of course. We note that in each of these ascriptions of relationality – coloniser/colonised, settlor/native, metropole/colony etc. – it is precisely the correspondence of a belonging-in-separation, and a separation-in-belonging, that is constantly named and (re)mediated through every invocation of these ascribed situations of beingness within a commensurate totality. To be coloniser is both to belong in a totality with the colonised and to be separated from the colonised within that totality.[18] Neither one is meaningful in the *World* without the other. Within this regulated intimacy does the specific content of the relations of *subjection* come to manifest.[19]

---

16 A similar intention towards a coherent understanding of the *World* as a totality can be found in E. Tendayi Achiume's argument that the 'European colonial project' be understood as a mandatory invitation to indefinite co-dependency; see 'Reimagining International Law for Global Migration: Migration as Decolonization?', *American Journal of International Law Unbound* 111, 2017, 142-46. I find this phraseology less effective however in conveying, and making explicit, the precise relational dynamic of *intimacy* which involves the oscillation between the enforcements of separation and belonging that operate in any given instance of (post)colonial (b)ordering.

17 For excellent essays that explore this intimacy in the context of the imperial formation of 'Englishness', see Catherine Hall (ed), *Cultures of Empire: Colonizers in Britain and the Empire in the Nineteenth and Twentieth Centuries, A Reader* (New York: Routledge, 2000); also Catherine Hall, *Civilising Subjects: Colony and Metropole in the English Imagination* (Chicago: University of Chicago Press, 2002).

18 I want to stress that I am not speaking here of the 'space' that interested *Bhabha* in which 'mimesis' and 'hybridity' arise; see Homi Bhabha, *The Location of Culture* (London: Routledge, 2004). My concern, to repeat the point, is not on the experience of beingness within these ascribed situations, but on the intimate correspondence of categories that inscribe subject-beingness in locations.

19 I employ the term 'intimacy' to describe two significant aspects of Colonial-Modern (b)ordering, neither of which are to do with 'affect' as it has come to be all the fashion in current 'critical theory'. Rather I use intimacy first, in the sense of categorical implicatedness similar to its use by Ashis Nandy in *Intimate Enemy: Loss and Recovery of Self Under Colonialism* (Oxford: Oxford University Press, 1983), and secondly, in the sense of material interconnectedness as described by Lisa Lowe, *The Intimacies of Four*

What I am setting out here is a connection long understood. At a simplistic
level, we know that, for example, many of the great 'Enlightenment' treaties of
politics and law were indeed fully in intimate correspondence with the burden
of belonging and separation, that is, of the actualities of the violent intimacies
of encounter, plunder and subjugation; simply, there would be no theories
of 'Whiteness' and the 'Enlightenment' without the bloody savagery of the
White-ing of folk as a claim to those *Black*-ed as matter of making the *World*.[20]
To know this alone, however, is insufficient. What is important is to recognise
the implications of this intimacy, as I am calling it, in precisely doing the work
of norm-alising the onto-epistemology authored by the violent *World-making*
imagination of 'White'-ness. By this I mean that our very understanding of the
categories of 'White' and 'non-White', coloniser and colonised, metropole and
(post)colony etc, each only meaningful in that it is utterly defined by its relationship as belonging to and with the other, and is by this belonging, formed as
being marked by an unbridgeable separation. The coloniser is nothing without
the colonised at the same time as s/he is Everything that is distant from the
colonised, utterly separated by an unbreakable intimacy of belonging.[21]

Consider the work of the *idea* of the 'colony', at least in so far as it pertains
to the operation of *World*-making in political-legal philosophy. I argued in
Chapter 2 that more than an empirical coherence, the idea of 'colony' has
served to provide a categorical situation for the framing of political-legal
relationalities as structure and discourse upon which the 'post-colonial' as
a subsequent situation is brought into imagination. It is the situation of the
colony after all that gives meaning to the purported ruptural situation of the
'post-colonial' as a *becoming-into-the-International*, as Vivienne Jabri understands it.[22] The colony becomes, as a reified philosophical situation and political category, regardless of the actuality of social relations that might prevail
in each individual place of subjugation, a *named* and (b)ordered location of

Continents (Durham: Duke University Press, 2015). The dual meaning of the term is significant in that
it makes explicit the *intimacy* of the Colonial-Modern philosophoscape with the (post)colonial Worldscape. Intimacy in my use therefore is not concerned with issues of *affective subjectivity* in the World
understood as a given, but rather with categorical and material *World*-making/(b)ordering within which
subsequent experiences of subject-beingness, and from this, affective responses, might arise.

20 For example, Susan Buck-Morss, *Hegel, Haiti and Universal History* (Pittsburgh: University of Pittsburgh Press, 2009).
21 It is of course this relationship, understood as dialectic, that occupied Fanon's and Memmi's studies on
the colonizer-colonised 'relationship', that has since come to define the basic structure of how we think
about the colonial and 'post-colonial' situations.
22 Jabri *The Postcolonial Subject*. We see the pervasive consequence of the *World*-making effect of the
colony also in Adom Getachew's World-making after Empire: The Rise and Fall of Self-Determination (Princeton: Princeton University Press, 2019).

subjection, named that is by reason of the intimate belonging engendered by the relation 'colony-metropole', and as such, structured and enforced as fundamentally and definingly separate.[23] But the 'colony' does something different in addition to this essentialising of situations; the colony also defines the *qualities* of the 'metropole' as an essentialised ontological category in/ of the *World*, given meaning and providence in *History*.[24] And here lies the significance of correspondence, of the intimacy that is *(post)colony-(Europe) metropole* as co-constitutive; together, in their intimate correspondence, *colony-metropole* forms the basic categorical foundation of (post)coloniality.

Recall the *Names* and *Places* that we referred to as constituting the basic structure of the 'post-colonial' *World*. We return to them here. Indeed, they are meaningful. They define the very sense of subject-beingness that we analyse and imagine in our critical endeavours to overcome what we see as the racialised (b)ordering of the *World*. These Names, and the meanings and imaginations that attach to them, these Places, all of these, derive, I argue, from the intimate correspondence of *Europe-Postcolony*. If it is the case that we are concerned to 'decolonise', to repudiate the norm-alities of 'border imperialism', then it is to these *White-Lies* that we need attend.

Europe is Not 'Theirs'

First, the Master Lie that births the Master Race: *Europe* as the origin story, mythological home and the spiritual foundation of the purported 'White-ness' of 'White'-folk. All begins here. Indeed, it is correct to say that *Europe* lies at the very centre of the *World*.

---

23 Ann Laura Stoler undertakes what is an intense examination of the conceptual work, and the many ambiguities, trajectories, and oscillations of 'the colony' as an imperial formation. This is impressive and as a rarity, subjects the assumed category to interrogation, exposing the work it does in establishing the multiple dynamics of the exercise of power, and the rationalisation of Empire; see Stoler, Duress, especially 69-121. But Stoler's focus is on the work of the 'colony' within the conceptual universe of the imperial mind, and in this, she is correct to identify the many and diverse functions of the colony (and its closely related ontological category of the 'camp') as sites of imperial governance and the ways in which these conceptual legacies persist and remain 'durable'. Stoler accepts the imperial, colonial location as separate from that of the 'colony', a location wherein the colony becomes its separated site of desire and abhorrence. My argument rather lies not simply in the commensurability of the 'colony' within the imperial formation as such, but of the coherence and commensurability of the imperial/ colonial metropole (*Europe* as I will call it) and the '(post)colony' operating together as a combined conceptual category. It is this *intimacy* that I regard as enabling the foundational philosophical work of normalising a particular imagination and enforcement of a *World*.

24 See Catherine Hall, *Civilising Subjects: Metropole and Colony in the English Imagination, 1830-1867* (Cambridge: Polity, 2002). Also, Robert Gildea, *Empires of the Mind: Colonial Pasts and the Politics of the Present* (Cambridge: Cambridge University Press, 2019); and Nadine El-Enany, *(B)ordering Britain: Law, Race and Empire* (Manchester: Manchester University Press, 2020). Interesting, El-Enany's recent work is a rare example that specifically identifies the operation of (b)ordering in the way that I speak of here, to understand that the 'metropole' – Britain in this case – is indeed a 'colonial space'.

Let us reconsider this idea of 'Europe'. And by *Europe*, I mean an *Idea*. I certainly don't intend it to mean that constituted artificiality that is now encapsulated by the name 'European Union' (although it is interesting that the EU fully depends upon this prior Idea for its ontological assertions.) The Idea of *Europe* is of wider, and deeper significance, and I use it here as an invention that gives ontological meaning also to those 'nation/states' that today we associate with 'Europeanness'. *Europe* in this sense provides a claimed civilizational coherence, a 'White racial frame' as Joe Feagin called it.[25] Be it in Samuel Huntington's recourse to the notion of 'Anglo-Protestant' values (speaking in the context of the 'American' national identity),[26] or in the assertions of (post-)'Enlightenment' philosophical traditions that purport to trace their origins from Greco-Roman antiquity right through to the 'French Revolution' and beyond, we see the work of a fabrication of *Europe* as a self-contained onto-epistemological category that is distinct, autonomous, indeed autochthonous, and significantly, superior to the Rest.[27] *White*-ness resides entirely in this invented History of *Europe*.[28]

We should note that, there is no shortage of knowledge now that refutes this mythologization of 'Europe'. We know that there existed no contiguous and bordered geographical space that can be so named as a matter of historical truth; we know that there is no singular cultural, religious or spiritual origin of the 'European' imaginary or identity; we know that there was shared no philosophical point of departure that could be fully assigned to the origins

---

25 See Joe Feagin, *The White Racial Frame: Centuries of Racial Framing and Counter-Framing* (New York: Routledge, 2013 (2nd edition)).

26 Samuel E. Huntington, *Who Are We? The Challenges to America's National Identity* (New York: Simon & Schuster, 2004).

27 See for example, Anthony Pagden, 'Europe: Conceptualizing a Continent' in Anthony Pagden (ed.), *The Idea of Europe: From Antiquity to the European Union* (Cambridge: Cambridge University Press, 2002), 33-54.

28 Barnor Hess is correct:

> In my view what race/modernity studies have so far neglected, conceptually if not historically, is the formative signifier of Europeanness, as a defining logic of race in the process of colonially constituting itself and its designations of non-Europeanness, materially, discursively and extra-corporeally. Since in both modern philosophical discourse and structural-historical modernity, the classifications and taxonomies of race though apparently framed as physical entities, are profoundly implicated in relationality. These normalized race relations were actually constituted through the colonial designations of Europeanness and non-Europeanness, in various assemblages of social, economic, ecological, historical and corporeal life. On this account the biologisation of the colonially constituted 'European'/'non-European' distinction and its territorialization on to diverse human bodies is but one historical symptom and political formation of race through modernity.

> Barnor Hesse 'Racialized modernity: An Analytics of White Mythologies' *Ethnic and Racial Studies*, 30(4), 2007, 643-663, 646.

of a 'European'-mind;[29] and as we have already seen, the skin-colour that has come to be assigned 'White' provided no essential point of reference nor unity; indeed we know all of these to be inventions, contingent and historical. All this has amply been exposed, but with little consequence, it seems. Similarly, in relation to the argument for the need to 'provincialise Europe',[30] to decentre it, to go beyond 'abyssal thinking' towards 'cognitive decolonisation',[31] notwithstanding such intentions, the Lie persists and powerfully so. These attempts to situate 'Europe' as a contingent and problematic assumption have not quite got to core of the problem, this is my argument. Important as their epistemic decentring efforts undoubtedly are, they retain still a privileged and autonomous ontology for the *Idea* of *Europe*. While it decentres 'Europe', it does not repudiate it. The flaw is nothing short of *World*-defining.

An example is useful to stress the point. Take Dinesh Chakrabarty's treatment of 'Europe'. While on the one hand his project of 'provincialisation' understands 'Europe' as a 'hyperreal' term,[32] for which scare quotes are adopted when 'Europe' is thus spoken of, on the other, great weight is given to 'European' thoughts, ideas and contributions – this is European and Europe without scare quotes – as if such a location of thought and being exist as given. Chakrabarty is quite certain of this latter 'truth' it seems:

---

29 See Kwame Anthony Appiah:

> If the notion of Christendom was an artefact of a prolonged military struggle against Muslim forces, our modern concept of western culture largely took its present shape during the cold war. In the chill of battle, we forged a grand narrative about Athenian democracy, the Magna Carta, Copernican revolution, and so on. Plato to Nato. Western culture was, at its core, individualistic and democratic and liberty-minded and tolerant and progressive and rational and scientific. Never mind that pre-modern Europe was none of these things, and that until the past century democracy was the exception in Europe – something that few stalwarts of western thought had anything good to say about. The idea that tolerance was constitutive of something called western culture would have surprised Edward Burnett Tylor, who, as a Quaker, had been barred from attending England's great universities. To be blunt: if western culture were real, we wouldn't spend so much time talking it up.

"There is no such thing as western civilisation", *The Guardian*, 9 November 2016, available at <https://www.theguardian.com/world/2016/nov/09/western-civilisation-appiah-reith-lecture> last accessed 18 November 2023.

30 Dinesh Chakrabarty, *Provincializing Europe: Postcolonial Thought and Historical Difference* (Princeton: Princeton University Press, 2000). See also the more recent turn to 'decolonial theory' which has given rise to a proliferation of critique against Eurocentrism and the advocacy of an 'ecology of knowledges'; see Walter Mignolo and Arturo Escobar (eds.), *Globalisation and the Decolonial Option* (Abingdon: Routledge, 2013); and Boaventura de Sousa Santos, *The End of the Cognitive Empire: The Coming of age of Epistemologies of the South* (Durham: Duke University Press, 2018).

31 Santos, *The End of the Cognitive Empire*.

32 Chakrabarty, *Provincializing Europe*, 28.

The phenomenon of "political modernity" – namely, the rule by modern institutions of the state, bureaucracy, and capitalist enterprise – is impossible to *think* of anywhere in the world without invoking certain categories and concepts, the genealogies of which go deep into the intellectual and even theological traditions of Europe. Concepts such as citizenship, the state, civil society, public sphere, human rights, equality before the law, the individual, distinctions between public and private, the idea of the subject, democracy, popular sovereignty, social justice, scientific rationality, and so on all bear the burden of European thought and history. One simply cannot think of political modernity without these and other related concepts that found a climactic form in the course of the European Enlightenment and the nineteenth century.

These concepts entail an unavoidable – and in a sense indispensable – universal and secular vision of the human. The European colonizer of the nineteenth century both preached this Enlightenment humanism at the colonized and at the same time denied it in practice. But the vision has been powerful in its effects. ...This heritage is now global.[33]

This is high accolade indeed. No equivocation here on 'Europe' in these statements of assignation, no scare quotes to accentuate its 'hyperrealness'. Quite the opposite, here 'Europe' stands fully formed, reaching out into the *World* of her *Others*, the only problem being that of 'double standards' as it were. Although treated mostly as a challenge to Europe, Chakrabarty's 'provincialisation' is more correctly an attempt to situate and understand the contextual imbibing of *European* values and ideas within locations of the 'colonised'. This indeed leaves the *idea* of Europe intact, arguably, reinforced. This, as I read the literature, is a common trait. For the many attempts of decentring 'Europe', such as Chakrabarty's, what is largely the preoccupation of the *post/decolonial* critic derives from the assumptions that the problem of *Europe* is a problem of *epistemology*; thus is understood the need for 'Europe' to be 'provincialised' and for the *Rest* to be 'pluriversally' recentred.

This is wrong. What this means is that, still, *Europe* remains fully intact, infinitely malleable in its 'post-colonial' self-perpetuation; we see this in all the recent 'nationalist' recovery projects of 'European/Western/White'

---

33 *Ibid*, 4 (emphasis in original, note omitted).

exceptionalism. A different correction is necessary, to drag the idea of *Europe* back from its apparent separateness form the *World* and to return it to the fold of a global totality from whence it originated. This is not simply an argument regarding historical wrongs committed by a rapacious 'Europe', not an argument against the purported violence inflicted by an historical, misguided, 'White-folk'. It is fundamentally about overturning the norm-alities of (b)ordering that entrenches the very Idea of *Europe* as a *World*-making Lie, that originates *White*-ness in the *World*.

We begin by taking 'Europe' apart, first and foremost, as a matter of material facticity. The Idea of *Europe* we shall see emerges precisely as a convenient smokescreen, to deflect attention from this material incoherence and thereby to assert the normality of the *World*.

Recall the insights of Fanon, Williams, Rodney; let us take these arguments seriously.[34] *Europe* is the creation of the 'Third World'. I am using shorthand here to encapsulate a range of substantive insights, but this shorthand suffices for my purposes. The point bluntly put is that *Europe* is fully a (post) colonial artefact, birthed first through the exigencies of colonial encounter and its rationalization, and subsequently by the (b)ordering of the 'post-colonial' settlement demarcating, as separate, the dual onto-epistemological categories of *Europe-Postcolony*. There is ample empirical evidence to demonstrate quite literally that *Europe* came to be entirely as a colonial creation, her cities and nations, her roads and buildings and institutions, her wealth and 'welfare' systems, all built on the loot of colonial dispossession and labour;[35] we note, of course, that the storytellers of 'Europe' prefer the sanitized terminology of 'trade' in describing this origin story. A different accounting of the 'ledgers of the world system', as Cedric Robinson called it,[36] reveals more accurately the extent and scope of its factual entries.

I make this point not simply as a matter for historical correction, not merely to repeat the arguments, for example, for reparations. We are familiar with indictments of the many wrongs of 'Europe' against the peoples of the worlds enslaved and colonised. Interestingly these facts of History are not

---

34 Frantz Fanon, *Wretched of the Earth* (London: Penguin Books, 1967), Eric Williams, *Capitalism & Slavery* (Chapel Hill: University of North Carolina Press, 1994); Walter Rodney, *How Europe Underdeveloped Africa* (London: Verso, 2018 (first printed in 1972).

35 See Utsa Patnaik, *A Theory of Imperialism* (New York: Colombia University Press, 2016). Also, Shashi Tharoor, *Inglorious Empire: What the British did to India* (London: Penguin Books, 2018) and El-Enany, *(B)ordering Britiain*.

36 Cedric J. Robinson, *Black Marxism: the Making of the Black Radical Tradition* (London: Zed Books, 1983), 111.

entirely rejected within 'European' circles; the historical record of subjugation and plunder, violence and cruelty, unjust enrichment, are all open for
repeated expressions of 'regret'. But this acknowledgement made, now, we
are told, the imperative of global solidarity is to address the urgencies of
contemporary 'development', 'Europe' and 'Postcolony' together, in 'partnership'. We know that this means little, offers little. The point however is
this: *Europe*, now deemed 'post-colonial', remains unquestioned in all of
these indictments of past atrocities, its mythology reinforced, its purported
separation from the *Rest*, reinforced. Indeed, it is so that the (b)orders that
perpetuate this separation serve as the defining issue of 'post-colonial' rene-
gotiations of 'justice' between *White*-ed and *Black*-ed lives, the negotiation
of differentiated access and redistribution of gains and losses the substance of
such appeals.[37] To *Europe*, against 'Europe', we complain. I argue differently.

The relevance of the invention of *Europe* is twofold: first, it serves literally
as the ground from which *White*-ness as an 'universal' onto-epistemology
of the 'rational-subject' is invented through 'political-legal philosophy'; and
consequently, it enables a global, diasporic assertion of such a superior 'race'
of people – as 'White-folk' – to flourish.[38] Taken together, *Europe* therefore
provides the frames and the languages that disguise what are at core relations
over *matter*, enabling instead a sanitised structure of rationalisation that
we now discourse as 'culture'; this the work of the invented 'disciplines' of
History, Anthropology, Sociology, Political-Legal Philosophy, as the 'sciences'
of the so-called 'social', to assert and mediate. To correct this misdirection of
attention, we recall that *White*-ness emerged as a mark, precisely an inscription, of differentiated 'racial identity' in the filthy mix of domination and
exploitation, fully as a name of *Licence* to subjugation of one over another.
In this encounter, as the exigencies of exploitation and control over diverse
peoples are confronted, we know that *White*-ing, a philosophical manoeuvre,
provided the rationalization of differentiated 'wages' in the sense that Du Bois
identified.[39] Thus were disparate communities united and separated, *White*-d
from *Black*-ed, the former as the Right-ful assertion, as 'subject', to *matter* as

---

37 For a recent reconsideration of the imperial legacies of the UK and France in this connection, see
    Robert Gildea, *Empires of the Mind: The Colonial Past and the Politics of the Present* (Cambridge:
    Cambridge University Press, 2019).
38 On the connection between the onto-epistemology of race, reason, and subjectivity, see Denise Ferreira
    da Silva, *Toward a Global Idea of Race* (Minneapolis: University of Minnesota Press, 2007).
39 W.E.B. Du Bois, *Black Reconstruction in America: Toward a History of the Part Which Black Folk
    Played in the Attempt to Reconstruct Democracy in America, 1860-1880* (New York: Russell & Russell,
    1962).

'property', the latter, as rightless *propertied-matter*, the very objects of appropriation. This encounter of violence: 'civilisation' they called it.[40] No doubt,
this was a long and arduous process of *World*-making, of a systematic accul-
turation into racialised socialities, but this is precisely its outcome: a *World*
made materially and categorically. And it remains thus, the Idea of 'European-Whiteness', now entrenched as a separate and autonomous existence in
the *World*, still the point of reference from which norm-ality and deviancy
is marked and judged. 'White-folk', regardless of complex pasts, originate in
and from this invented place, 'Europe', this the fantasy that anchors *White*-d
souls to their assumed and claimed place upon the *World*. Whether for the
'White-folk' in the many 'nations' of contemporary 'Europe', or in the Americas North and South, or in the southern settlements of 'South Africa' or
'Australia' or 'New Zealand', *Europe* provides an origin story which frames,
even if not quite cleansing, the historical record, a narrative Lie of self-ascribed
'race' and 'place'. The Lie of 'White-folk': a homogenous and autochthonous
'History' of *a priori* origins, *Europe*.[41] From here, the *World* is 'discovered',
the *Rest*, invented.

The truth is radically different.

This we must assert emphatically: it was not 'Europe' that sailed the
'World' and placed her many flags upon the territories of the 'discovered', not
'Europeans' that inflicted their violence on the peoples encountered; *Europe*
was the obscene outcome of the material relations that so ensued, *Europeans*,
the *White*-being-ness of entitlement, invented in violent encounter. Such is
our error: we point the accusatory finger at Europe and Europeans as if they
exist as an entity and an identity prior to plunder and enslavement, prior to
the colonial subjugation and differentiated categorisations of peoples, prior
that is to the materiality of violence that prompted the invention of the Idea,
and the enforcement, of its norm-ality. This is to go along with the lie that
'Europe' is as we know it, 'White', rich, (b)ordered in the 'World', against the

---

40 See Theodore W. Allen, *The Invention of the White Race* (New York: Verso, 2012); Roediger, *The
  Wages of Whiteness: Race and the Making of the American Working Class* (London: Verso, 1991); Nell
  Irvin Painter, *The History of White People* New York: W.W. Norton, 2011).

41 And for this reason we see the enormous effort expended by 'nationalist' politicians concerned to
  protect 'White-folk' who resort to some form or other of nostalgia for a homeland now under siege
  by the invading hordes of outsider-'migrants', especially urgent now with the portend of 'climate
  refugees'; see for example, Andrew Telford, 'A threat to climate-secure European futures? Exploring
  racial logics and climate-induced migration in US and EU climate security discourses', *Geoforum 96.*
  2018, 268-277. For too long we have misunderstood these racialised 'populist' discourses as matters of
  'racism'. But as we have seen in Chapter 3, we might more usefully understand such recourse to 'race'
  and 'nation' as the constant reassertion of (b)orders of mythologised belonging and exclusions; they
  are in other words the discourses of 'property' that is of the *matter* of the *World*.

'Rest'. It is to accede to the argument – and it is an utterly preposterous argument at that – as we shall see below, that the 'White-European' retains still the Right to (b)order the *World*, to define the enclosed borders of *White*-ness and to claim exclusivity over possession of the matter therein, matter as we have seen is fully forged through the flesh and blood of *Black*-ed bodies. How is it that in all of our imaginations of 'decolonisation', this fundamental tenet of colonial philosophy remained such that the 'post-colonial' actuality of the *World* is fully amenable to the fantasies of invented *White-European-ness*? Indeed, it is with the 'post-colonial' settlement that separated 'Europe' from the 'Postcolony' that *White*-ness becomes fully entrenched as a total-izing system of reality. With the purported passing of the colonial into the 'post-colonial', the original violence that was the invention of *White*-ness in the *World*, which named *Black* in the *World*, becomes now norm-al-ised, redeemed as a universally validated category of a '(provincialized)race' within a racialised global sensibility. This is indeed a cleansing, where colo-nial relations of differentiation, once clear in their manifest violence, are now transformed, sanitized as an aberration, a 'racism' solely committed by the proverbial 'bad apples' amongst an otherwise innocent 'White-folk'. Appar-ently, it is the case now that 'Europe' is entirely and fully against 'racism', fully for universal dignity, rights, and democracy, fully for Humanity. Stupendous. This is surely a 'discovery' yet to be made by the *un-White* of the World. No, 'Europe' must not so easily be let off the hook.

It is time that we understand this: 'Europe' does not belong to 'them', the so-called 'White'-European. 'They' – those who insist on abiding by the structural assertion of being that is being-White-folk – have no claim to enti-tlement to this (post)colonial artefact; Hamid Dabashi was right to argue, when commenting on the 'refugee crisis' that so perturbed 'Europe', that "[t]hese refugees are liberators. They are liberating Europe from the deadpan myth of "the West"".[42] I would go further. And let me stress that this is not a matter of inserting 'Black History' into the story of 'Europe' or of appealing for greater generosity of 'bordering' practices. This is a matter of overturning the Idea of *Europe* entirely. So, this is *Our* moral, philosophical, political responsibility as the global un-*White* to unapologetically assert: 'Europe' as place, denied its Lie, *Europe*, is entirely *Ours* to claim, whether *they* like it or not.

---

42 Hamid Dabashi, "Europe is the creation of the Third World", *Al Jazeera*, 26 June 2016, <https://www.aljazeera.com/opinions/2016/6/26/europe-is-the-creation-of-the-third-world/> last accessed 25 August 2020).

The *Postcolony* is not 'Ours'

As *Europe* is asserted, so the *Postcolony* is invented as a meaningful category in and of the *World*.

I use the term *Postcolony* in a specific sense. Not in the commonly assumed sense of the 'post-colonial' state-place as a location-in-the-International but as a specific (b)ordered category of subjection within a global totality of name-ing and place-ing.[43] Recall that the Idea of *metropole* is utterly derived from its coeval ontological *Other*: *metropole* and *colony* conjoined as a categorical point of departure that is the precursor to the 'post-colonial' resettlement of the *World*. The same understanding of *intimacy* applies to the situation of the *Postcolony*.

For my purposes, what is significant is that the *Postcolony* remains of, in, and with *Europe*, intimately so notwithstanding the apparent rupture of the old into the new. My argument is that it is critical that *Postcolony* and *Europe* be read together as *World*-making categories, co-constitutively and coevally. They are meaningless otherwise. It is precisely this *intimacy* that the 'post-colonial State', as a political-legal category that normalises the resettlement of the (post)colonial *World*, operates to obscure and sever. An understanding of *Postcolony*, however, opens the situation to full view; the *Postcolony* serves as the horrific onto-epistemological reflection that projects *Europe* into the *World* as the (*White*-)norm-ality that continues both to admonish and haunt the *Black*-ed wretcheds of the Earth. This is not just a matter of the mind, it is also a matter of *matter*, that is to say, the *Postcolony* defines the material spaces and places that are marked upon the Earth as the *World* is divided and ruled. Simply, *Postcolony* (with *Europe*) serves as the technology that (b)orders the *World* as a discursive and material actuality.

By the affirmation of 'decolonisation' through the evental moment of the 'declaration of independence', with the purported ruptural transformation of the *colony* 'becoming-into-the-'International'' as *Postcolony,* the completion of *World*-making is materialised. The colony, that situation entirely defined by the assertion of intimate belonging-separation to metropole, however problematic and abusively so, is now, as *Postcolony,* utterly bereft; as it remains still wholly *of Europe*, belonging entirely to a totality defined both materially and philosophically by its intimacy to 'European memory' and imagination, it is

---

43 For a related critique of 'limited statehood' as a recent fashion in critical political theory, see Andrew Brandel and Shalini Randeria, 'Anthropological Perspectives on the Limits of the State', in Thomas Risse, Tanja Borzel and Anke Draude (eds.), *The Oxford Handbook on Governance and Limited Statehood* (Oxford: Oxford University Press, 2018) 68.

now (b)ordered as entirely separate, made *Other-ed*.[44] This, in its essence, is the 'post-colonial' deceit: *Postcolony* and *Europe*, even as they remain categorically and materially intimate, are simultaneously constructed as ontologically separate, and thereby are they mutually *liberated* from the 'colonial' situation. By this manoeuvre, the ontological foundation of the architecture of the *World* as a (post)colonial totality is secured.

All this, to repeat, is known; it is not as if we have been short of a clear and uncompromising view of the perversions of the 'post-colonial' condition.[45] The many and diverse histories of 'post-colonial' experiments of 'liberation' from imperial embrace have abundantly been chronicled and commented upon. The question however is: what have we done with this knowledge, what have understood by this realisation?[46]

In this connection, let us recall the significance of Fanon's insights and prophesies of the 'pitfalls of nationalism'; it precisely portends an impossibility of the 'post-colonial' situation. *Independence*, as Fanon foresaw, as Gandhi realised from the outset, as Sankara and Cabral sought to overcome in their efforts to govern the 'struggle', as Nyerere struggled to reconcile in his intent towards 'nationalism' and 'Pan-Africanism',[47] has come to mean little

44 See Ngũgĩ wa Thiong'o, *Secure the Base: Making Africa Visible in the Globe* (London: Seagull Books, 2016).

45 From the most cited early repudiation of the 'pitfalls of the national consciousness' by Fanon, to the most intense dissection conducted by Achille Mbembe in his *On The Postcolony*, and his more recent restatement in *Necropolitics*, the 'postcolony' has received much critical, attention. In most of these critical examinations, attention has focussed on the specific 'post-colonial' state, and/or 'international' contexts, critique often concentrating on the many betrayals, cooptions, defeats, of the 'post-colonial' imagination and effort under conditions of global capitalism and imperialism. This type of literature is much repeated. A different, one might say 'systemic', analysis of the 'post-colonial' global rearrangement, from early optimism to subsequent domestication can found in Vijay Prashad's *The Poorer Nations: A Possible History of the Global South* (London: Verso, 2012). The point I am stressing here is simply that the critical analysis of the 'postcolony', understood as a 'post-colonial' state and state-system, has been abundantly done. My interest and understanding of the *Postcolony*, however, is differently focussed. I understand the *Postcolony* not simply as a 'political' fact, but as a philosophical category.

46 In this connection, I am thinking of the rich and plentiful literature which speaks to the persistent global struggles against both the imperial reach of continuing coloniality and more specifically the violence of 'post-colonial' states. Again, these are commonly treated as exposes and denunciations of state and imperial violence. My view is that such actualities of struggle point to a philosophical situation, not simply a factual one. For examples; see Dominique Caouette and Dip Kapoor (eds.), *Beyond Colonialism, Development and Globalization: Social Movements and Critical Perspectives* (London: Zed Books, 2016); Peter Dwyer and Leo Zeilig, *Africa Struggles Today: Social Movements Since Independence* (Chicago: Haymarket Books, 2012); Sam Moyo and Paris Yeros (eds.), *Reclaiming the Nation: The Return of the National Question in Africa, Asia and Latin America* (London: Pluto Press, 2011); Francois Polet (ed.) *The State of Resistance: Popular Struggles in the Global South* (London: Zed Books, 2007). These are but a selection, any number of others may be cited. The question, I repeat, is what lessons do we learn from these insightful and inspiring accounts of refusal, resistance, and regeneration?

47 This tension is eloquently addressed by Nyerere in this 1966 speech at the University of Zambia, 'The Dilemma of the Pan-Africanist', at '(1966) Julius Nyerere, 'The Dilemma of the Pan-Africanist'', *Black Past*, 7 August 2009, <https://www.blackpast.org/global-african-history/1966-julius-kam-

more than a renegotiation and resettlement of the configurations of material belonging-separation following the *Reason* and exigencies of appropriation, and thereby, subjugation. The painful lessons of the various substantive
'nationalist' experiments is that the *Postcolony*, as an artefact of the 'post-colonial' settlement, remains the possession of *Europe*. Indeed, I regard it as
uncontentious to make the point that it was always intended thus. In the
most obvious sense, we see this evidenced by the numerous claims of *Europe*
regarding the proper conduct of the *Postcolony*; the many assassinations of
disobedient 'post-colonial' upstarts from the very early days of the 'post-
colonial' settlement, and the resulting ubiquity of 'regime change' deemed
amenable to the desires of *Europe*, have been little more than the unexcep-
tional, even banal, exercise of *White*-right.[48] Today, little has changed. This
same assertion of *Right* now goes by the names of 'self-defence' (increasingly,
'anticipatory' and 'preventive' in adoption),[49] of 'humanitarianism' and
'Human Rights', and if ever there was a perversion of an idea, of the 'responsibility to protect'; so many new-fangled names to describe the assumption
of civilisational *Right* over the peoples deemed subject to *White*-tutelage
and discipline. We might protest incessantly, and incessantly we do, but
no amount of 'post-colonial' outrage of these normalised infringements
of 'sovereignty' bears weight in the reality of the (post)colonial ways of the
World. Indeed, the constant complaining of such infringements is to utterly
misunderstand the fundamental reality of the (post)colonial situation. On
this there can be little argument: *Postcolony-Europe* remain fully in intimate
correspondence of *belonging-separation*.

All this should be obvious, the complaint of the violence that continues
to be inflicted on 'post-colonial States' are, after all, a recurrent theme in
critiques of 'International Relations'. But there is a more significant and
deeper sense in which this conspiracy of intimacy operates. Here it is neces-

---

barage-nyerere-dilemma-pan-africanist/≥ last accessed 22 December 2021.
48 The violence of the 'West' over the 'Rest' has been much documented. A classic of this genre remains
the early exposés of Noam Chomsky and Edward Herman, theirs demonstrating not just the interventionary proclivities of the US regime but the fundamental materiality underpinning the intimacy
of imperial rule and 'Third World' fascism as a mode of regulatory terror. See Noam Chomsky and
Edward Herman, *The Washington Connection and Third World Fascism: The Political-Economy
of Human Rights Vol.1* (London: Pluto Press, 2015). I return to a reconsideration of 'violence' in
Chapter 6.
49 As I undertake the final preparations of this manuscript for publication, incessant is the utterly repulsive assertion of, and demand for, exactly this *White*-right of 'self-defence' that in its full and bloody
reality means the massacre by 'Israeli defence' forces of the civilians in Gaza and other occupied-terri-
tories. I discuss the situation of Palestine in Chapter 5, the arguments put there all the more urgent in
light of what are on-going atrocities by the 'State of Israel'.

sary to point to what is a common misunderstanding. By my assertion that the *Postcolony* remains the possession of *Europe* I don't mean to repeat the common complaint of a 'neo-colonial' arrangement where it is observed that the 'metropole' retains effective control and power over the 'post-colonial' State. This would be an incomplete understanding of the (post)colonial totality borne out of what I have called 'methodological post-colonialism'. Yes, and we know it well, such influence, and indeed overbearing domination, persists but this is not the insight of significance. The *Postcolony* remains the possession of *Europe* in that both categorically and structurally, the *Postcolony* preserves the *World* made-(*Black*-ed)matter born out of *White*-Reason. And by this reason is (post)colonial subjugation reconfigured in the 'post-colonial' arrangement, its pedagogical and epistemological grounds reframed and refined with the domestication, even if not the negation, of the ruptural threat of the anti-colonial assertion, the *Postcolony* functioning fully now as the intimate accomplice of *Europe* in their *World*-(b)ordering functions.[50] 'Border imperialism', we see, is not an outcome of the imperial-colonial relation, it is quite centrally the very *Reason* of global coloniality.

Thus is the structural, regulatory, coherence of the 'post-colonial' settlement. The 'post-colonial' State exists within a totalised *World*-scape of *Postcolony-Europe*, (b)ordered and regulated as a systemic whole. Fundamental to this coherent operation is the obvious, but largely misunderstood, function of the 'State-place' as a territorial configuration. At its most fundamental, the *Postcolony* serves two functions:

1) to contain subjected-bodies, to literally keep bodies-in-their-(Right-ful/less)Place(s);
2) to territorially organise and regulate the appropriation and distribution of commodified 'resources', 'natural' and 'human', and to facilitate the smooth operation of this *Licence* of global capital by all means necessary.

Simple as that. All fancy meditations on '(limited-)sovereignty, 'constitutionalism' and 'citizenship', on the problems of political-belonging and exclusions, on the perplexities of Human Rights(lessness), all descriptions of land/property rights regimes, of 'economic' regulation, etc, all boil down to these two essential operations of the *Postcolony* as a territorialised technology

---

50 On this, Arif Dirlik's suggestion that the term/concept 'postrevolutionary' better encapsulates the impact and argument of 'postcolonial' perspectives is correct in my view; see Arif Dirlik, *The Postcolonial Aura: Third World Criticism in the Age of Global Capitalism* (Boulder: Westview Press, 1997), especially 163-185.

of containment and regulation/enforcement. I emphasise coherence in this regulatory totality, not aberration or double-standards, or any such assumption of dissonance between the *Reason* of 'State' and its phenomenological actuality. On this, let us turn to Achille Mbembe:

> In truth, the problem is neither the migrants nor the refugees nor the asylum seekers. Borders. Everything begins with them, and all parts lead back to them. They are no longer merely a line of demarcation separating distinct sovereign entities. Increasingly, they are the name used to describe the organized violence that underpins both contemporary capitalism and our world order in general – the women, the men, and the unwanted children condemned to abandonment; the shipwrecks and drownings of hundreds, indeed thousands, weekly; the endless waiting and humiliation in consulates, in limbo; days of woe spent wandering in airports, in police stations, in parks, in train stations, then down onto the city pavements, where at nightfall blankets and rags are snatched from people who have already been stripped and deprived of virtually everything – bare bodies debased by a lack of water, hygiene, and sleep. In short, an image of humanity on a road to ruin.
>
> In fact, everything leads back to borders – these dead spaces of non-connection which deny the very idea of a shared humanity, of a planet, the only one we have, that we share together, and to which we are linked by the ephemerality of our common condition. But perhaps, to be completely exact, we should speak not of borders but instead of "borderization". What, then, is this "borderization", if not the process by which world powers permanently transform certain spaces into impassable places for certain classes of populations? What is it about, if not the conscience multiplication of spaces of loss and mourning, where the lives of a multitude of people judge to be undesirable come to be shattered?[51]

This is powerfully stated, the description both literal and metaphysical of the 'road to ruin'. But not just of ruin, also of unspeakable enrichment and this we must not overlook. The truth of Mbembe's account of 'borderisation' however is not that it speaks of an aberrant 'Europe' in relation to the outcast and destroyed souls of the *Postcolony*, but that it reveals *Europe* and *Postcolony*,

---

51 Mbembe, *Necropolitics*, 99.

conjoined, intimate in belonging-separation, precisely as the descriptive registers of this reality. Simply, this is *Europe-Postcolony* in its discursive and material fullness. Borderisation. Mbembe does not see it, instead, the anguish, common to many, derives from a disillusionment, precisely the error I speak of. For Mbembe, all this is an aberration; thus he laments that borders "are no longer *merely* a line of demarcation separating distinct sovereign entities. ... they are the name used to describe the organized violence that underpins both contemporary capitalism and our world order in general". As if it ever were thus, 'merely'. This is to accord the *European* imaginary some reified mythological original content, to not see the centrality of "spaces of loss and mourning" to the very *Reason* of *Europe-Postcolony*. This error is plain in the following passage:

> It must be repeated that this war (which aims to hunt down, capture, round up, process, segregate, and deport) has only one end goal. It is not so much about cutting Europe off from the rest of the world or turning her into an impenetrable fortress, but rather *about granting Europeans alone the privilege of the rights to possession and free movement across the whole of the planet – a planet on which, in truth, we should all have the same entitlements.*
>
> Will the twenty-first century prove to be the century of assessment and selection in the bias of security technologies? From the confines of the Sahara, across the Mediterranean, the camps are once more on their way to becoming the last step in a certain European project a certain idea of Europe in the world, her macabre emblem... *One of the major contradictions of liberal order has always been the tension between freedom and security. Today the question seems to have been cut in two. Security now matters more than freedom.*[52]

What is *Europe* if not precisely that privilege of the 'right to possession and free movement'? Where in the material *History* of the World is the evidence for any assumption that "we should all have the same entitlements" to the 'planet' as *matter*?[53] Fundamentally, the entirety of Mbembe's eloquent commentary on the misery of the 'Postcolony', seen now as consumed by the ruins of *necropolitical* unreason, is informed by this error: there is, in brutal actuality, no contradiction whatever in the 'liberal order'; 'security' – as a

---

52 *Ibid*, 103 (emphases mine).
53 *Ibid*.

condition and situation that is (global) *Europe* – always matters more than (universal) freedom. To fail to understand this original *Reason* of *White*-ness as naturalised in the Idea of *Europe* is to forever be afflicted with heartbreak, the result of a miscomprehension of the reality of this global constitution of abomination. But this is precisely what we must understand. The *Postcolony* is precisely the necessary deformity that defines the beauty of *Europe*, and ever, against the *Postcolony* must *Europe* be (b)ordered, enforced, and protected as such. This is just so.

I concentrate on Mbembe here because his is a valuable telling of the politics of *Europe-Postcolony*; necropolitics, if you will, is what I have called the fundamental *Reason* of coloniality that brought into the *World* the onto-epistemological categories of *Black*-ed lives as *White*-matter. All else is so much philosophical chicanery.

In saying this, let me be clear. I am not dismissing the significance of the 'national liberation' of colonial territories in the historical contexts of anti-co-lonial struggles. Exactly the opposite. In my view, this historical expression and particular manifestation of *anti-colonial* praxis was absolutely and unqualifiedly a struggle of revolutionary importance. At the most funda-mental level, it gave explicit audibility to the philosophical assertion of the 'anti-colonial' as a situation of being-thinking that serves as a potent disruptor of any attempt at the universal assertion of parochial desires. And it is by this anti-colonial imaginary that we understand the significance, and the limits, of the 'revolutionary' assertion of 'national liberation'. By 'revolutionary' in this connection, we limit our description to the frames of comprehensibility contained within a particular 'political' imagination, context and time-spe-cific, necessary but entirely unfinished. The 'national liberation' imagination and expression was just that, an expression of the anti-colonial situation. Particular to time and context. A great distance however separates the imag-ination and hope that was invested in the struggle against the subjugation by 'colonial' *White*-normality of *Black*-ed bodies, than is contained within the closure of the 'post-colonial State' as a 'political' institution constituted by a 'nationalist' imagination.[54] This distance between the anti-colonial as

---

54 As Issa Shivji pointedly put it:

> as the trajectories of Bandung and Pan-Africanism show, they were led by the bourgeois tendency that sought to install an auto-centric capitalist accumulation within their countries and nations. This proved to be its failure as peoples' projects. The bourgeoisies in Asia and the proto-bourgeoisies—private or state—in Africa were eventually compra-dorised ... [from this] the most important lesson to draw, nations still want liberation and people still want a revolution.

situation and praxis, and the *Postcolony* as technology of regulation is precisely the anti-colonial *frontline* I am interested to describe here.

We return to my central claim: the *Postcolony* is not 'Ours'. I make this claim to counter a fundamental assumption, and critical operation, of the 'post-colonial' situation as 'settled'.

We are familiar with the terrible normalities of the situation. Aijaz Ahmed some years ago described it as the 'neo-fascist' pathology of power of the 'Third World' State.[55] This phraseology encapsulates the full range of the human experiences of ('post-colonial') suffering. Here is the disappointment, even disdain, of the 'post-colonial' intellectual despairing of his compatriots who have been unable to take up the burden of 'freedom' as one would have expected.[56] Here are the human debris perceived as despoiling the virgin lands of *Europe* with the stain of *Black*-ness and all its vile and incalcitrant expressions of exotic debasements that needs so to be controlled if must, expelled if possible.[57] Here is the assumption of *eminent domain* as unfettered State-rights to dispossession and murder.[58] Here is the norm-alised corruption of meaning that perverts dissent against the avarices of racialised, casteist, power as 'sedition', as 'anti-national', as 'treason', here the full terror of capricious 'national security', of the violence of 'gulag 'constitutionalism' in the face, and in the service of, a global economic constitutionalism'.[59] Here is the materiality of regulation that enforces 'private indirect government' and

Issa Shivji, "Whither Africa in the Global South? Lessons from Bandung and Pan-Africanism.", Keynote address to the International Seminar on The Global South – From Bandung to the XXI Century (September 28-30, 2015), Universidade Federal São Paulo, at Issa Shivji, 'Whither Africa in the Global South?: Lessons of Bandung and Pan-Africanism, *Black Agenda Report,* 11 November 2015, <https://blackagendareport.com/lessons_bandung_and_pan-africanism> last accessed 20 February 2022).

55 Ahmad's is fully a description of the *Postcolony*, exactly so, (b)ordered and regulated to the 'neo-fascism' that Ahmad succinctly describes. It remains apt to the present actualities of (post)coloniality; Eqbal Ahmad, "The Neo-Fascist State: Notes on the Pathology of Power in the Third World", *Arab Studies Quarterly* 3(2), 1981, 170-80.

56 For an excruciating example, see Albert Memmi, *Decolonisation and the Decolonised* (Minnesota: University of Minnesota Press, 2006).

57 Accounts of such encounters of imperial blowbacks are plentiful; for an early example, see Paul Gilroy, *There Aint no Black in the Union Jack: The Cultural Politics of Race and Nation* (London: Routledge, 2002). For more recent discussion, see Gildea, *Empires of the Mind;* and El-Enany, *(B)ordering Britain.*

58 A particularly brutal example of this, all the more so for its being reminiscent of Apartheid-era violence, was the so-called Marikana massacre in South Africa; see Sam Adelman, 'The Marikana Massacre, the rule of law and South Africa's violent democracy', *Hague Journal on the Rule of Law*, 7(2), 243-262.

59 See Upendra Baxi,'The (Im)possibility of Constitutional Justice: Seismographic Notes on Indian Constitutionalism', in Zoya Hassan, E. Sridharan and R. Sudarshan (eds.), *India's Living Constitution: Ideas, Practices, Contoversies* (Delhi: Permanent Black, 2002), 31-63; Also, Oishik Sircar, 'Spectacles of Emancipation: Reading Rights Differently in India's Legal Discourse', *Osgoode Hall Law Journal* 29(3), 2012, 527-73.

the 'privatisation of sovereignty'.[60] Here is the original site of the 'camp',[61] between the many Saharas and Mediterraneans that contain the multitudes of outcasts horded from their road to ruin, deemed disposable to 'Humanity'.[62] Etc., etc., etc.; 'post-colonial' appropriations of the 'Colonial Master's' violent reasoning and technologies, now proudly, unashamedly, bandied as 'Law' and 'Order', 'Development' and 'Security'. All this is the burden borne by the so-called 'post-colonial subject'. Imagine that, such absurd norm-alisations of the perverse!

What is this *World* that is asserted to be imprinted upon our imagination as fixed, (b)ordered, a totality of Names and Meanings? Who ordained it as such? On what wager of unknowable futures? Yet, so we have it, it seems, and for that we, that is to say, most of us critical commentators of the *World*, even as we agonise over its cruelties and horrors, we repeat the same Names, infer the same Meanings: of *Europe*; of *Postcolony*. No surprise, therefore, that the *World* remains secure, *this* World, a totality of Names and Meanings that renders the Idea of *Humanity* little more than an obscene and debased construct. I do not accept that we face here the limit of the 'anti-colonial' as a refusal to abide by a degenerate *World*. To see clearly this system of reality is the first step in reclaiming the original anti-colonial assertion that the *World* is not predetermined nor predestined. A different knowing of the present is necessary. I offer the following understanding: quite simply, the *Postcolony* freezes time and space, imagination and futures, it imprisons people – in subjugation, as *subjects* – and transmogrifies sacred lands – mountains, rivers, valleys, burial-sites, memory-lines, spirit-worlds – into *matter*, fungible, made-profane as 'property', as commodity. Here, the 'post-colonial' subject resides, is emplaced, contained, sometimes in relative comfort and security if obedient, otherwise in spaces/places of violence in the undersides of *Europe*, both *here* and *there*, the territories of the *(post)colony* and the *metropole*, as ghosts and zombies, visible yet metaphysically *inexistent*, the antithesis to the

---

60 Mbembe, *On the Postcolony*, 54-79; wa Thiong'o, *Secure the Base*.
61 Stoler is right to understand the 'camp' and 'the colony' as being of a 'conjoined conceptual matrix'; both born out of a reason of containment, of incarcerations of different sorts but of the same *Reason*; see Stoler, *Duress*, 76-78. This connection provides a crucial corrective to what I consider to be a misguided preoccupation with 'the camp' as an ontological location of 'exception'. All such fixations with 'exception' presume an otherwise 'normal' situation of 'Law', of the 'political' mythologised by the universalist conceits of 'Enlightenment' philosophies. I understand the camp, in its multiple institutionalisations, as wholly an essential *border* technology that conjoins *Postcolony-Europe*. In this way might we also understand the 'camp' fully as a *frontline*.
62 See generally, Zygmunt Bauman, *Wasted Lives: Modernity and Its Outcasts* (Cambridge: Polity, 2004); Brad Evans and Henry Giroux, *Disposable Futures: The Seduction of Violence in the Age of Spectacle* (San Francisco: City Lights Books, 2015).

thesis. In this sense, the *Postcolony* is a reminder both of perversion and abjection that remains the situation of *Black*-ed beingness original to the *White-Reason* of the invented/'discovered' *World*, requiring still civil-isation, a situation still of incompletion, a not-quite-yet-*Europe*, never-quite *Europe*, ontologically, categorically less-than *Europe*. Just so.

A totality of intimate belonging-separation; this is the *World* of *Europe-Postcolony*, of the continuation of *White-licence* in (post)colonial places as 'post-colonial' *subjects* are (b)ordered within places of containment or abandonment, of the marking and surveilling of *Black*-ed enclaves, be they ghettos or camps of various descriptions and architectures, in the places of 'Europe' for the protection and preservation of *White* cultures and futures. And precisely this *World*, of philosophoscapes and *World*scape, of words and matter, is the matter of anti-colonial *frontlines*. And for this reason, my assertion: the *Postcolony*, this idea and artefact of brutality and shamelessness invented by the *Reason* of *White*-ness, and imposed now as the limit of anti-colonial imagination, is precisely what I say is NOT 'OURS'.

The Persistent (Extra)Ordinariness of the *Anti-Colonial*

As I have said repeatedly, we are familiar with the complaints against *this* World. So, what to do?

Let me restate my argument: *Europe-Postcolony* are categorical inventions that make the *World* as a (post)colonial totality. It provides the ground from which the foundational Words and Meanings of the (post)colonial totality are generated, norm-alised, and enforced as the *World*. Through these registers of meaning do we – most of us political-legal philosophers contemplating the 'post-colonial' condition – understand and analyse the present situation. We see the problem as one of separation, of exclusion from the *World*. I see it differently.

It is vital that we understand that the onto-epistemological (b)ordering categories of *Europe-Postcolony* do not equate with the material geographies of what was previously *metropole-colony*. The latter certainly imposes a meaning on the latter, but they do not correspond. The 'post-colonial' settlement in this regard did not merely herald the becoming-into-the-*International/World* the 'liberated' territories/States now 'decolonised' but created a resettled and re(b)ordered geography of *Europe-Postcolony* as a global totality, that is a *World* wholly commensurable. The façade provided by 'methodological post-colonialism' perfectly obscures the totality of this material, racialised system of reality. Thus, the significance of reclaiming the anti-colonial assertion in the present.

To reclaim *Europe* as not *Theirs* is to repudiate the mythology of 'White' autochthony and originality that is sought to be attached to the lands of the 'metropole'; it is to reclaim the materiality of the *World* indeed as an intimate totality, unimaginable without the intimacy of belonging-separation that birthed it. To renounce the *Postcolony* as not *Ours* is to refuse the (b) ordering of permanent subjection as *Black*-ed-matter. It is to refuse enclosure, both materially into territorial enclaves of dispossession and categorically as 'post-colonial'. It is to refuse to abide by a 'post-colonial' settlement enforced as an imagination finalised, a hope terminated. It is, in other words, to understand and assert that both these lands now assigned as *of-Europe* and *of-Postcolony* – and thereby, the whole *World* itself – remain open to be reclaimed.

Saying this, let me emphasise the following point. I am not concerned to provide a critique of the many 'injustices' that persist as such. There is nothing exceptional, or particularly interesting, about the fact that there is domination and subjugation in all places. This is the way of the *World*, we might say. It is also a fact that worlds of hope, of struggle, of refusal, of imagination, are all still around us. We, critical types – and I here specifically address all those of us who regard ourselves as intellectuals of the 'South', the critical commentariat let us say – are abundantly familiar with writings on 'resistance'; this is bread and butter for our many theorisations after all. I want, however, to do more with this evidence. I want to attach a greater significance to this actuality than to merely employ the evidence for empirical or narrative purposes. What is of consequence, as a matter of philosophy, and, therefore, as a rationalisation of actions one way or another, is how these truths are ascribed meaning, articulated through which words, through whose voices. These are matters of 'location' and 'locatedness', of philosophical positioning and judgement, indeed of the doing of philosophy itself as *encounter*. To say this and that about the horrors of the *World*, as we so often do, is undoubtedly important as a matter of reportage, but little else is achieved. We have become expert at critically commenting on the *World* with great theoretical sophistication and analytical innovations, and, in the process, with saying very little, our grandiose imaginations for revolutionary transformations usually adorning the 'conclusions' we proffer in our commentaries. Let us be more daring than that and begin instead to take the risk of saying what such critical insights necessarily entail by way of implication and response. I suggest we begin by giving full meaning specifically to this anti-colonial assertion that *Europe* is not *Theirs,* the *Postcolony*, not *Ours*.

While it might appear so, this assertion is not so outlandish. It is evidenced by the everyday actuality of struggles in 'post-colonial' places. Encounters against the rapacious enforcements of the *Reason* of coloniality are everywhere (extra)ordinarily present. Precisely this (extra)ordinariness of the everyday I understand as *anti-colonial* praxes, reclaiming *frontlines* now from asserted and enforced *(b)orders* of *Europe-Postcolony*. Understanding the present in these terms of the 'everyday' enables a far more potent philosophy, one in which the asserted claim of the *Postcolony* to our bodies, minds, souls, are rendered derisible, where dissent is liberated from the (post)colonial regimes of judgements – *they* call it treason, sedition, anti-nationalist and other such like – and reaffirmed as entirely the lived projects of hope, anti-colonial, unceasing.

Consider the following. Raul Zibechi in surveying the diverse struggles of social movements in Latin America, identifies four shared characteristics of refusal and renewal:

- the reterritorialization of the movements: the recovering of spaces from state-capital enclosures for the regeneration of social and economic (re)production.
- the assertion of autonomy from the state and institutionalised political systems; the recovering of social organisation and decision-making practices.
- the valorisation of culture and the affirmation of identities and differences: the recovering of (dangerous) names of being(otherwise) from the emptiness of "citizenship".
- the formation of independent intellectuals: the recovering of knowledge-systems and its processes.[63]

What implications for philosophy? How might we understand, 'read', these struggles? Perhaps, as a 'post-colonial' politics of 'civil society' within the state? Perhaps, as strategies of 'participation' and 'empowerment'? Perhaps, as instances of 'dissensus' towards a 'becoming-political'? Or might we understand them as having an altogether different philosophical significance?

---

63 Raúl Zibechi (trans. Ramon Ryan), *Territories in Resistance: A Cartography of Latin American Social Movements* (Oakland: AK Press, 2012), 14-16. For similar analyses of grassroots resistance to political and developmental closures, see also Raul Zibechi, (trans. Ramor Ryan), *Dispersing Power: Social Movements as Anti-State Forces* (Oakland: AK Press, 2010); Gustavo Esteva and Madhu Suri Prakash, *Grassroots Post-Modernism: Remaking the Soil of Cultures* (London: Zed, 1998); Marina A. Sitrin, *Everyday Revolutions: Horizontalism and Autonomy in Argentina* (London: Zed Books, 2012).

I take the view that what Zibechi describes is a fundamental situation for philosophical recovery:

> Non-citizens – those stripped of their citizenship in neoliberal society – are opening up their own spaces in a process of struggle ...; spaces that they create, design and control. Understanding this requires reversing one's perspective: rejecting the negative and state-centred viewpoint – that defines people by what they lack – and adopting another way of looking that starts with the differences that they have created in order then to visualize other possible paths.[64]

We are presented here with a description of the present, that is, I assert, of an *anti-colonial* present. What Zibechi identifies as the four characteristics of refusal can be differently stated as follows:

- a reclaiming from enclosure of the meaning and workings of 'territory' as lived-place.
- the assertions of *desubjectification* otherwise than inscribed by the 'political-legal' registers of enforced meanings.
- the reaffirmation of onto-epistemologies of beingness.
- the formation of *anti-colonial philosophers*, and the regeneration of the praxes and pedagogies of thinking-knowing.

My intention in reformulating Zibechi is to demonstrate a different understanding that results from an anti-colonial philosophical orientation and perspective. How we 'read' the descriptions of everyday truths of resilient and rebellious human being-ness in located-worlds is precisely the work of doing philosophy as encounter, against *(post)colonial* philosophies of subjection, *anti-colonial* philosophies of refusal and recovery. Indeed, Zibechi's injunction to reverse one's 'perspective', to adopt 'another way of looking' to 'visualise other paths' points precisely to the necessary provocation for philosophy. Gustavo Esteva makes the point more bluntly:

> While academia continues with the exploration, conceptualization, and interpretation of social reality, tending time and again to reduce it to the 'old truths' of modernity, people by the millions are creating new social realities with corresponding social paradigms, leaving behind the social paradigm within which they were colonized, enclosed, exploited, marginalized, and oppressed.[65]

---

64 Zibechi, *Territories in Resistance*, 66.
65 Gustavo Esteva, Salvatore J. Babones, and Philipp Babcicky, *The Future of Development: A Radical*

There is nothing 'to-come' about any of this. This not some some forlorn philosophy of *passing* and of the *passerby*, of a broken subject, of "the figure of a human out to make great strides up a steep path" on a journey of 'trans-figuration' towards a humanity to come.[66] It is not an instrumental squeezing of the social actualities of struggle and the regeneration of life-worlds into a refinement of post-structural philosophies of 'excessive subjectivity',[67] not a portend of some liberated future of a 'decolonial' epistemological pluriverse.[68] It does not make grandiose claims of 'World' transformation in any sense; this is quite the hubris of philosophies that seek to walk in the purported steps of *Europe*, assuming the majesty of *Europe's* pretensions.[69] This under-standing of 'new social realities' is about actualities that are messy, uncertain, often precarious, often defeated, but for all that wonder-fully hopeful, (extra) ordinarily resilient. Importantly, they are grounded in the material and social conditions of their time and place. We ought to be reminded that there is nothing exceptional in all of this. But we can be assured that the 'spirit of revolution' is well-nurtured in these grassroots communities, their everyday

---

Manifesto (Bristol: Policy Press, 2013).

66   See Mbembe, *Necropolitics*, 186-87.

67   See Michael Neocosmos, *Thinking Freedom in Africa: Toward a Theory of Emancipatory Politics* (Johannesburg: Wits University Press, 2016) 437-38.

68   See Savelo J. Ndlovu-Gatsheni, *Epistemic freedom in Africa: Deprovincialisation and Decolonisation* (Boca Raton: Routledge, 2018).

69   This kind of aspiration, one might call it, is a feature of much radical work, wonderfully insightful in repeating the critique of coloniality, yet resorting to grand platitudes always by way of 'conclusion'. An example is Aaron Kamugisha's intensely scholarly *Beyond Coloniality: Citizenship and Freedom in the Caribbean Intellectual Tradition* (Bloomington: Indiana University Press, 2019), in which the concluding paragraphs tells us:

> My reading of Caribbean thought suggests that its urgent belief is that the Caribbean must recreate itself anew. This transformation will mean a different political economy, political arrangements beyond the reification of petty bourgeois dominance, and an entirely different structure of feeling in the realm of our public and private citizens' lives. Caribbean solidarity in the interests of self-determination and human freedom, like its sibling black solidarity, has never existed outside a labyrinth of contradictions, persistently troubled by the ongoing reproduction of coloniality. We are reminded, though, that the black survival of coloniality is the ultimate beyond. It is a future dreamed of and struggled toward by the black radical tradition that each generation has to learn anew. 214 (reference omitted).

We recall Kehinde Andrews, discussed in Chapter 3; a similar claim to a vague solidarity is here, again, invoked. This might excite critical scholarly sensibilities but says very little about the materiality of the situation. As it decries the 'reification' of 'petty bourgeois dominance', it fully suffers from a reifi-cation of 'Caribbean thought' and its imagination of a 'Caribbean' recreated anew. Indeed, the crux of the matter is the matter of 'a different political economy, political arrangements ... and an entirely different structure of feeling', but this requires far greater an examination of the material conditions of the 'Caribbean', not just as a reification of (post)colonial Names and Meanings but of the material actuality of the 'Caribbean' as a configuration in the *World*, and of the complex social realities as lived and struggled for. I am less confident about any claim to a 'learning anew' of 'Caribbean thought'; this sounds to me, dare we say it, as a kind of 'thought and thinking' aspired to by a particular social strata, *our*s, that we might recognise as indeed 'petty bourgeois', at its most 'critical' best.

struggles fully the stuff of the "seismic ethico-epistemo-ontological shift" that Drucilla Cornell and Stephen Seely call for.[70] Of one thing we might be certain; everyday communities of struggle certainly do not need any grand gestures from philosophers of 'resistance' to "think liberation' or "emancipation", or indeed of '(b)orders' and 'frontlines', on their behalf.[71] Their articulations are clear and powerful in their own right, their struggles sufficiently full and rich with located knowledges of liberation, of beingness in actual *frontlines*. Now, in making such a claim as this, it is conventional to provide substantiation, from 'the field' (what colonial imaginary, this!) as it were, to prove the point. So here, below, a few; they are not in themselves of any great unique significance, simply reflective of located 'philosophies' that can be found in any 'place' we might look to find:

> Our autonomy doesn't need permission from the government: it already exists.[72]

> What do we have to ask forgiveness for? What are they to "pardon" us? ... Who should ask for forgiveness and who can grant it?[73]

> We need to get things clear. There definitely is a Third Force. The question is, what is it and who is part of the Third Force? Well, I am the Third Force myself. The Third Force is all the pain and the suffering that the poor are subjected to every second in our lives. The shack dwellers have many things to say about the Third Force. It is time for us to speak and to say, 'this is who we are, this is where we are, and this is how we live.[74]

---

70 Drucilla Cornell and Stephen D. Seely, *The Spirit of Revolution: Beyond the Ends of Man* (Cambridge: Polity Press, 2016), 130.

71 See for example the project of Michael Neocosmos, which he describes as follows:

> How are we to begin to think human emancipation in Africa today after the collapse of the Marxist, the Third World nationalist as well as the neo-liberal visions of freedom? How are we to conceptualise an emancipatory future governed by a fidelity to the idea of a universal humanity in a context where humanity no longer features within our ambit of thought and when previous ways of thinking emancipation have become obsolete Neocosmos, *Thinking Freedom in Africa*, xiii.

Neocosmos is of course wholly wrong to think that 'humanity' no longer features in contemporary thought, his error is to assume that the 'universal idea' of humanity is one designed to portend universal liberation rather than to facilitate differentiated subjugation. As we see on a daily basis, the recourse to Humanity is ever present in every interventionist assertion of power in the *World*. This is not a perversion of the Idea, but its very *Reason*.

72 The words of a Tzetzal woman from Morelia region in Mexico, as quoted in Shannon Speed, "Dangerous Discourses: Human Rights and Multiculturalism in Neoliberal Mexico," *PoLAR: Political and Legal Anthropology Review* 28(1), 2005, 29.

73 Statement of the FZLN rejecting the offer of 'pardon' by the Mexican government soon after the 'Zapatista' insurrection in 1994, quoted in Esteva and Prakash, *Grassroots*, 182-83.

74 S'bu Zikode, 'The Third Force', *Journal of Asian and African Studies* 41(1/2), 185-89, 186. See also,

I suggest we hear these voices uttering such words in every location of asserted and enforced (b)orderisation, on indigenous and peasant-lands, in urban settlements, in policed/militarised zones of surveillance and incarceration, in pathways and seaways of migration, in 'camps', in all these places and more. The above are simply some examples of such words. For their lack of exceptionality, even simplicity, they are powerful. And I am admittedly reading them in this way that I assert, as statements of anti-colonial *frontlines*, articulations of refusal and regeneration that renders the *World* of *Europe-Postcolony* as chimera even as it is utterly violent. My point is that only such a reading, such a re-cognition of the everyday, makes possible the beginnings of a philosophical repudiation of the perverse *White-Lies* of *Europe-Postcolony*, of a material challenge to the perverse norm-alities of global coloniality.[75] For this I make no apology. Indeed, precisely such a philosophical act of 'sedition' is necessary. Recalling the 'principles' of anti-colonial praxis outlined in Chapter 2, it is quite the affirmation of judgement, authorship, control and action that we find articulated in these examples, that we find asserted in the everyday repudiations by peoples in struggle.

One further point might be usefully cleared up here. It might be obvious that in making my argument, I am not perturbed by Gayatri Spivak's much quoted insight that 'the subaltern' cannot speak?[76] Spivak's was indeed an insight that shed light on the pretensions of liberation/emancipation assumed available within 'liberal-Modern' structures, processes, and

---

Zikode's denunciation of South African 'democracy' in "Twenty Years of Hell in Shacks: Presentation to the DDP Conference on 'Twenty Years of Local Democracy in South Africa', Durban, 20 & 21 October 2014', available at *Abahlali baseMjondolo,* 20 October <http://abahlali.org/node/14413> last accessed 17 February 2022.

75 A refreshing and rare example of what I am here calling the doing of philosophy as *encounter* is found in Nadine El-Enany's recent work, *(B)ordering Britain,* where she argues for 'irregular migration' to be understood in terms of 'anti-colonial resistance':

By calling for a reconceptualisation of irregularised migration as anti-colonial resistance, I am not arguing for a reformist strategy that would rely on nation-states or international organisations to introduce measures that might facilitate a more redistributive migration regime. ... Rather the reconceptualisation I offer ... is primarily intended as a counter-pedagogy to that of law. Rather than being seen as rightfully at the mercy of legal status recognition processes, racialised people must both be understood, and understand themselves, as being collectively entitled to the reclamation of wealth accumulated via colonial dispossession. (226-227)

Of course, what is relevant, and difficult, following from such an important statement of a philosophical position is what that 'counter-pedagogy' entails, and how such resistance might encounter the full violence of *Europe-Postcolony* which will undoubtedly be provoked in response. That, indeed, are the very real matters that pertain to the very real contexts and locations of *being*-anti-colonial. On the question of 'violence' in the connection of the *encounter,* see below, Chapter 6.

76 Gayatri Chakravorty Spivak, 'Can the Subaltern Speak?' in Cary Nelson and Lawrence Grossberg (eds), *Marxism and the interpretation of culture* (Basingstoke: Macmillan Education, 1988).

discursive registers. It pertains to a problem that arises within an assumed totality, a 'problem' only manifest if we were to accord (post)colonial normality a presumed totalising reality and 'sovereign' authority. Minus this assumption, we might understand such 'speech' differently, radically so, as utterly significant. Indeed, we must read 'cannot' in Spivak's formulation both categorically and injunctively; the 'subaltern' as a category of subject/ion is one disabled politico-juridical 'speech', and those made thus-subject, *cannot* be permitted speech/voice. Understood in this dual sense that gives coherence to the *philosophoscapes* and *Worldscape* of *Europe-Postcolony*, we might learn from these assertions of presence as precisely statements of a philosophical situation that smashes open the *World*. And with every utterance in every humble location in which it seeks to manifest, the totality of the *World* indeed is repudiated.

This, I suggest: we might understand such invocations of *beingness-otherwise-than-subjected* by those who appear stubborn and oblivious to their 'subaltern' silence, to see in such assertions from the grounds of struggle, precisely the ground of *anti-colonial* actualities of philosophy and action.[77] And from this realisation, from this understanding of the philosophical situation, we might also learn that it is our conceptions of the *World* inherited fully from *colonisation*, its norm-alities and its categories of 'political' beingness-voicings, that are not fit for purpose, and more than that, are duplicitous and deceitful.[78] Those on the *frontlines* of struggle are, I suspect, less hindered by their purported *subaltern* status, less impressed by their apparent incapacities of speech and action. Let us rest assured that they speak, and act, as they wish, their judgements defining the when, and the how of it. Whilst the

---

77 I read Issa Shivji's efforts to reclaim an imagination of a Pan-Africanism of the 'working people' as a similar work of a contemporary anti-colonial formulation of struggle and hope; see 'Pan-Africanism or imperialism? Unity and struggle towards a new democratic Africa' in Issa G. Shivji (Godwin R. Murunga ed.), *Where is Uhuru? Reflections on the struggle for democracy in Africa* (London: Fahamu Books, 2009), 196-207; and 'The Concept of the Working People', *Agrarian South: Journal of Political Economy*, 6(1), 2017, 1-13.

78 Unfortunately this is seldom the case, philosophers of the 'Global South' mostly appear to reinforce extant categories of the World even as they bemoan its coloniality, its racialised parochiality; it is telling that most 'theorisations' of such persistent insistences of refusal to subjection continue to be fixated with 'post-colonial' presumptions, either as struggles for Human/Citizenship Rights for those inclined to 'civil society'-type analysis and prescriptions, or as ruptural *Events* of becoming subject/ Citizen for those with 'critical-(post)Enlightenment', 'post-structuralist' inclinations. Neither move far from the underlying coloniality of methodological post-colonialism. In these claims of the work of 'theory', of the responsibility (and right) to read the philosophical situation of the present, the anti-colonial locations and pasts of thought and vision appear absent, or readily discarded, a short, disruptive philosophical interruption now returned to Eurocentric familiarities of 'Enlightenment'-based thought and action; see Jayan Nayar, 'Some Thoughts on the '(Extra)Ordinary': Philosophy, Coloniality, and Being Otherwise', *Alternatives: Global, Local Political*, 42(1), 2017, 3-25.

philosopher and the 'coloniser' might aspire to conquer the totality of 'Being' through the inscriptions of their universal categories, let us not assume that peoples are everywhere so colonised, even as they might be *conquered* under extant (post-)colonial regimes of (b)ordering.[79]

All this said, let us not get carried away – as so often is the case in many a contemporary excursion into 'critical' thought under the fervour of a newly discovered 'decolonial' turn. I want to stress the tentative *anti*-colonial quality of philosophical praxes as I present it here. On the one hand, this is to emphasise the contingent and contextual nature of all thinking, as well as the incompleteness, and unknowability (in the abstract, out of time and place), of the substantive actualities of 'decolonisation' that rely upon located experience and experimentation, not professionalised intellectual presumptions.[80] On the other, it is to precisely and firmly assert the fundamental situation of repudiation that is at the heart of anti-colonial praxeology.

The articulations of refusal such as those quoted above, such articulations that I argue must be read as a repudiation of *Europe-Postcolony*, point to no immediate solution to the problems of coloniality and *White-Reason*. Neither do they promise any redemption, their successes in overcoming the predatory impositions of the *Reason* of coloniality are perhaps far outnumbered by their defeats. This may well be the fate of many struggles and we cannot pretend otherwise. What is significant, however, is that they demonstrate the persistence of thinking-being against the asserted totality and finality of 'post-colonial' settlements, whatever the outcome in any contingent present. As such they point to a philosophical situation not terminated by *colonisation* nor the 'post-colonial' settlement. This is to say that, regardless of (post)colonial assertions of totality and finality, persisting in the *World*, as thinking-being in worlds, are other onto-epistemologies of beingness-otherwise existing in rebellious persistence with names and meanings not forgotten, memories and imaginations not erased, voices and songs not

---

79 James C. Scott's work amply demonstrates this lesson: see, for example, *Weapons of the Weak: Everyday Forms of Peasant Resistance* (Yale: Yale University Press, 1987); and *Domination and the Arts of Resistance: Hidden Transcripts* (Yale: Yale University Press, 1992).

80 For too often, critical 'post-colonial' thinkers have sought to place too heavy a burden upon past articulations of anti-colonial refusals and imaginations – we think of the immensity of reinterpretations (of (re-)interpretations) and disputations that are conducted and published under the academic enclave of 'Fanonian Studies', or the various celebrations and denunciations of Gandhian thought, for example of scholarly practice. In this, what were located and experiential thought, with all the inconsistencies and limitations and biases and fallibilities that attach to these greatly inspiring works, are argued over as if to discern the truth of some answers to the colonised condition! I prefer to understand these past works as being great in their context not for offering any answers that point to *decolonisation* but for opening up to us invaluable questions and insights on the anti-colonial struggle to think being-otherwise.

silenced. That is all. It is this affirmation of a *philosophical situation*, incessantly pointed at by the persistent struggles of rebellious communities worldwide, that I stress is necessary work of anti-colonial philosophy, to deny the author-ity of 'post-colonial' *(b)orders* and repudiate the perverse and cruel norm-alities of the (post)colonial present that they enforce.

Radha D'Souza provides a useful reminder:

> The conflation of individual life with social institutions is a hallmark of liberal thinking. We have inherited rights-based institutions. Do we need to, for that reason, demand rights, struggle for them and place our futures in its power of promise, knowing the promises are empty for most people most of the time? What did the socialists and the freedom fighters in the anti-colonial movements do? They demanded the real thing- food not right to food – national independence not right to independence, peace not right to peace, debt-repudiation not forgiveness.[81]

Demanding 'the real thing'! This perfectly describes the substance of anti-colonial praxes. And this is all that can be said in general terms about *(b)orders* and *frontlines* as the structures of *Europe-Postcolony* are sought to be variously dismantled. The rest is a matter of uncertain struggles in real times and real places.

---

81 Radha D'Souza, *What's Wrong with Rights? Social Movements, Law and Liberal Imaginations* (London: Pluto Press, 2018)

5

*On the Situation of Palestine and the Problem of Zionist-Israelism**

Edward Said famously posed the 'question of Palestine.'[1] The 'question', we are aware, remains fully open, unresolved, intractably so it would seem.[2] Crucially, it is a question that goes to the heart of the normalisation of *Europe-Postcolony* as a totalising frame of global (b)ordering. But this is not so often understood. For all that is argued on the matter, it is revealing that the work of a colonial philosophscape, fully in operation, inflicts both as fact and imagination a system of reality entirely constructed from an asserted, and indeed, enforced closure of thought. We have become accustomed to it. So effective is this closure, this asserted totalisation of a system of reality, that we appear unable to deviate from what can and cannot be said in terms of 'Israel' and 'Palestine'. Any challenge to this norm-alisation of the 'problem' is now subject, it seems, to an increased severity, and temerity, of response.[3] Not without good reason.

---

* This chapter was written before the events of 7 October 2023 and the subsequent campaign of sustained military bombardment of Gaza by the so-called 'Israeli Defence Forces'. As I undertake final revisions of the manuscript for publication in December of the same year, I observe the abject shamelessness with which Palestinian lives are deemed disposable even as 'regret' is sanctimoniously expressed. The arguments and positions I advance in this chapter, although written prior to these events, are reinforced by these blatant assumptions of civilisational supremacy and *Right*.

1 Edward Said, *The Question of Palestine* (London: Routledge and Kegan Paul, 1980).

2 For a recent statement on the on-going question, see, Amnesty International, *Israel's Apartheid Against Palestinians: Cruel System of Domination and Crime Against Humanity* (London: Amnesty International, 2022).

3 We are only too familiar with the constant policing of 'anti-semitism' that inevitably follows any critical discussion of 'Israel' and its Zionist policies; for a personal account of a sustained campaign and academic sacking, see Steven Salaita, *Uncivil Rites: Palestine and the Limits of Academic Freedom* (Chicago: Haymarket, 2015). See also, on the policing of 'self-hating Jews', Cynthia Levine-Rasky,

In this chapter, I do not speak of the "Israel-Palestine' conflict as a geopolitical problem to be solved. I do not focus on the periodic indictments of *Israeli* breaches of International Law and violations of Human Rights. Nor am I concerned here to explore the feasibility of any 'two-state solution' or to analyse the repeated 'diplomatic' movements and stagnations on these matters. So much on all of this has been documented and analysed.[4] There is no purpose in repeating the familiar complaints that ensue. Given that so much is known, I am conscious of this question always: what else is there to say on the matter, especially so when it seems little more *can* be said to affect the impunity with which the negation of the Palestinian peoples continues.[5] This, notwithstanding the current environment of critical scholarship and political commentary that appears to have found greater courage in naming 'Israel' a 'settler colonial' and Apartheid state.[6] But scholarly vehemence on the cause of 'justice' for Palestine, and the wrongs of 'Israel', is of little consequence, it seems, to the material actualities that prevail on the ground of Palestine. What more can be said? What more needs be said that goes beyond the mere consolation of repetition?

In what follows, the 'state of Israel', as such, is not addressed as if it were a given ontological category and fixed political-legal artefact in the *World*. I begin with a view that the preoccupation, or more accurately, the distraction, of *Israel* obscures the fundamental issue of the colonial situation of relevance. Given what we know on the intentions and effects of the *Zionist* project, my concern is to argue for an anti-colonial response. And towards

---

"Jewish Whiteness and Its Others", *Journal of Modern Jewish Studies*, 19(3), 2020, 362-381. I will return to the issue of 'anti-semitism' later in the discussion.

4 For a succinct introduction to many of the central issues of assertion and contention as they are usually played out; see Ilan Pappe, *Ten Myths About Israel* (London: Verso, 2017). For a thorough contemporary study of the political-legal issues, and a thoughtful analysis of possibilities for 'decolonisation', see Noura Erakat, *Justice for Some: Law and the Question of Palestine* (Redwood City: Stanford University Press, 2019).

5 Erakat's analysis provides a full picture of this comprehensive negation of Palestinian hope by the global (post)colonial political-legal order. Notwithstanding the numerous declaratory statements of the United Nations calling for a correction, the present prospects appear ever more distant, the colonial settlement in Palestine today enforced with full complicity of the contemporary political 'leadership' of the so-called Palestinian Authority. Noura Erakat maintains some hope in the solidarity movements as exemplified by the 'Boycott, Divest and Sanction Movement' (BDS) but in her deeper consideration of what decolonization might entail, there is a clear sense of uncertainty and distance; see Erakat, *Justice For Some*, 211-242.

6 We should remember of course that long before this current wave of interest in the settler colonial framing of the situation, Fayez Sayegh, in 1965, had already said what needed to be said, succinctly and plainly in *Zionist Colonialism in Palestine* (Beirut: Research Centre Palestine Liberation Organization, 1965). Sayegh employed the 'settler colonial' terminology in his analysis but his treatment on the issues, in my opinion, is somewhat different from its contemporary emphases, consistent with what I am here arguing to be the 'colonial situation'. Sayegh is not concerned as such with a settlement with Israel as a settler colonial state, but with Palestine and liberation from the settler colonial Zionist state that is Israel. This is a crucial difference.

this end, I do not accept the conventional wisdom that names as 'post-colonial pragmatism' the closure of anti-colonial repudiation and correction.

By way of concluding her deeply thoughtful analysis, Noura Erakat asks:

> What possible futures can Palestinians build for themselves as well as for the Jewish-Israelis that currently dominate them that would make this tortured history a chronicle of hope rather than one of mourning? This path is not well-paved; in fact, it does not even exist. Embarking upon it is a commitment to build new possibilities for decolonization and freedom more generally. It is primarily a commitment to ask different questions. The future of Palestine has the potential to provide new models for humanity, including legal orders that can make us whole, ones that Europe has not been able to deliver.[7]

What does it mean to ask different questions in this context? How might we maintain a commitment to this imperative of hope?

This is my position. I do not regard that the situation of Palestine is one on which 'Europe' has not been able to deliver. Exactly the opposite, it is one where we precisely witness the materialisation of *Europe* as *World'*-making imagination; *Israel-Palestine* is fully *Europe-Postcolony* in operation. I argue that what is commonly regarded as the context of 'Israel-Palestine' remains a continuing, incomplete, and precarious colonial enforcement of (b)orders through the genocidal violence of *Zionist-Israelism*.[8] My focus is to reveal the

---

7 Erakat, *Justice for Some*, 240-41.

8 I coin this term, *Zionist-Israelism*, rather than adopt the term *Zionism*, as is common, to bring attention to the historical facts that *Zionism* as an imagination of Jewish regeneration was variously theorized and advocated, there being nothing inevitable about the racialized state-form that transpired, or more accurately, conspired, to become. I discuss this below. On the assignation of 'genocide' to the situation, I do not use this term lightly. That it has come to be entrenched as a legal category with very limited practical application is clear, and yet, and particularly so in this context, it is necessary to return to the intention contained in its original, and raw, articulation as a philosophical naming of the incorrigible limit, the extreme cruelty, of human relationality. We remind ourselves of this naming of a crime of 'genocide' by Raphael Lemkin:

> it refers to a coordinated plan aimed at destruction of the essential foundations of the life of national groups so that these groups wither and die like plants that have suffered a blight. The end may be accomplished by the forced disintegration of political and social institutions, of the culture of the people, of their language, their national feelings and their religion. It may be accomplished by wiping out all basis of personal security, liberty, health and dignity. When these means fail the machine gun can always be utilized as a last resort. Genocide is directed against a national group as an entity and the attack on individuals is only secondary to the annihilation of the national group to which they belong. – Raphael Lemkin, "Genocide: A Modern Crime", *Prevent Genocide International*, available at: <http://www.preventgenocide.org/lemkin/freeworld1945.htm> (accessed 9 February 2022).

nature of this situation from an anti-colonial philosophical perspective and to reaffirm the reality of 'Palestine', still unsubsumed, still unsubdued, still a frontline of struggle against the norm-alisation of the (post)colonial assertion of *The State of Israel*, still open for the recovery of what Ariella Aisha Azoulay evocatively calls 'potential history'.[9] It is also my intention to address head on the usual and frequent resort to regimes of silencing, enforced specifically through perverse accusations of 'anti-semitism', that are an insult to the real suffering of decimated peoples across the times and spaces of the Colonial-Modern present.

Let me also make this introductory clarification. My position is not intended as an attempt to persuade those supporters of *Zionist-Israelism* that the Palestinian cause is one that is 'just', and worthy of dignity in resolution. The peoples of Palestine, and those in solidarity with them, fully know this. As such, this is not an argument that pretends any form of objective calculation of options for a 'solution'. As I see it, and as it has been evidenced repeatedly, this is (post)colonial folly.[10] The argument here does not seek accommodation within a (b)ordered totality asserted as 'Israel-Palestine'. It is unequivocal in its affirmation rather of the anti-colonial understanding of Palestine as an integral whole. What comes of this, comes of it; this is a matter of struggle and judgement by the peoples of Palestine, all. Mine is simply a restatement of the relevant philosophical situation as a point of departure for praxis.

With this understanding, the following need still be said.

Situating the (Anti)Colonial in Palestine

Recent critical attention has focussed on speaking of 'The State of Israel' as a 'settler colonial state'.[11] I acknowledge the vitality of engagement this

---

We note that what provoked this expression of outrage was undoubtedly a matter of 'European' sensibility, the persistent *White* inflictions upon *Black*-ed populations not contemplated as such. Nevertheless, the sentiment remains. The subsequent refinement that came with the juridification of 'genocide' under 'International Criminal Law' so-called, can be understood as so much machination of *White* philosophy to disqualify *Europe* as ever, 'legally', culpable for its *norm-alised* inflictions of brutality and cruelty. But this is beside the point. What is interesting is that this judgement of genocide against 'Israel' is not new; much legal analysis and argument making this case is available. As again, what is shockingly lacking is any clear statement on the implications of this knowledge as a matter of consequence. For a recent summary of the many legal views against 'Israeli' perpetration of 'genocide', see 'The Genocide of the Palestinian People: An International Law and Human Rights Perspective', *Centre for Constitutional Rights*, 25 August 2016, available at: <https://ccrjustice.org/genocide-palestinian-people-international-law-and-human-rights-perspective> (accessed 20 February 2022).

9 Ariella Aisha Azoulay, *Potential History: Unlearning Imperialism* (London: Verso, 2019)

10 For a sharp analysis of the content and implications of 'diplomacy' in the 'Israel-Palestine' context, see Joseph Massad, "The rights of Israel", *Al Jazeera*, 6 May 2011, available at: <https://www.aljazeera.com/opinions/2011/5/6/the-rights-of-israel> (accessed 12 February 2022).

11 For a useful statement on the 'settler colonial' frame of understanding and analysis, see Patrick Wolfe, "Settler Colonialism and the Elimination of the Native," *Journal of Genocide Research*, 8(4), 2006, 387-409.

scholarly frame of analysis and critique has generated, but I am not so certain of its real utility. With regard to Palestine, I find the 'settler colonial' view inadequate, and, more than this, obscuring.[12]

For my purposes, 'The State of Israel', as such, is of secondary importance. I don't mean by this that it is immaterial, but that the material reality that is relevant from an anti-colonial understanding is not the effects of 'Israel' – as a 'settler-colonial state' – in its actions against 'Palestine' – as 'occupied lands' – but of the integral *colonial* situation of Palestine past to present. As I see it, there is an underlying and fundamental difference in quality between the two situations. And the implication of this difference is significant, between, on the one hand, a concession to (post)colonial (b)orders, and on the other, an assertion of anti-colonial frontlines. Three specific aspects are of relevance.

First, as a matter of ontological assumption, the 'settler colonial' frame assumes a definitive ontological quality that attaches to the categories of 'settler' and 'native' in the constitution and performance of the 'colonial' relationship. The significance of the categories 'settler' and 'native' is that they denote, as constitutive, a relationality that defines the situation, that is to say, the subsequent 'colonial' situation of differentiated subjection arises as a material encounter between the 'settler' who appropriates lands occupied by the 'native'. Not before. And this is the critical point; the assignation of 'settler-native' is precisely the prefiguration of subject-beingness that originates the colonial relationship as 'coloniser'-'conquered' in such contexts. The particular content of the colonial structure, both material and discursive, therefore, follows from, and is defined, by this encounter, that is, by the consequence of the outcomes of the specific conflicts between 'settler', being-'settler', and 'native', being-'made-native', in time and place.[13]

Secondly, what is commonly referred to as 'settler colonial states' is descriptive of 'settled (post)colonial arrangements, not of situations that remain essentially unresolved.[14] From an anti-colonial standpoint, it is imperative that this

12 For reasons other than mine, but also critical of the 'settler-colonial' frame of analysis, see; Ann Laura Stoler, *Duress: Imperial Durabilities in Our Times* (Duke University Press, 2016), 37-67; Brenna Bhandar and Rafeez Ziadah, "Acts and Omissions: Framing Settler Colonialism in Palestine Studies", *Jadaliyya*, 14 January 2016, available at: <https://www.jadaliyya.com/Details/32857> (accessed 8 August 2023); Yara Hawari, Sahrri Plonski and Elian Weisman, "Seeing Israel through Palestine: Knowledge Production as Anti-Colonial Praxis", *Settler Colonial Studies* 9(1), 2019, 155-75.

13 Patrick Wolfe is careful to make clear this context of settler-colonial situations, see *Traces of History: elementary structures of race* (London: Verso, 2016) 203-238.

14 On this point, I note Ann Stoler's description of incompletion:

   Settler colonialism is no more fixed and given than any colonial formations that assert their illegitimate claims. Settler colonialism might better be understood not as a unique "type," but as the effect of a failed or protracted contest over appropriation and dispossession that is not

understanding is not diluted by the apparent conciliation to asserted 'facts'. In most analyses of 'settler colonial states', what is revealed is that the fundamental (b)orders of the situation are in material terms fixed, their settlement as *(b) orders* more complete, and from this, the conquest of the 'native' by the 'settler' more entrenched as (post)colonial *norm-ality*. Notwithstanding ongoing struggles, 'settler-colonial' state-situations exist in the form of 'constituted' political-legal entities encompassing both the coloniser and conquered populations in its constitutional frame of 'recognition-subjection', even if such recognition entails the material subjugation of the 'native' populations. When we speak of the usual culprits – the United States, Australia, New Zealand, Canada, South Africa – this quality of the situation is evident. I do not intend to suggest by this that the struggles to overturn the colonial norm-alities of these 'state' situations is insignificant, or that they bear no consequence to the material realities of subjection. However, it remains that the questions that arise in these contexts, the subjects of 'indigenous' struggles – a categorisation that is itself an inscription of subject-beingness under an already settled situation – are more involved with issues that pertain to a 're-settlement' of (b)ordering, that is, of a renegotiation of the (post)colonial arrangement, be it in the form of onto-epistemological recognition – of name, identities, histories and cosmologies etc – and/or of the material redistribution of resources in the form of compensatory reparations, or distributions of authority and jurisdiction of 'delegated sovereignty'. No radical ontological challenge of the (b)ordered institution of the 'state' is fundamentally at issue in these circumstances; the essential (b)order of the situation remains intact.

And, thirdly, the location of the colonial situation in 'settler colonial states' is the (b)ordered space of the asserted totality named as 'State'. Within these (b)orders are frontlines of repudiation understood and asserted; 'colonial settler' and 'conquered native', now as constituted 'subjects' under the (post)colonial fiction of 'citizenship', here stand in intimate relationality of belonging-separation within a coherent structure of (post)coloniality. From this situation of encounter, as a settlement of this encounter of (b)order/ frontline, is the shape and content of the *World*, as a totality of (post)colonial settlement, in turn configured.

over when the victories are declared, killings are accomplished, and decimation is resolved as the only "solution." Settler colonialism is only ever an imperial process in formation whose security apparatus confirms that it is always at risk at being undone. – *Duress*, 60-61

In my view, this is an overstatement of the spaces available for contestation within what is usually regarded as 'settler colonial' state formations. This notwithstanding, Stoler's description is perfectly apt in the case of *Zionist-Israelism* in Palestine.

We return to the 'question' of Palestine; a different situation persists altogether, such that to assign it as one of being subject to a 'settler colonial state' is diminishing rather than enforcing of an anti-colonial understanding. My argument is this:

1) 'Israel-Palestine' was not originated, defined, or constituted by the relationality of a 'settler-native' situation but rather by a prior assertion and enforcement of colonial (b)orders, that of 'Mandate Palestine', on which continuities of dispossession and elimination were entrenched.

2) The colonial encounter was never transformed into a 'settler colonial state' situation whereby the prefigurative relationality of 'settler-native' is reconfigured into a regime of recognition under (differentiated) 'citizenship' within a (b)ordered 'State' totality. 'Israel' remains a precarious categorical assertion, unfinished and unfixed, even if it's materiality of violence is exaggeratedly pronounced.

3) The location of the colonial situation, past and present, is not located within, and confined to, the (b)orders/frontlines of 'Israel-Palestine'. It is not the internal settlement of 'Israel-Palestine', as a settler-colonial state, that defines and configures the contours of a 'post-colonial' *World*. Exactly the opposite is true, it is entirely the case that it is the various configurative settlements of the (post)colonial *World* – in their calculations and machinations of (b)ordering – that defines the precise (b)ordering of the on-going situation of Palestine. In this way, how we understand the 'question' of Palestine goes to the heart of the philosophical and material situation of the *World* as (post)colonial actuality itself.

All this needs elaboration.

Manoeuvres of Origination

It is of critical importance that we locate *Zionist-Israelism* as an imagination,[15] and indeed as a sustained project of elimination, entirely originating within a prior colonial situation. Not just as a matter of historical interest, but, as a continuing determinant that maintains the unsettled situation of Palestine. It is well documented that the process of Jewish 'settlements' – usually

---

15 This point that the entire basis of the claim to a 'Jewish People' in relation to a Land – *Eretz Israel* – is premised on an imagination transformed into an invention is of critical importance. For a comprehensive tracing of the contested ideas that preceded the particular invention of the 'nationalist' imagination and project that was to become the Idea and violent materialization of 'The State of Israel'; see Shlomo Sand (trans. Yael Lotan), *The Invention of the Jewish People* (London: Verso, 2020). See also, Wolfe, *Traces of History*; Illan Pappé, *Ten Myths about Israel* (London: Verso, 2017).

spoken of in terms of Zionist 'settler colonialism' by critical commentators, or as the (Five) *Aliyas* in the mythologisation of *Zionist-Israelism* – was never an assumption of an original situation, never an independent and organic construction of a relational encounter, between 'Jewish-settler' and 'native-*fellahin*'.[16] It was instead, from its beginnings in the late 1800s, a process of migrations and institutionalised settlements entirely dependent upon the facilitation and protection of a colonial structure already in place, first under the joint arrangements of the Ottoman and British authorities, then under the sole auspices of the imperial-colonial structure of the so-called 'Mandate Palestine'. It was, in other words, not the 'settler-native' encounter that gave rise to the colonial situation, it was the colonial situation, already institutionalised, that originates the differentiated relationalities of *subjection*, of incursions and expulsions. While the fact of 'legality' this patronage conferred might, under the conventional colonial terms of understanding, be regarded as strengthening the argument for 'validity of title', exactly the reverse is true when understood from an anti-colonial perspective.

Crucial in this architecture of colonial myth-making is the infamous and much commented-on *Balfour Declaration* of 1917. Its significance is as Said stated it:

> What is important about the Declaration is, first, that it has long formed the juridical basis of Zionist claims to Palestine and, second, ... that it was a statement whose positional force can only be appreciated when the demographic or human realities of Palestine are kept clearly in mind. That is, the declaration was made (a) by a European power, (b) about a non-European territory, (c) in a flat disregard of both the presence and the wishes of the native majority resident in the territory, and (d) it took the form of a promise about this same territory to another foreign group, so that this foreign group might, quite literally, *make* this territory a national home for the Jewish people.[17]

I linger on the Declaration, and on Said's reading of it, for a moment. Not to recount, again, a linear historical record of the 'conflict' that is defined as pitting the 'Jews against the Arabs', but to consider the assumption, and assertion, that underpins it, and its subsequent implication from an anti-colonial perspective. These are significant insights of Said. They point to the

---

16 For an elaboration of this argument, see Wolfe, *Traces of History*; Illan Pappé, *Ten Myths about Israel*.
17 Said, *The Question of Palestine*, 15-16 (emphasis in original).

fundamental character, as a matter of ontological foundation, of the colonial situation. Unfortunately, Said stops there, not quite addressing the radical implications of these insights in ways useful to an anti-colonial correction to the *Zionist* project of 'Israel'. Quite the reverse, he concedes to the very colonisation of 'reality' that he sought to question in this work:

> There is not much use today in lamenting such a statement as the Balfour Declaration. It seems more valuable to see it as a part of history, of a style and set of characteristics centrally constituting the question of Palestine as it can be discussed even today. Balfour's statements in the declaration take for granted the higher right of a colonial power to dispose of a territory as it saw fit.[18]

Two points stand out: 1) the presumed and assumed right of the colonial power (this we well know), and 2) the consequence of defining the 'question of Palestine as it can be discussed even today'. The combined effect of these two consequences is to entrench what we are purportedly to regard as the prevailing system of reality, that is 'Israel-Palestine' bifurcated, from which any subsequent discussion on the matter is to originate. Said is correct to point this out. However, Said makes the error of downplaying – as nothing more than a 'part of history' – the contemporary significance of the Balfour Declaration. In my view, this is to inadvertently acquiesces to the very erasure of the anti-colonial as a situation for philosophy, and to accept the foundational assertion of the (post)colonial settlement that is 'Israel-Palestine' ontologically separated, again, the structure *Europe-Postcolony* entrenched. From this (post)colonial originary settlement, all subsequent erasure, still ongoing, is enabled:

> [t]he fact of the matter is that today Palestine does not exist, except as a memory, or more importantly, as an idea, a political and human experience, and an act of sustained political will.[19]

So was lost an opportunity, as a commentator that had a platform in *Europe* (the United States), to re-state the anti-colonial present at a critical juncture of the struggle. Said's was a forceful indictment of the 'absenting' of Palestine by the 'interpretive' acts of 'Israel', but as I read it, he located the 'question' within the (b)orders already asserted, already entrenched, as 'Israel-Palestine'. This, the error. I understand Said's intention to emphasise the potency of

---

18 *ibid*, 16
19 *ibid*, 5. The sentiment, we see, is repeated, in the present time, by Erakat, *Justice for Some*, 23-60.

'memory' as a vibrant consciousness of the political movements of 'Palestine' towards self-determination' and international recognition. We might regard this as a pragmatic political argument which Said later stressed as an imperative of 'Palestinianism' understood as a "political movement that is being built out of the reassertion of Palestine's multicultural and multi-religious history."[20] But, in my view this is to concede everything. To accede to 'History' as a fixing of a (post)colonial settlement relinquishes precisely that which is fundamentally the crux of the anti-colonial position. Writing in 1992 after the betrayals of the 'Camp David' process, Said, retained a hope of a reconciliation, perhaps as a result of his location, and a nod to his audience; he closed his book with this statement:

> In 1988, we Palestinians as a people took a giant step towards reconciliation and peace. We now await a corresponding gesture from the Israeli people and its government.[21]

It was not forthcoming. 'Palestinianism' brought no fruition to the aspiration of liberation and a bi-national state, culminating in what Said later described as the "protracted, disorderly, hypocritical, and undignified surrender" that was the settlements of the 'peace process' in Oslo.[22] As we learn from the more recent restatement of the *Question* by Erakat, pragmatism, brought little corresponding movements towards reconciliation.[23] This is not, in my view, a matter of failure, not merely a consequence of cynicism and bad faith, nor of missed opportunities and betrayals. It is also not for an inadequacy of effort that can be corrected if only we could be more strategic, more sophisticated, more nuanced and confident in our engagements with the law as a political site of struggle. My argument is that there can be no resolution of a conflict which sustains both 'Israel' and 'Palestine' as if these were commensurable ontological categories. A different quality intrinsic to the colonial situation instead pertains, and we are familiar with its operation; what is at work here, again, is the assertion of a philosophoscape to entrench a desire of *Europe* making a *World*.

The Balfour Declaration is critical to my understanding as it serves as a point of origin for a series of inventions that construct a colonial reality, as Said understood, all of which imagined by the assumption of authorial

---

20 Edward Said, *The Politics of Dispossession: The Struggle for Palestinian Self-Determination*, 1969–1994 (New York: Pantheon, 1994), 3.
21 Said, *The Question of Palestine*, 244.
22 Edward Said, *The End of the Peace Process* (New York: Pantheon, 2000), 18-19.
23 See Erakat, *Justice For Some*, Conclusion.

Right. From this moment, and only as a consequence of this original authorial *World*-making assumption, we see a coherent and self-referential continuity runs through the architecture of constitutive articulations – from the
Balfour Declaration, to the United Nations Partition Plan (Res 181(II), 29
December 1947), to the 'Declaration of the Establishment of the State of
Israel' (May 14, 1948) – that gives meaning to, and entrenches, the (post)
colonial assertion of (b)ordering that has the name 'Israel-Palestine'. Thus, we
speak of 'Israel-Palestine' today as the accumulative result of these assertions
of invention; we speak of it ubiquitously the result of the entrenchment of
thought as a matter of (post)colonial discursive closure. Every further point
in the historical evolution of the colonial situation of Palestine has been built
upon this norm-alisation of the continuity of colonial (b)ordering;[24] from the
genocidal expansion of *Zionist-Israelism* as legally sanctioned by the 'Declaration of Independence' of 1948, via 1967 and the 'Six Day War', through to
the present day (post 'peace processes' of Camp David and Oslo) extensions
of the logics of 'walls' and 'check-points' and 'camps' of racialised differentiation and segregation, the thread of colonial continuity runs coherently.

   All of this has of course been subject to in-depth examinations, of the
meaning and implications of each of these moments understood to be
constitutive of the 'Israel-Palestine' conflict. But, perhaps at a cost of diluting
the fundamental issue. As a matter of philosophical consequence, what this
sequence of constitutive events demonstrates is but the elaboration of an
underlying and coherent structure of the colonial assertion, the record of
its detail archivally important but less so as a qualitative statement on the
situation as such. Invention upon invention built on colonial structures;
these are the foundations of the 'State of Israel'. While the (colonial) settler
mythology of a return Home – *Eretz-Israel* – serves to construct an immemo-
rial divine beginning, the much more mundane, and vulgar, origins of 'Israel'
as a materialisation in territorial form of *Zionist-Israelism* was continuously

---

24 Much of the discussion on the 'history' the 'Israel-Palestine conflict' centres around the long and
   sordid account of political-legal wranglings in the United Nations. It is notable that in these defining
   junctures of (b)ordering, there is little involvement of the peoples of Palestine, nor substantive descriptions of their sensibilities. It is of course of critical significance that throughout these machinations,
   the ensuing 'settlements' were refused by the Palestinian representatives; see Erakat, *Justice for Some*,
   especially 61-94. Also, Ran Greenstein, *Zionism and Its Discontents: A Century of Radical Dissent in
   Israel/Palestine* (London: Pluto Press, 2014). It is noteworthy, of course, that the official Palestinian
   positions, in line with that of the so-called wider 'Arab World', have since become much more concilia-
   tory. This might be read as a marker of a 'post-colonial settlement' on the essential issue of the (b)order
   that is 'Israel-Palestine', of the *fact* of a 'pragmatic' present. I do not however make this concession to
   the question of the philosophical situation.

a matter of opportunism and colonial manipulation.[25] I don't point to this as a complaint; the colonial philosopher, as I have maintained, has every entitlement to rationalise such efforts, no doubt, but it is quite a nonsense to presume that peoples who are sought to be thus conquered into subjection are to thereby abide by such colonial fantasies of compliance. From an anti-colonial view what is of significance is that these inventions remain fragile. Facts of History, perhaps, but frontlines, still.

Fragile (B)orders and Precarious Settlements

Naming indeed matters. Thus are (b)orders of imagination asserted and sought to be 'settled', discursively and materially. In this way, the naming of a situation is precisely the critical philosophical manoeuvre that erases a past, rendering a colonial situation as (post)colonial norm-ality. 'Israel' is precisely this move of erasure. Yet it remains unfulfilled, its claim to be fixed upon the *World* inherently precarious. While it might not appear so from the sheer amassment of its record of violence, the assertions and inventions of *Zionist-Israelism* are characterised not by a firmness of conviction, but by a fundamental ontological uncertainty. Nothing is more revealing of this desire, even need, for perpetual reassurance, than the semantics of the 'Right to Exist' that defines the 'political' stance of righteous intransigence that the 'State of Israel' so insists on.

This is indeed a peculiar 'political' characteristic; unique in its absurdity, the vehemence of its insistence on (repeated) universal acknowledgement appears to be correlated to increases in the militaristic expansion of its desires. It is unmistakeable; the more 'Israel' operates as an organisation of dispossession and mass-killing, the greater its appeal to vulnerability and victimisation, the responsibility of the *World* to respect and protect. Such is the claim: 'Israel's Right to Exist' is to be 'recognised' unequivocally, precisely the condition of engagement, with no reciprocal assurances of responsibility. There is no need here to repeat the arguments made that there exists no such State 'right to exist' in 'International Law';[26] this is beside the point. The point rather is that we observe as a defining feature of *Zionist-Israelism* precisely the trope of the exceptionalism of the (divine) fragility of *White*-supremacy.[27]

---

25 I will argue below that a different significance attaches to the mythology of 'Eretz-Israel' in the formation of *Zionist-Israelism*.

26 For a review of the debates, see Anthony Carty "Review: Israel's Legal Right to Exist and the Principle of the Self-determination of the Palestinian People?" *The Modern Law Review* 76 (1), 2013, 158-177.

27 That White'-ness, rather than Judaism or Jewishness *per se* underpins the *Zionist* Project is argued by Noura Erakat, "White as Property in Israel: Revival, Rehabilitation, and Movement", *Harvard Journal on Racial & Ethnic Justice* 31, 2015, 69-104.

In the 'State of Israel', we find this expressed at its limit.[28] Joseph Massad explained it perfectly:

> Zionism and Israel are careful not to generalise the principles that justify Israel's rights to colonise, occupy, and discriminate, but are rather vehement in upholding them as subsets of an exceptional moral principle. It is not that no other people has been oppressed historically, it is that Jews have been oppressed *more*. It is not that no other people's cultural and physical existence has been threatened; it is that the Jews' cultural and physical existence is threatened *more*. This quantitative equation is key to why the world, and especially Palestinians, should recognise that Israel needs and deserves to have the rights to colonise, occupy, and discriminate. If the Palestinians, or anyone else, reject this, then they must be committed to the annihilation of the Jewish people physically and culturally, not to mention that they would be standing against the Jewish God.

This is an accurate description of the politics, and its attendant discourse, of entitlement and exceptionalism that is pervasive in discussions on the so-called 'Israel-Palestine conflict'. The important question, however, is not whether 'Israel' is justified in demanding this positional privilege; this, as we are familiar, only gives rise to an incessant back and forth of claim and counter-claim. This is both distracting and pointless. What is instead important to understand is the operation of this claim, that is, to consider, as a matter of philosophical consequence, the foundation and effect of this assertion of exceptionalism. The question of significance is this: what is the underlying motivation that determines this particular overt anxiety that translates into an asserted claim to incontrovertible right to violence? From this, we better understand the discursive effects that have come to define the politics of what is regarded as the possible in relation to 'Israel-Palestine'.

The obvious assumption, or more accurately, the defining error, that dominates the majority of commentary on the ontological anxiety of 'The State of Israel' is that we witness here a lingering trauma of historical Judeophobia culminating in the *European-Judeocide* committed in Nazi extermination camps, now filtered through the more recent experience of 'Arab' hostility; much has been invested in this particular myth in the discourse on and of 'Israel'. It bears a reminder, of course, that this is a matter entirely of *Europe*, the

---

28 Massad, "The Rights of Israel"

Jewish Question and its *Final Solution* originating in the context of the birth-pangs and poisonous auto-construction of *European White*-ness.[29] But as we shall see later in this chapter, this is a truth that is radically re-settled by this invention of 'Israel' with profound consequences to our understanding of the situation of Palestine. For now, what is critical is simply to note that it is from this point of departure, of an asserted victimhood to 'eternal anti-Semitism', that the contemporary problem of 'Israel-Palestine' is presented as a matter of a 'conflict' seeking resolution. I suggest a different understanding of the ontological anxiety that pervades the imagination and intention of 'Israel'.

The claim to exceptionalism is essential in that it is fundamental to the very assertion of *Zionist-Israelism*. It is not the trauma of experience that lies at the heart of this offensive stance against challenge; saying this is not to diminish the horrors inflicted by German Nazism upon peoples deemed unworthy of human life. But it is to accord its proper significance in the larger scheme of the situation. As a start, we remember that the aspirations of *Zionist-Israelism* preceded Nazism and its racialised perversions both in origination and practical realisation. Indeed, the *Shoah* served to provide a discursive trump in the negotiations of the post-War settlements of the United Nations, but the assertion itself was fully born out of a prior Idea of racial exceptionalism.

To be clear, *Zionist-Israelism* originates from a position that is, from its very foundations, precarious in that its underlying intentions, blatantly profane, were draped in a convenient mythology literally of biblical scope and scale. Now, we know that the assertion of a 'People' 'returned' to a hereditary land from exile is entirely built on fictions.[30] And yet, precisely this manoeuvre of mythological embedding is fundamentally necessary for the invention of the link between Jewishness and *Zionist-Israelism*. Not because it is upon its truth that the security of the claim to 'Eretz-Israel' in the lands of Palestine lies. But because the biblical story – of the exceptionalism of a chosen people of *Return* – provides a distracting cover for the more profane exceptionalism that defines the material and worldly roots and aspirations of *Zionist-Israelism*. Setting aside the controversies that surround the 'History' of the 'Jews', the real matter at issue is the invention of *Zionist-Israelism* as an expression of *White*-exceptionalism.

---

29 Hannah Arendt's discussion remains profoundly instructive, *The Origins of Totalitarianism* (London: Penguin Books, 2017, 1951), Chapter 2. Similarly, and for the use of term 'Judeocide', see Arno J. Mayer, *Why Did the Heavens Not Darken* (London: Verso, 2012); Wolfe, *Traces of History*, Chapter 3.

30 For accounts of the hyper-sensitive and overtly aggressive policing of the origin stories of Jews as a cohesive and unitary people of Biblical lineage; see Wolfe. *Traces of History* 239-252; Sand, *The Invention of the Jewish People*, 250-313.

This is well-documented, the evidence repeatedly presented. From Sayegh, Sands, Said, Wolfe, Pappé , Erekat etc, we are fully aware that the history of 'Zionism' as it emerged in 'Europe' – that is to say in a *Europe* emerging – is intimately connected with the entrenchment of *White*-ness as a structure of the *World*. "[T]he Jewish state was born out of sin", and this Pappé demonstrates clearly.[31] We are not short of documentation, of course, on the violence, the 'sins' past and continuing, inflicted by the 'State of Israel'. However, and again, it is necessary to situate the question of origins in a different place than commonly assumed. It is not the sin of the 'Dalet Plan' and the resulting Nakba that serves as the foundation on which the 'Jewish state' was built. No doubt, it is essential that these are recognised as significant events for judgement, as Pappé insists "from our present vantage point, there is no escape from defining the Israeli actions in the Palestinian countryside as a war crime. Indeed, as a crime against humanity."[32] But, the 'sin' has a deeper meaning and implications, and it is essential that we make this clear, to put an end to what is perhaps the gravest *Lie* that underpins *Zionist-Israelism*.

This is that the 'State of Israel' is an artefact of a global Jewry carrying the burden of suffering and memory of the *Shoah*. It is convenient, and powerful, to project the undeniable horrors of Nazi 'death-camps' as the backdrop and defining context that constructs and informs the consciousness manifest as the 'State of Israel' but this would be to engage in a perversion. The evidence suggests differently. The 'State of Israel', as a political-legal-territorial artefact of *Zionist-Israelism*, was born not of *European-Judeocide* but of a racialised elite desire for *'European-Whiteness'*. We know that 'Zionism' is a recent expression of Jewish consciousness, born out of an elite and minority 'Ashkenazi-Yiddish' articulation of secular regeneration.[33] Even so, even as a minority assertion of racial 'Self-hood' it was contested and open to differing imaginations of possible Jewish futures. The 'national' imagination, was but one, adopting as it understood the prevailing trope of *European* exceptionalism, the assumption of racialised supremacy and privilege. The burden for the emergent secular 'Zionist' was the affront that they remained Other-ed, insufficiently *White*-d within their *European* locations of acculturated

---

31 Pappé, *Ten Myths About Israel*, 64
32 Pappé, *Ten Myths About Israel*, 63.
33 For discussions on the contestations around the imagination of Jewishness and Zionism; see Sand, *The Invention of the Jewish People*; Alan R. Taylor, "Zionism and Jewish History", *Journal of Palestine Studies*, 1(2), 1972, 35-51.

habitation.[34] A new 'national home' was necessary. And an 'old home' –
Eretz-Israel – was discovered/invented. There is no uncertainty about this
fact; the assertion of Jewish exceptionalism that I call *Zionist-Israelism* was
in every aspect an assertion of White-ness corresponding to the solidifying
self-rationalisation of *Europe* in its colonial self-invention. As Wolfe put it:

> Zionism ... was a conscious exercise in auto-racialisation. It embraced
> European colonial discourse, including race, nationalism and even,
> albeit strategically, antisemitism itself. In short, Zionism ... is 'the
> product of Europe, not of the ghetto'[35]

And so we see, not Jewishness as religion but as *race* – following in the
dominant Reason of *Europe* – defined this imagination.[36] This connection to
an Idea of *Europe* is critical to an understanding of the situation we currently
confront. Wolfe's explanation is useful:

> On the one hand, Zionism sought to be internal to Europe. It aimed
> to build a civilised, territorially defined nation-state that would be
> thoroughly European in culture and allegiance. On the other hand,
> however, as a project that laid claim to a Palestinian inheritance,
> Zionism situated itself outside Europe, an exteriority that found
> expression in the diasporan narrative of temple-destruction and
> ensuing exile. Culturally, in other words, Zionism sought to belong

---

34 For a clear statement of this fact, see Theodore Herzl, *The Jewish State* (New York: Dover Publications,
    1988), 76:

> We have honestly endeavored everywhere to merge ourselves in the social life of
> surrounding communities and to preserve the faith of our fathers. We are not permitted
> to do so. In vain are we loyal patriots, our loyalty in some places running to extremes; in
> vain do we make the same sacrifices of life and property as our fellow-citizens; in vain do
> we strive to increase the fame of our native land in science and art, or her wealth by trade
> and commerce. In countries where we have lived for centuries we are still cried down as
> strangers, and often by those whose ancestors were not yet domiciled in the land where
> Jews had already had experience of suffering. The majority may decide which are the
> strangers; for this, as indeed every point which arises in the relations between nations, is
> a question of might. I do not here surrender any portion of our prescriptive right, when
> I make this statement merely in my own name as an individual. In the world as it now
> is and for an indefinite period will probably remain, might precedes right. It is useless,
> therefore, for us to be loyal patriots, as were the Huguenots who were forced to emigrate.
> If we could only be left in peace....

> But I think we shall not be left in peace.

Indeed, the entire pamphlet that sets out Herzl's dream might be read as an enticement to the slighted
Jewish capitalist classes to seek security in a 'Jewish state' first settled and worked upon by the lower
classes of Jews who have nothing but their impoverished despair to lose, the latter requiring some
further reassurances to 'transplant' their economic interests.

35 Wolfe, *Traces of History*, 107 (reference omitted)

36 And it is this error that is fundamental to a correction of what is understood by 'anti-Semitism'; see
    below for an elaboration.

to Europe while, ancestrally, it laid claim to an Oriental provenance.
... The great lack that defined life in the European diaspora for Zionists was a territorial basis with which their pre-existing 'Jewish nation'
could combine to form a state, understood as demo-territorial unity.
The is the point at which we can appreciate the full utility of the notion
of return. Jews were by no means the only identifiable community in
Europe that lacked a territory of its own, nor the only one to claim a
primordial inheritance .... Why, then, should Jews be intrinsically entitled to colonise Palestine? The answer that Zionism provided was that
the Jewish lack was different to those of other communities, since it
had come to pass not by happenstance but through the unredeemed
injustice of expulsion (at the hands, moreover, of the Romans, from
whom Western European nations claimed succession).[37]

This passage contains insights that are of critical significance to an understanding of the present; the connection between *Zionist-Israelism* and
the invention, and imposition, of *Europe* as an ontological and militaristic
category in the *World* more profound than usually appreciated. My interest
here lies precisely in the connection between the desire, founded on the
'culture of race', we might call it, of/for *Europe*, and the (biblical/Roman)
claim to inheritance of Palestine. Upon this assertion, consolidated and
cloaked subsequently in the claim to the perpetual trauma of the *Holocaust*, is
grounded the entire basis of exceptionalism that defines the (b)ordered situation of Palestine. The following becomes clearer to view.

'Israel' is an *Idea* and political formation born out of *European-White*-ness.
Now, there is a great deal of confusion that is observed in discussions pertaining
to this fundamental point; it is often taken to mean that this is to claim that
Jewish peoples are now charged with the 'postcolonial', 'Critical Race Theory'
taint of 'White-guilt'.[38] I cannot speak for other commentators on the subject

37 Wolfe, *Traces of History*, 245-46 (reference omitted)
38 See for example, Paresky, 'Critical Race Theory and the 'Hyper-White' Jew', Sapir 1, 2021, 18-27
available at: <https://sapirjournal.org/social-justice/2021/05/critical-race-theory-and-the-hyper-
white-jew/> (accessed 8 August 2023). See also, Brian Blum, "Jews are not white: Race and identity
in Israel and the US – Opinion", *The Jerusalem Post*, 18 November 2021, available at: <https://
www.jpost.com/opinion/jews-are-not-white-race-and-identity-in-israel-and-the-us-opinion-685368>
(accessed 8 August 2023); Leil Leibowitz, "No Jews Aren't White", *Commentary*, July-August 2021,
available at: <https://www.commentary.org/articles/liel-leibovitz/jews-are-not-white/≥ (accessed
8 August 2023); Hen Mazzig, 'Op-Ed: No, Israel isn't a country of privileged and powerful white
Europeans, *Los Angeles Times*, 20 May 2019, available at: <https://www.latimes.com/opinion/op-ed/
la-oe-mazzig-mizrahi-jews-israel-20190520-story.html≥ (accessed accessed 8 August 2023). Contrast,
Kwame Anthony Appiah, 'I'm Jewish and don't Identify as White. Why Must I Check that Box?'
The New York Times Magazine, 13 October 2020 (Updated 19 May 2021), available at: <https://

but my argument, bluntly put, has nothing to do with Jews as people nor with Jewishness as an asserted racialised ascription. It is entirely focussed on 'Israel' as an invention of *Zionist-Israelism*. This I do emphasise: Zionist-Israelism is wholly premised on a claim to *White*-entitlement whereby Jewishness, as Wolfe and others have amply demonstrated, is attached to *European* civilisation as both in origins and futures. There is great consequence to this association, and this I will return to shortly, this intimacy of *Europe-Postcolony*. For present purposes, this original motivation for the imagination of *Eretz-Israel* defines the precarity, and anxiety, that confronts the 'Israeli'-psyche; the anxious claim by *Zionist-Israelism* to the 'right to exist' in the precarious reality of the 'Middle-East' – of the precarity of the 'only democracy in the Middle-East' – must be understood as corresponding coherently to what is the supremacist's ontological terror of 'White-Replacement'. This is a perfectly understandable fear; there is no greater terror for a system of reality built upon a Lie than its simple repudiation after all. 'Israel' is precarious by vicarious reason that *Europe* is a fragile virtue in the (Kaganian) 'jungle' of the World.[39] And as such, a further correspondence pertains that is the claim to the absolute *Right* to supersession, that is to say, the *Right to Destroy*, with impunity, as divinely ordained and sanctioned. There is no equivocation on this point. The fragility intrinsic to the genocidal character of *White*-ness as a *European World*-making structure demands this, and so it is for the assertion that is 'Israel'-in-the-*World*. Seen in this light, through the lens of ontological fragility, as it were, *Zionist-Israelism* is built upon a paranoia that is necessary as an intimate and essential companion to its assertion of presence. Simply, 'Israel' *is*, while 'Palestine' *cannot, must not*, be. And for this reason, the perpetual war against the invented 'Arab' threat, no matter child or adult, 'civilian' or 'terrorist', embodied in the figure of the 'Palestinian'.

So, when the shrill of 'political-legal' argumentation on the 'conflict' are rendered quiet, when all the distraction of debates regarding the 'History' of the situation is set aside, this is the hard reality of the situation of Palestine as a (b)ordered norm-alisation of a precarious assertion of *Zionist-Israelism*: The Idea of 'Israel' is premised upon a claim to ontological exceptionalism, which translates into the material reality of genocidal violence as a 'right' to 'self-defence' against a perpetual and essential existential fragility. I see no incoherence or perplexity here, the tormented (post)colonial actuality of

---

www.nytimes.com/2020/10/13/magazine/im-jewish-and-dont-identify-as-white-why-must-i-check-that-box.html≥ (accessed 8 August 2023).

39 See Robert Kagan, *The Jungle Grows Back: America and Our Hostile World* (New York: Alfred A. Knopf, 2018).

Palestinian suffering is precisely the necessary and corresponding fact of the exceptionalism of *Zionist-Israelism*. As such, this fear, this constant knowledge of a fragility of 'existence' as 'The State of Israel', for all its absurdity in international law, is absolutely warranted; both as the *Idea*, and as a violent manifestation upon the lands of the peoples of Palestine, 'Israel' remains precarious because it is, quite simply, by definition, by imagination, so. I do not say this to validate or assuage this anxiety even as I acknowledge fully its premise. Exactly the opposite, this is, and must remain an anxiety that is fully and justifiably brought to bear. As I argued in Chapter 3, it is precisely *White*-replacement that is necessary and integral to an anti-colonial correction of the prevailing system of norm-ality. It is imperative, that is if we take seriously the intention to address the situation as a matter of anti-colonial correction, that we are clear on the situation as such.

All this, remains, precisely precarious. And this is understood by the protagonists of *Zionist-Israelism* as the *Idea* of 'Israel' is sought to be entrenched as 'post-colonial' norm-ality. The violence that is 'Israel' is commensurable to its precarity. This for the simple fact that notwithstanding the materiality of 'Israel' as an assemblage of violence, Palestine remains. I am not here minimising the immensity of the human consequences of this militarised creation, unimaginable as it is in its daily cruelty. Still, *Palestine* exists, unconquered, precisely as a spectre that stubbornly repudiates 'Israel' as a claim to the *World*. Not the original plan of decimation that defined the origins of *Zionist-Israelism*, nor the inter-generational trauma of the *Nakba*, erases the original presence of Palestine in the Israeli imagination.[40] Not the complete debacle of the various 'Peace Processes',[41] nor the apparent renewed sense of impunity for planned programmes of surveillance, encampment and killings conducted under the constant appeal to 'security' against 'terrorists', diminishes the 'threat' of this spectral presence of Palestinian resistance. Not the complicity of the utterly *colonised* contemporary 'political leadership, nor the apparent global resignation to the 'post-colonial' settlement of 'Israel' and 'Occupied Palestinian Territories', none of these normalisations of *Zionist-Israelism* subdues the essential refusal of the Palestinian peoples to be (b)ordered, to relinquish the frontline that is *Palestine*.[42] It is, I would argue, still as Sayegh maintained:

---

40 For an understanding of the Nakba not as historical event but as a structure of continuing dispossession and negation, see Elias Khoury, "Rethinking the *Nakba*", *Critical Inquiry* 38(2), 2012, 250-66.
41 For a detailed account of the Oslo Process, see Erakat, *Justice for Some*, Chap. 4
42 For rich descriptions and analysis of the meanings and implications of sacrificial resistance in this connection, see Nasser Abufarha, *The Making of a Human Bomb: An Ethnography of Palestinian Resistance* (Durham: Duke University Press, 2009).

those sacrifices were not in vain. For they safeguarded the Palestinian national rights and underscored the legitimacy of the Arabs' claim to their national heritage. Rights undefended are rights surrendered. Unopposed and acquiesced in, usurpation is legitimized by default. For forfeiture of its patrimony, the Palestinian generation of the inter-War era will never be indicted by the Palestinian generations to come. It lost indeed – but not without fighting. It was dislodged indeed – but not for want of the will to defend its heritage. Nor has the people of Palestine retroactively bestowed undeserved legitimacy upon the Zionist colonization of Palestine by recognizing the fait accompli after the fact. ... But the people which had remained, thirty years undaunted by the combined power of British Imperialism and Zionist Colonialism, and which subsequently refused to allow the seizure of its land and the dispersal of its body to conquer its soul also, knew very well how to resist those siren-calls. ... [T]he people of Palestine has remained loyal to its heritage and faithful to its rights.[43]

And as stated more recently, in total defiance of the recognised complicities of the 'Palestinian Leadership', the following by the collective Palestinian Youth and Students Organizations:

Let history bear witness to the crime, the ongoing Nakba that has continued since 1947-48 and, at the same time, testifies to the ongoing Palestinian resistance that continues until victory, despite all of the sacrifices and lengthy years of struggle.

No to the path of surrender and liquidation! No to the project of the "self-rule government" and "administrative autonomy!"

Yes to the path of return and liberation. Yes to the resistance and intifada until victory!"[44]

Perhaps such affirmations of presence and refusal are naïve, futile. This is not the issue however, not as a matter of philosophical trenchancy. This continuity of memory and of assertion is pertinent precisely because it marks the anti-colonial situation that remains *uncolonized*, not subsumed into a (post) colonial norm-ality as (b)ordered, as settled. The recovery of a philosophical

43 Sayegh, *Zionist Colonialism in Palestine*, 47-48.
44 "It's time for the 'Palestinian Leadership' to go", *Palestinian Youth Movement*, 7 May 2020 available at: <https://palestinianyouthmovement.com/statements-b/2021/3/2/it-is-time-for-the-palestinian-leadership-to-go> (accessed 10 August 2023) (emphases in original).

situation in this connection is of utmost importance as it fundamentally overturns the 'political-legal' assumption that defines much of the response to the 'problem' of 'Israel-Palestine'. When understood and articulated as an anti-colonial frontline, we see that we are not dealing here with a problem requiring, or is amenable to, a settlement of conflicting rights as if the 'conflict is one that is commensurable under a frame of mutual 'recognition' between 'Israeli' and 'Palestinian'. My argument is that the *Reason* of *Zionist-Israelism* cannot contain such a possibility. Incommensurability is precisely the fundamental quality of the situation. There is no other available conclusion based on the shameful evidence we abundantly possess. The 'State of Israel' is, categorically, the name of a global (post)colonial settlement that concedes, as disposable, the peoples of Palestine. As such, the 'conflict' of relevance is not one between 'Israel' and 'Palestine', as two antagonists of categorical commensurability quarrelling over the security of unsettled 'borders', but as an incommensurable encounter between an anti-colonial reclaiming of an unceded, unrepentant Palestine against a continuing, rampant, and genocidal *Zionist Israelism* as a (post)colonial formation. To this frontline we must return.

The 'Post-Colonial' Settlement as (Post)Colonial Manoeuvre

We arrive here at the crux of the matter, that is to understand the situation of Palestine as being fully located within a structural totality of *Europe-Postcolony*. A failure to understand the situation in this light is to miss the essential quality of the problem. It is not without reason that the apparent 'conflict' between 'Israel-Palestine' remains protracted, impossible seemingly to settle one way or the other, so evocative of such intense passions of entitlement couched in imaginaries of belonging and 'Return'.

We observe that a frequent complaint from the protagonists of the 'State of Israel' is that the world obsesses about the 'alleged' – they would assert – 'Israeli' infractions not equalled in other situations of conflict.[45] This, for them, proof of the 'anti-Semitism' inherent in such criticisms of 'Israel', for, after all, the situation warrants no special attention; is it not the case that the problem of 'Israel-Palestine' is simply – as if this were ever an appropriate term for the human condition of suffering – just another context of 'conflict', as are so many others? I want to pause on this point.

---

45 For a discussion, see William Eichler, "Singling out Israel: A perspective from the left", *Open Democracy*, 2 June 2015 available at: <https://www.opendemocracy.net/en/north-africa-west-asia/singling-out-israel-perspective-from-left/> (accessed 10 August 2023).

It is clear that critical commentators, particularly those with 'postcolonial' inclinations, have been much exercised by the undoubted suffering of the Palestinian people. We have already seen that the frame of 'settler-colonialism' provides a useful point of critique which has generated much of the recent attention on the problem. And yet, how exactly do we understand the significance of the issue? What do we make of the following statement, albeit in somewhat pressured circumstances, by Achille Mbembe:

> Israel is not the main object of my work. I have written books, articles, thousands of pages and Israel appears in them maybe two or three times – not even Israel but Palestine and that is in part of my work peripherally... It wouldn't even occur to me to contest Israel's right to exist, that's something for me that is self-evident. If you ask me whether I'm for Israel's right to impunity, that's something else. And that's as valid for Israel as it would be for South Africa, Cameroon, the USA, France and the rest.[46]

Mbembe clarifies that the issue of concern is that of impunity, nothing further, equal to that in any other situation of concern. It may, of course, be understood that this qualification was made under the duress of the accusation of 'anti-Semitism'. Regardless of the context, however, Mbembe's explanatory statement is in substance fundamentally mistaken, once again, serving as a concession to the (post)colonial situation of Palestine specifically, and to the 'post-colonial' deceit more generally. And this is precisely the point I make. Contrary to Mbembe's qualification, the situation of Palestine, that is, the (b)ordering of 'Israel-Palestine' as a duality in the *World*, is indeed at the heart of the global resettlement of (post)coloniality. It is not peripheral, or incidental to the structure of the *World*. Quite the opposite. We address here a question that is beyond explanation as a 'conflict' between two peoples, territories, and borders, one that exceeds questions of accountability and impunity, serious as these are. What is at stake is indeed more significant and profound, defining, in quite a fundamental way, the operation of the 'post-colonial' philosophoscape of global coloniality.

I want to focus attention here on two aspects of this (post)colonial manoeuvre, the first, expressed in the realm of what might be taken as practical, geopolitical calculations of norm-alisation, the second, more significant and profound, a matter of philosophical (b)ordering at its core.

---

46 For the context of the incident behind this statement, see Tymon Smith, "The Metamorphosis of Achille Mbembe", *New Frame*, 10 June 2020 available at: https://www.newframe.com/long-read-the-metamorphosis-of-achille-mbembe/ (accessed 10 August 2023).

With regard to the first, an obvious reality of the situation of Palestine is the apparent 'betrayal' of the anti-colonial cause and the norm-alisation of 'post-colonial' accommodation. This we know. After the early days of solidarity, the contemporary refrains of outrage against 'Israeli occupation', periodic and performative, is coupled with the more mundane and 'pragmatic' calculations of geopolitical, economic, and 'security' exigencies which lend towards an accommodation with the situation as it is. The recent 'agreement' reached by the United Arab Emirates and Bahrain with 'Israel' for the normalisation of economic and diplomatic relations has been greeted with the accusation of 'Arab Betrayal',[47] but this is nothing radically new; indeed the facts of the global accommodation with the 'post-colonial' order settled by the partition of 'Israel-Palestine', then with the 'de facto' re(b)ordering of 1967 through to the present actualities of 'settlements' and checkpoints and the 'Wall', all testimony of this accommodation long in practice, more induced by the gains of 'cooperation' with imperialism than with 'Arab solidarity.[48] The 'post-colonial' *World*, it seems is far travelled from its anti-colonial imagination, 'Occupied Palestine' now a settled feature of the 'State of Israel', a subject of diplomatic protestations as the occasion might warrant but not overly affecting of the 'security' and economic imperatives of the 'post-colonial' settlement as a global totality of (b)ordering. Interestingly these shared priorities are very much targeted against precisely the 'threats' posed by anti-colonial remnants; the 'cooperation' between that old champion of anti-colonial struggle – India – and 'Israel', in matters of 'security' and 'defence' ample proof of this more pragmatic actuality of 'post-colonial' relations.[49] The point simply is this: notwithstanding the regular gestures and

---

47 See for example, "The Great Betrayal of Palestine by the Arab Ruling Classes", *Socialist Worker (Features)*, Issue 2914, 29 July 2014, available at: <https://socialistworker.co.uk/features/the-great-betrayal-of-palestine-by-the-arab-ruling-classes/> (accessed 10 August 2023); Iqbal Jassat, "Normalisation and the Betrayal of Palestine by Arab Despots", *Middle East Monitor*, 1 October 2021, available at: <https://www.middleeastmonitor.com/20211001-normalisation-and-the-betrayal-of-palestine-by-arab-despots/> (accessed 10 August 2023); Shadi Hamid, "A Separate Peace: What the Gaza Crisis Means for Arab Regimes", *Brookings: Order from Chaos*, 16 May 2021, available at: <https://www.brookings.edu/blog/order-from-chaos/2021/05/16/a-separate-peace-what-the-gaza-crisis-means-for-arab-regimes/> (accessed 10 August 2023); Oliver Holmes *et al.* "'We Feel Betrayed': Palestinians Fear Cost of Arab States' Deals with Israel", *The Guardian*, 22 September 2020, available at: <https://www.theguardian.com/world/2020/sep/22/we-feel-betrayed-palestinians-fear-cost-of-arab-states-deals-with-israel> (accessed 10 August 2023).
48 See, Abu-Manneh Bashir, "Israel in the U.S. Empire", *Monthly Review*, 58(10) 2007, available at: <https://monthlyreview.org/2007/03/01/israel-in-the-u-s-empire/> (accessed 12 August 2023); Mehmood Hussain, "The Palestine Liberation Movement and Arab Regimes: The Great Bterayal", *Economic and Political Weekly*, 8(45), 1973, 2023-28.
49 See Goldie Osuri, "Kashmir and Palestine: itineraries of (anti) colonial solidarity", *Identities*, 27(3), 339-356. For accounts and details of the development of such cooperation, see for example, Harsh

exhortations of support and solidarity with the cause of Palestinian plight and against 'Israeli' aggression, there is in all of this little of consequence insofar as political, economic and diplomatic matters are concerned. Indeed, for all of the ink expended within the United Nations system on the 'question of Palestine', all we have by way of actual action with any material consequence is the Boycott, Divestment and Sanctions movement which remains, as it is, almost entirely a non-governmental movement of public judgement and action.[50]

This is a hard reality of the 'post-colonial' betrayal of the peoples of Palestine. But it is not, I argue, the most significant aspect of what I am calling the 'post-colonial manoeuvre' with respect to the situation of Palestine. What we see as the accommodation of the 'State of Israel' is merely symptomatic of a more profound (b)ordering which goes to the heart of what it means, philosophically speaking, to understand the *World* as a (post)colonial system of reality. And here lies the essence of the problem, understood properly as a problem only when seen through an anti-colonial philosophical lens.

As I have argued in the previous chapter, 'post-colonial' norm-ality is defined by the assumption and assertion of an underlying structure of *Europe-Postcolony*. We return to this analytical frame. My argument is this: the situation of Palestine contains within it the pivotal (b)order/frontline of the global system of (post)colonial reality, bringing together the operation of *Europe* – of *White*-ness, of *Rights of licence* – and of *Postcolony* – of the

V. Pant and Ambuj Sahu, "Israel's Arms Sales to India: Bedrock of a Strategic Partnership", *ORF Issue Brief*, 311, September 2019, Observer Research Foundation, available at: <https://orfonline.org/wp-content/uploads/2019/09/ORF_Issue_Brief_311_India-Israel.pdf> (accessed 12 August 2023); Alvite Singh Ningthoujam, "India-Israel Defence Cooperation", *BESA Center Perspectives Paper*, 236, 27 January 27 2014, available at: <https://besacenter.org/wp-content/uploads/2014/01/perspectives236.pdf> (accessed 12 August 2023). For an account of similar cooperation with African states, see, Toi Staff, "Israel's diplomatic thrust into Africa spearheaded by military training", *The Times of Israel*, 4 March 2019, available at: <https://www.timesofisrael.com/israels-diplomatic-thrust-into-africa-spearheaded-by-military-training/> (accessed 12 August 2023).

50 See 'BDS: Freedom, Justice, Equality', available at: <https://bdsmovement.net> (accessed 12 August 2023). Indeed, there is a great deal of indignant backlash by the 'defenders' of 'Israel' against the purported anti-Semitism of the movement; for a flavour, see Yermi Brenner, 'Germany's BDS movement and the paradox of anti-Semitism', Aljazeera, 21 April 2016, <https://www.aljazeera.com/features/2016/4/21/germanys-bds-movement-and-the-paradox-of-anti-semitism> (accessed 12 August 2023); David M. Halbfinger, Michael Wines and Steven Erlanger, 'Is B.D.S. Anti-Semitic? A Closer Look at the Boycott Israel Campaign', *The New York Times*, 27 July 2019, <https://www.nytimes.com/2019/07/27/world/middleeast/bds-israel-boycott-antisemitic.html> (accessed 12 August 2023); Sheryl Gay Stolberg, 'House Overwhelmingly Condemns Movement to Boycott Israel', The New York Times, 23 July 2019, <https://www.nytimes.com/2019/07/23/us/politics/house-israel-boycott-bds.html> (accessed 12 August 2023); ''The New Antisemites': New Report Uncovers the Dangerous Connection Between BDS and Antisemitism', *Stop AntiSemitism*, 16 December 2019, <https://www.stopantisemitism.org/new-anti-semites-report> (accessed 12 August 2023); 'BDS Israel boycott group is anti-Semitic, says US', 19 November 2020, *BBC*, <https://www.bbc.com/news/world-middle-east-54999010> (accessed 12 August 2023).

civilisational obligation of *contained/abandoned* subjection – all in one point of understanding. Indeed, the *Idea*, and presence, of 'Israel' is heavily invested with a reconfigured imagination, and norm-alisation, of 'post-colonial' *Europe*. Concomitantly, in this 're-settlement' of the (post)colonial *World*, 'Palestine', as a (b)ordered place of containment given meaning through the offer of *beingness-in-subjection*, is made simply *Postcolony*. We see the evidence.

Consider this, the profound transformation of *Europe* and, correspondingly, the global redemption of *White*-ness.

Understood from an anti-colonial vantage point, there is no lack of certainty that the emergence and entrenchment of *White*-ness, as a racialised category of norm-ality in the *World*, is responsible for the abjection of humanity made less-than, other-ed into non-Beingness and subjected as such not simply as an instance of violent subjugation but as a systemic totality. This is the 'colonial' system of reality, much acknowledged and accorded a great deal of fanfare in purportedly corrective gestures. Equally, we know that *Europe* was precisely the meaning attached to an ontology of *Rightful* domination and appropriation; with *Europe*, as a philosophical naming, thereby is constructed as norm-ality the *Colony* as an onto-epistemological situation and a phenomenological actuality. All this was the hard work of anti-colonial philosophy to reveal and repudiate. And yet, with the blink of a figurative (and philosophical) eye, a magical transformation: from enslaver and coloniser, 'post-colonial' *Europe* is transformed as liberator and redeemer, now the bulwark and, indeed, *frontline*, of the 'civilisational' values of 'Human Rights', 'democracy', 'freedom', 'peace' – we are familiar with the refrain. This is quite something, this shift, precisely the manouever that re-makes the World, now 'post-colonial', once again in the image of *Europe* as civilisational *norm-ality*, as *normative* 'Humanity'.

How so, this redemption, this absolution of the sin intrinsic to the category *European-Whiteness*, under our very (anti-colonial) noses? The answer, an obscene appropriation of suffering, of an evil perpetrated by *Europe*, and its reinscription as *White*-victimage/salvation. In this connection we understand the *exceptionalisation* of the *Holocaust* as the fundamental category of (post)colonial *World*-making.

To repeat the fact: modern Judeocide is fully the experience of *Europe*, the asking of the question "The Jewish Problem" and its answer of the "Final Solution" with its pogroms and extermination 'camps', expressions of an extreme desire of perverted purification born out of an integral *European* assertion of racial supremacy and paranoia. Then, the 'post-colonial' transformation: the invention, as a philosophical point of exceptionalism, *Shoah-become-Holocaust*. With this naming of a horror made exceptional beyond description and comprehension, and of a (*White-d*) victim now embraced by the same *Europe* that inflicted this racialised denigration upon its Jewry, is engineered the radical transformation, profoundly significant as a moment of 'post-colonial' *World*-making. It is as Henryk Broder – speaking specifically of the German appropriation of the *Holocaust* but true more significantly when understood as a *European* manoeuvre – put it: "We have turned a mark of shame into a badge of honor. Isn't it fantastic, the way we stand by our sins?"[51] Fantastic indeed. With it, washed of its colonial sins by its categorical reinvention as liberator of (*European*) Jews, the *Idea* of *Europe* is made anew in the 'post-War' imagination of global norm-ality structured through the architecture of the 'super-power' settlement that becomes, with its sanitised nomenclature, the order of the 'United Nations'. I stress here the double operation of exceptionalism that inheres in this (post)colonial manoeuvre:

1) the assertion of *European-White*-ness as exceptional liberator and protector of Humanity;

2) the assertion of a *White-d*, *Europeanised* Jewry as exceptional victim of incomparable suffering.

Both liberator and victim in *the* pivotal situation – the *Holocaust* – that marks the *World* re-made, how magnificent this redemptive transformation from that historical category of *coloniser*. With the combined scenes of 'Allied' troops marching into the concentration camps abandoned by the defeated Nazis, and the images of desperate and grateful inmates – rendered 'White' in this regime of imagery – thereby liberated, *Europe* as a value and virtue is returned to the centre stage of History. In this light we see that the lasting legacy of the 'Second World War' exceeds that of a peaceful resolution of conflict; more than its *World*-making effect through the creation of the United Nations architecture of 'global (b)ordering' it is the evocation of the paradigmatic victim and saviour that renders the post-War settlement (one might say, metaphysically) profound.[52] In this way, the *Holocaust* is indeed a radical moment, but not by

---

51 Henryk Broder, "We Invented the Holocaust", *Transition* 89, 2001, 74-87, at 79

52 The point is especially pertinent for the specific rehabilitation of Germany into the *European* fold. A striking feature of post-War German foreign policy indeed being the total and unwavering support of 'Israel' with near total silence on the violence inflicted on Palestinian peoples; see, Daniel Marwecki, *Germany and Israel: Whitewashing and Statebuilding* (Oxford: Oxford University Press, 2020); Anonymous, "Palestine Between German Memory Politics and (De-)Colonial Thought", *Journal of*

reason of the utter inhumanity that originated its *naming*, but in its *named* effect to (b)order and regulate 'suffering' in the *World*.[53]

It is important to understand the effect of this assertion of contemporary 'post-colonial' exceptionalism on the actual operation of the present (post)colonial normality. Ann Stoler makes the following observation while commenting on the apparent hesitation in past years for 'postcolonial studies' to engage fully with the issue of 'Israel':

> [I]t is the very availability of those analyses [of 'Israel' being a coloniser state] and the cumulative knowledge they represent that was censored, as if an invisible *cordon sanitaire* was around Israel, as though acknowledgement of Israeli aggression and recognition of the familiar and unique forms in which it was manifest would diminish and demean the sacrosanct History of the Holocaust as **the** genocide that has most mattered in, and to, "our" world. Again it is not ignorance that is at issue but self-censorship and a regime of truth-telling that made Israeli aggressions appropriate to ignore."[54]

Stoler makes no further point following this insight, her focus rather on the tentativeness of engagement, on the self-censorship that afflicted early 'postcolonial studies'. This is true, of course, but it is not so interesting. More important is the understanding, stated in passing and as a matter of fact, of the simple fact: "the sacrosanct History of the Holocaust as **the** genocide that has most mattered in, and to, "our" world." I have no doubt that Stoler is not affirming such claims of uniqueness and exceptionalism. Nevertheless, they remain, as such, simply stated, as such. I think it more significant and revealing. Consider, what makes this particular History 'sacrosanct'? Why did this particular genocide matter most? By what reason of accounting, of morality or essential value, this judgement of exceptionalism, especially so after Aimé Césaire's intervention?[55] It seems to me we have simply taken it to be so, this assertion. My argument is that it is precisely the entrenchment of this *norm-ality* that lies at the heart of (post)colonial *European-White* exceptionalism, the manoeuvre of philosophical absolution, the result of the

Genocide Research, 23(3), 2021, 374-82; Broder, "We Invented the Holocaust".

53   The apparent assumption of primacy of the *Holocaust* as the 'gold standard' in determining the validity or otherwise of claims of 'genocide' and of the reparatory implications that might follow is perverse proof of its regulatory power; for an example of such deliberations, see John Torpey, ""Making Whole What Has Been Smashed": Reflections on Reparations", *The Journal of Modern History*, 73(2), 2001, 333-58.

54   Stoler, *Duress*, 52 (emphasis in original)

55   Aimé Césaire (trans. Joan Pinkham), *Discourses on Colonialism* (New York: Monthly Review Press, 2000)

dual and combined ascriptions of *victim/liberator* being essential and foundational in defining the structure of 'our' *World*. The ascription of ultimate
and exceptional evil to the fact of the gas chambers was indeed a philosophical moment. With it, all attention returns to *Europe*, altogether remade,
reinvented, as a 'post-colonial', 'post-racial' category in the *World*. In this
transformation, 'Israel'-in-(partitioned)Palestine, seals the deal; it is the *Idea*
made worldly with name and meaning as *the* place of redemption for the
archetypal victim and the site of absolution for the sinner-turned-liberator.
Here, victim and saviour coalesce to realise the re-settlement of the ontological, and indeed, epistemological, (post)colonial system of reality.[56] And
once again a 'Declaration of Independence',[57] marks the moment; indeed, we
might regard this the first such declaration under the UN Charter system that
claims for itself the ontological status of 'post-colonial'. As we see, the place
of 'Israel' in the structure of the (post)colonial *World* is far from peripheral,
this exemplified by the centrality of the territorial protection of 'Israel' fully
as a *European* bastion amidst *Oriental-Arab* savagery in the *Postcolony*. This
is precisely as Theodor Herzl imagined it, after all, and the exact proposition
that he put to the 'anti-Semitic' allies that he envisaged would support the
ideal of the 'Jewish state':

> We should there form a portion of a rampart of Europe against Asia,
> an outpost of civilization as opposed to barbarism. We should as a
> neutral State remain in contact with all Europe, which would have
> to guarantee our existence. The sanctuaries of Christendom would
> be safeguarded by assigning to them an extra-territorial status such
> as is well-known to the law of nations. We should form a guard of
> honor about these sanctuaries, answering for the fulfilment of this
> duty with our existence. This guard of honor would be the great
> symbol of the solution of the Jewish Question after eighteen centu-
> ries of Jewish suffering."[58]

---

56 The invention of the mythological civilisational bond of 'Judeo-Christianity' being the epistemological key in this connection; see, Gil Z. Hochberg, ""Remembering Semitism" or "On the Prospect
of Re-Membering the Semites", *ReOrient*, 1(2), 2016, 192-223. For an opposite, uncritical, affirmation of this invention, seen as an emergent frame of cohesion and solidarity, see Debrah Dash Moore,
"Jewish GIs and the Creation of the Judeo-Christian Tradition", *Religion and American Culture: A
Journal of Interpretation*, 8(1), 1998, 31-53.
57 Declaration of Independence, Provisional Government of Israel Official Gazette: No. 1; Tel Aviv 5 Iyar 5708,
14 May 1948, previously available at: <https://main.knesset.gov.il/en/about/pages/declaration.aspx>
(accessed 20 August 2023, now, denied, 24 December 2023) Alternatively, at <https://ijs.org.au/
israels-declaration-of-independence-14-may-1948/> (accessed 24 December 2023).
58 So much after all was precisely the dream of Theodor Herzl: Herzl, *The Jewish State*, 96.

No, not a matter peripheral to the 'post-colonial' situation, 'Israel-in-Palestine' is fundamental to the (re)bordering of the *World*; it is the pivotal manoeuvre that returns *European-Whiteness* as the central *Reason* that defines the *World-as-norm-ality* and the *norm-ality-of-the-World*. As such 'Israel' is indeed sacred ground where *Europe* is reborn, returned from 'exile', redeemed perversely to sin, righteously, once again. The rest is a matter of management, as we have seen, of the regulation of licence, containment and abandonment in 'occupied Palestine' as *Postcolony*. In this situation, (occupied-)'Palestine' is to comply as it is demanded of them, its subjection precisely its condition of being as the necessary and *intimate* negation essential for the assertion of 'Israel'.

And the work of (post)colonial philosophy here? This is what is so often neglected in critical discussions on the 'question of Palestine', an examination of the situation not simply as a question of 'settler-colonialism' but, first and foremost, as a philosophical matter. Understood in this light, precisely the meaning and implications of the discourse on exceptionalism comes to focus. I speak here of the norm-alisation of 'anti-Semitism' as a fundamental philosophical manoeuvre that defines narrative exceptionalism, determining what is permissible and what is forbidden in any discussion regarding questions of culpability and victimhood,[59] and of any possible futures that might thus be imagined, for *Israel(-Palestine)*.

Returning 'Anti-Semitism' to Anti-Colonial Praxis

By way of reiteration, let me state plainly the anti-colonial position:

- The situation in Palestine persists as an open and unresolved assertion of a racialised enforcement of colonial conquest and subjugation notwith-

---

59 Neil Caplan provides an interesting discussion of the intractability of the competing sense of victimhood, of the *Shoah* and the *Nakba*, in addressing any resolution of the 'conflict':

> Far from the absurd expectation that either party will agree to re-educate its people to see themselves in the role of victimizers, it may be more realistic to hope that critical scholarship may help decrease, in however small increments, the level of self-righteousness and closed-mindedness with which both Israelis and Palestinians cling to their narratives of victimhood. This, as many dialogue attempts illustrate, is no easy task; even among the most enlightened parties to this conflict it is difficult to admit much merit in the rival's national narrative, or that" the Other" may also have some cause to feel victimized. Yet movement in this direction would seem to be a prerequisite for making some of the tough compromises required if there is ever to be a workable solution to the protracted conflict.

Neil Caplan, "Review: Victimhood in Israeli and Palestinian National Narratives", *Bustan: The Middle East Book Review*, 3(1), 2012, 1-19, 19 (reference omitted). What is ignored in this discussion is the simple fact that this is no ordinary 'conflict' between two commensurable protagonists. The structural inequality – of *Europe-Postcolony* as I have demonstrated – that defines the situation renders this not an equal exchange of 'dignity' but the utter demand of the exhaustion of one to the primacy of the other as the pre-requisite for any conversation of 'resolution'. The result of this is a denialism of the worst kind that presents itself as thoughtfulness.

standing the 'post-colonial' attempts of norm-alisation via the United Nations Partition Plan (Res 181(II), 1947), the 'Declaration of the Establishment of the State of Israel' (1948), the UNSC Resolution 242 S/RES/242. 1967) etc.

- As such, the so-called 'State of Israel' remains little more than a colonial assertion repudiated by the peoples of Palestine. Any claim of its 'right to exist' as a 'post-colonial' State is therefore utterly meaningless.

This much is clear and incontrovertible: I say this fully aware of the usual assertions otherwise by the proponents of *Zionist-Israelism*. This alone however is not the end of the matter. A further anti-colonial correction needs affirming, and this, we observe, is less prominent in the literature. It is, however, I maintain, the critical move to recover an anti-colonial philo-sophical *frontline* from a persistent move of usurpation designed to foreclose, indeed, to colonise, the discursive spaces open to contestation:

- The assertion of the 'State of Israel' is both by intention and effect 'anti-Semitic' in that it 1) implicates all of Jewry in the infliction of a White-supremacist assertion of racialised violence against other imaginations of Jewish-beingness and, 2) is premised on the subjugation, if not elimina-tion, of 'semitic'-Arab peoples from Palestine.

In this argument, I am going beyond the understanding, as clearly presented by Joseph Massad, for example, that Zionist-Israelism has from its origins been aligned with 'anti-Semitic' forces in 'Europe' to realise its racialised ambition for a 'national state'.[60] It is usually the case that this mutual affinity, past and present, is understood in perplexity as if it were somehow a rela-tionship marked by a contradiction of sorts. As an example of this apparent intimacy, and it appears hard on the eye and to the heart, no doubt, that Benjamin Netanyahu is seen in affectionate handshake with Victor Orban.[61] But contrary to common representations of this relationship between Zion-ist-Israelism and the 'European Far-Right,' there is nothing surprising here.

---

60 See Joseph Massad, 'Pro-Zionism and antisemitism are inseparable, and always have been', *Middle East Eye*, 9 May 2019, available at: <https://www.middleeasteye.net/opinion/pro-zionism-and-an-tisemitism-are-inseparable-and-always-have-been> (accessed 21 March 2022).

61 Indeed, the 'liberal' press is much at pains to recover 'European values' from this unholy alliance as if there were some categorical difference between the 'liberal' and the 'populist' forces when it comes to the essence of *Europe-in-the-World*; see, as examples; Zeev Sternhell, "Why Benjamin Netanyahu Love the European Far-Right", *Foreign Policy*, 24 February 2019, available at: <https://foreignpolicy.com/2019/02/24/why-benjamin-netanyahu-loves-the-european-far-right-orban-kaczynski-pis-fidesz-visegrad-likud-an-tisemitism-hungary-poland-illiberalism/> (accessed 28 March 2022); Oren Liebermann, "Why Netanyahu is cozying up to Europe's renegades", *CNN*, 19 July 2018, available at: <https://edition.cnn.com/2018/07/19/middleeast/netanyahu-europe-israel-intl/index.html> (accessed 28 March 2022).

That is, if we understand that at the heart of the intention of Zionist-Israelism is precisely the affirmation of a supremacist denigration of the 'semitic' peoples deemed lesser, precisely the affliction that Zionism was intended to correct – the creation of the 'new Jew' as Pappe put it – through the assertion of a European selfhood as a (White-ed) Jewish nation.[62]

For the (post)colonial project of *Zionist-Israelism*, two simultaneous manoeuvres operate, the result of the assertion of *Zionist-Israelism*-as-Jewishness: 1) the liberation of (*White-d*) Jewishness from its denigrated 'Semitic' ascription; and 2) the usurpation and weaponisation of 'anti-Semitism' as meaning to apply to the beingness of 'Israel' as the territorial embodiment of Jewry.[63] I want to stress here the correspondence rather than any distance, in the *World*-views of *Zionist-Israelism* and the '*White*-nationalism' of the so-called 'European/North American Far-Right'; both envisage a *White*-supremacist (b)ordering of the *World* – a 'Judeo-Christian' alliance as it were – against the hordes of (un-*White*) Semitic-races that form the shared existential enemy to be eliminated. It is as Sayegh understood it quite some time ago, a shared aspiration of *World-making*:

---

62 Pappe, *Ten Myths About Israel*, 29, Indeed, we might regard the early proponents of Zionist-Israelism as the original 'self-hating Jews' as their nationalist project was precisely to depart from the 'traditional' and the 'orthodox' ways of Jewish-beingness in Europe.

63 Principal in enforcing this interpretation of 'anti-Semitism' are the highly influential proponents of the International Holocaust Remembrance Alliance (IHRA) definition; see, 'What is antisemitism: Non-legally binding working definition of antisemitism', *Remembrance Alliance*, available at: <https://www.holocaustremembrance.com/resources/working-definitions-charters/working-definition-antisemitism> (accessed 28 November 2023). The sustained application of this weapon of 'anti-Semitism' against Jeremy Corbyn as Leader of the Labour Party in the United Kingdom is an example of both the potency of this discursive appropriation, more so for the apparent normalisation of its unquestioned wielding; for a discussion see, Les Levidow, "Bad Consciences: Projecting Israel's Racist-Settler Aggression onto Labour Party "Antisemitism"." *Free Associations*, 81/82. 2021, 65–93; Jamie Stern-Weiner, "Jeremy Corbyn hasn't got an 'antisemitism problem'. His opponents do.", *Open Democracy*, 27 April 2016, available at: <https://www.opendemocracy.net/en/opendemocracyuk/jeremy-corbyn-hasn-t-got-antisemitism-problem-his-opponents-do/> (accessed 28 November 2023); Emily-Rose Baker, "The Weaponization of Antisemitism: Naomi Wimborne-Idrissi's Suspension from the UK Labour Party", *Jewish Women's Archive*, 17 December 2020, available at: <https://jwa.org/blog/weaponization-antisemitism-naomi-wimborne-idrissis-suspension-uk-labour-party> (accessed 28 November 2023). As a counterpoint is the recent initiative of the 'Jerusalem Declaration on Antisemitism' by concerned academics and commentators, its intention explicitly to limit the use of 'anti-Semitism' as a weapon; 'The Jerusalem Declaration On Antisemitism, *JDA*, available at: <https://jerusalemdeclaration.org/≥ (accessed, 28 November 2023). While the Jerusalem Declaration has attracted much attention especially in university circles concerned with issues of 'academic freedom' – this includes my own institution, the University of Warwick – it remains however inadequate, still seemingly bound by the unquestionable adherence to the norm-ality of the state 'right to exist' in the discourse on 'The State of Israel'; see in respect "examples that, on the face of it, are antisemitic", Art. 10: "Denying the right of Jews *in the State of Israel* to exist and flourish, collectively and individually, as Jews, in accordance with the principle of equality." (emphasis, mine) This retains what is a unique claim of 'state right' recognised, as we have seen, in no other situation.

The Zionist concept of the "final solution" to the "Arab problem" in Palestine, and the Nazi concept of the "final solution" to the "Jewish problem" in Germany, consisted essentially of the same basic ingredient: the elimination of the unwanted human element in question. The creation of a "Jew-free Germany" was indeed sought by Nazism through more ruthless and more inhuman methods than was the creation of an "Arab-free Palestine" accomplished by the Zionists: but behind the difference in techniques lay an identity of goals.[64]

Clearly the aspiration to eliminate the 'unwanted human element' remains mutual to both protagonists. The 'handshake' is a reaffirmation of this connection of *White*-ness, where Netanyahu stands not as a 'Semite' of the past but as fully *Whitewashed*, equally a warrior and stalwart against the incursions of the 'Arab'. But more than simply a shared 'anti-Semitic' hatred, what is unique about the present situation is that this unity is obscured, disguised as an aberration, reasserted as an error, both of the *Ideas* of 'Israel' and 'Europe'. It is precisely this philosophoscape of (ab)norm-ality that is at issue. I am not concerned with the perversities of the 'European Far-Right' here, or more accurately, I see little difference in such a categorical distinction in the *Idea* of 'Europe', as I have already argued. The norm-alisation of the anti-Semitism' of 'Israel' on the other hand certainly deserves attention.

As I have stated, this is the critical move that re-*Orientalises* the shared 'Arab' enemy: *Zionist-Israelism* 'liberates' Jewishness from its 'Semitic' stain in *Europe* simultaneously as it claims a monopoly over the wrong of 'anti-Semitism' as solely pertaining to its victimisation. In this dual gesture, the 'Arab' now stands stripped of 'Semitic' status as their persecution is intensified. If once 'anti-Semitism' was the ascription of degeneracy and inferiority that united the Arab and the Jew as 'Europe's' *orientalised* other against which both Arabs and Jews combined in joint repudiation,[65] now it stands renewed as the exceptional (post)colonial category for universal protection preserved solely for the 'Jew' of *Zionist-Israelism* as perpetual victim of 'anti-Semitic'

---

64 Sayegh, *Zionist Colonialism in Palestine*, 26-27
65 This important argument is made in Gil Z. Hochberg, "'Remembering Semitism" or "On the Prospect of Re-Membering the Semites'", *ReOrient*, 1(2), 2016, 192-223. Also, Yoni Furas, "We the Semites: reading ancient history in mandate Palestine", *Contemporary Levant* 5(1), 2020, 33-43; Jonathan Judaken, "Introduction: Rethinking Anti-Semitism (AHR Roundtable)", *American Historical Review* 123(4), 2018, 1122-38. It is important to note, as Furas rightly argues, that there are good reasons for discarding of this category altogether, 'Semite' being precisely a racialised, Orientalist invention. But this is a different debate. For our present purposes, so long as 'anti-Semitism' remains brandished as a discursive weapon, this argument for an anti-colonial reappropriation is a necessary correction.

vulnerability. In this re-(b)ordering of suffering and vulnerability, of victim-hood and accountability, 'Israel-as-perpetrator' against the Semite-Arab asserts for itself categorical impunity, for it must be so that under this regime of exceptional beingness-in-the-*World* the 'Jew' cannot, by definition, be 'anti-Semitic'. I say this, but this is not quite so; a refinement is necessary. An 'Israeli/Zionist-Jew' cannot, by definition, be 'anti-Semitic', unless, that Jew *per chance* reveals themselves to be a 'self-hating Jew' who deigns to be in opposition to *Zionist-Israelism*. In such cases, we understand that 'Israel' trumps 'Jew' as properly the victim of 'anti-Semitism'. And 'anti-Semitism' as understood to be attached to the vulnerability of *Zionist-Israelism*, trumps all other imputations of racism. Such is the fantastical power of (post)colo-nial philosophical sophistry asserted as the norm-ality of the *World*.

The power of this perverse assumption of exceptionalism lies in the fact that its operation is apparently accepted as somehow *normal*, and I regard this an utter failure of anti-colonial philosophical work. It is indeed to the credit of the philosophers of *Zionist-Israelism*, proof of their success in defining categories of contestation, that we find any effort at an interrogation of their premises striking, even daring. Consider these words of Lawrence Davidson:

> Those who assert that Zionism is the tuest [sic] form of Judaism must dismiss or discredit the critics of Israeli policies. ...they must be rendered 'irrelevant to the world Jewish community.' It would be interesting to see how today's tribal Zionists would react to the statement made in 1961 by the great Jewish philosopher Martin Buber. Essentially ... Buber asserted that "Only an internal revolu-tion can have the power to heal our people of their sickness of cause-less hatred....Only then will the old and young in our land realize how great was our responsibility to those miserable Arab refugees in whose towns we have settled Jews who were brought here from afar; whose homes we have inherited, whose fields we now sow and harvest; the fruits of whose gardens, orchards and vineyards we gather; and in whose cities that we put up houses of education, charity, and prayer...." Buber concluded that the situation was so morally reprehensible that "it is bound to bring complete ruin upon us." Buber too would now have to be labeled (sic) "irrelevant in the world Jewish community.

The continuing disagreement as to what constitutes the real values of the community has, in effect, split Judaism into majority and minority parties. The majority element, which controls the religion's institutional manifestations, openly identifies itself and its ethics with the expansionist, brutalizing policies of the Israeli tribal state. They have given themselves and their religion over to the Zionist dream of a Jewish state. What they have inherited, however, is the very worst aspects of nationalism that comes when nationhood is pursued not in a pluralistic spirit, but in a tribal one: chauvinism, aggressiveness, and xenophobia. As a result there has been *a militarization of the Jewish mind, the Passover ritual and other Jewish celebrations have been turned into paeans of nationalism, imperialism and colonialism, and Zionist nationalists have invented (as a vicarious act of fratricide) the category of "self-hating Jew" for those who share their religion but not their politics.*"[66]

Davidson's is an example of an important statement of conscience by critical Jewish voices against the assertions of *Zionist-Israelism*. These are many but they remain, as Davidson acknowledges, fringe to the now dominant assertion of 'Jewishness-in-the-World', matters of internal debate, at best, lending towards positions of influence or 'irrelevance' in the 'Jewish community'. Important as such statements are, they are wholly insufficient from an anti-colonial standpoint: simply, they do not address the core of the situation. What remains in these efforts to return conscience to the 'Jewish mind' is still the assumption of 'Israel', the question being one limited to its nature and tendencies, not its ontological assertion. There is no Palestinian involvement

---

66 Lawrence Davidson, "The Zionist Attack on Jewish Values", *Issues*, Winter 2009 available at: <http://www.acjna.org/acjna/articles_detail.aspx?id=520 > (accessed 28 November 2023) (emphases mine). Similarly, this anguished statement by Judith Butler:

> If we think that to criticise Israeli violence, or to call for economic pressure to be put on the Israeli state to change its policies, is to be 'effectively anti-semitic', we will fail to voice our opposition for fear of being named as part of an anti-semitic enterprise. *No label could be worse for a Jew, who knows that, ethically and politically, the position with which it would be unbearable to identify is that of the anti-semite. The ethical framework within which most progressive Jews operate takes the form of the following question: will we be silent (and thereby collaborate with illegitimately violent power), or will we make our voices heard (and be counted among those who did what they could to stop that violence), even if speaking poses a risk?* The current Jewish critique of Israel is often portrayed as insensitive to Jewish suffering, past as well as present, yet its ethic is based on the experience of suffering, in order that suffering might stop.

Judith Butler, "No, it's not anti-semitic", *London Review of Books*, 25(16), 2003 available at: <https://www.lrb.co.uk/the-paper/v25/n16/judith-butler/no-it-s-not-anti-semitic> (accessed 28 November 2023) (emphases mine), That this question is even asked, that this is the pressure experienced in balancing the assertion of 'Israel' and the weight of silence', such is the utter absurdity of the 'anti-Semitic' discourse. See also, Judith Butler, "Bari Weiss's Unasked Questions", *Jewish Currents*, Fall 2019 available at: <https://jewishcurrents.org/bari-weisss-unasked-questions> (accessed 28 November 2023).

in these quests for the soul of 'Israel', of course, their 'presence' in such deliberations of (in)justice are limited, appearing only as either worthy victims or
unworthy trespassers. For all the notable solidarity with the suffering of the
'occupied' peoples of Palestine expressed, such remain a coloniser's discourse
arguing about the scope and breath of the meaning of 'anti-Semitism' in the
face of 'Israel's' impunity. Two assumptions of pertinence remain entrenched
in these 'Jewish' admonishments: 1) the existence (as of *Right*) of the 'State
of Israel'; 2) the intrinsic validity of 'anti-Semitism' as attached to anti-Jew-
(ishness). An anti-colonial understanding of the situation begins differently.

If it is the case that the term 'anti-Semitism' is to have any semblance of
coherence of meaning then this I repeat: the assertion of the 'State of Israel'
is, both by intention and effect, 'anti-Semitic' in that it 1) implicates all of
Jewry in the infliction of a White-supremacist assertion of racialised violence
against other imaginations of Jewish-beingness and,[67] 2) is premised on the
subjugation, if not elimination, of 'semitic'-Arab peoples from Palestine.
Against this, an anti-colonial recovery, a reclaiming of 'anti-Semitism' as
anti-colonial praxis against the (post)colonial assertion of impunity by the
global proponents of *Zionist-Israelism*. The 'weapon', so to speak, needs
to be returned to anti-colonial possession as a uniting philosophy of 'Arab-
Jewish' (and Canaanite, Ethiopian etc) 'pan-Semitic' solidarity against the
(post)colonial intentions of *European-Whiteness*.[68] Not defensively, not apol-
ogetically, but defiantly as anti-colonial praxis.[69]

---

67 This point is poignantly made by Azoulay by way of her refusal, "to be an "Israeli", to think like an
    Israeli, to identify myself as an Israeli, or to be recognized as an Israeli. I refuse partly because being an
    Israeli means being entitled to stolen lands and the property of others"; *Potential History*, xii.
68 For useful discussions of, and sources for, such early articulations of the re-unification between
    Jewish and Arab 'semitic' traditions against the *European* anti-Jewishness of the 'Zionist' movement,
    see Arie Dubnov & Hanan Harif, "Zionism: Roads not Taken on the Journey to the Jewish State",
    Ma'arav: Online Israeli Art and Cultural Magazine, 9 June 2012, available at: <http://maarav.org.il/
    english/2012/04/29/zionisms-roads-not-taken-on-the-journey-to-the-jewish-state-arie-dubnov-han-
    an-harif/> (accessed 27 March 2022). See also, Furas, "We the Semites"
69 As an example of this self-acknowledged trepidation:,
        Why is denying Israel's right to exist objectionable in the first place? Did not anticolonial
        movements (seek to) dismantle colonial states? Did they not uproot European settlers
        from their lands? It is important to remember that when the PLO first drafted its charter
        Israel was but twenty years old. In living memory Israel did not exist. The experience of
        exile for 750,000 refugees was not just new. It was raw and passionately suffered and felt.
        At that historical moment it was unimaginable that Israel was here to stay. It was incon-
        ceivable that, in contrast to all the successful anticolonial independence movements of
        the past few decades, Palestine would – could – be lost. For Palestinians, recognizing
        Israel meant – and, for many still means – ratifying their own dispossession. The refusal
        to recognize Israel was a refusal of Israel's self-representation as a counter-history. It
        was a demand to recognize Israel as a colonial state. It was a commitment that history
        could and must be otherwise. Let me be clear. I am not arguing that Israelis should be
        uprooted. (Note: I too am interpolated by the command to 'recognize Israel'.) Nor am I

In this connection, the following I state as the anti-colonial understanding of the situation of Palestine:

- Palestine remains uncolonized, even if temporarily conquered and
  subjected to (post)colonial domination.
- 'The State of Israel', as an invention of *Zionist-Israelism*, is an anti-'Semitic',
  'White'-supremacist institution, enforced as a (post)colonial territorial
  (b)ordering of conquest and subjugation of the (Semitic) peoples of Palestine.
- Being so, the 'State of Israel' possesses no absolute or incontrovertible
  claim to any 'Right to Existence' as such, it's enforcement as an organised,
  militarised structure of (post)colonial subjugation precisely the *frontline*
  of anti-colonial repudiation.
- All actions of the 'State of Israel' against the peoples of Palestine – be they
  Arab, Christian or indeed Jewish – are actions of colonial violation and,
  thereby, stand repudiated. All actions in support of the 'State of Israel' by
  reason of the 'post-colonial' settlement are equally so repudiated.
- All actions undertaken in opposition to the assertions of *Zionist-Israelism*,
  both within the territorial space of Palestine, and globally, are validated by
  the affirmation of anti-colonial solidarity in struggle.

All this, of course, might be regarded as an 'impossibility' within the norm-
ality of the global architecture and militarised enforcement of the (post)
colonial settlement. That it might well be, but not as a matter of a philosophical surrender of the situation. Recalling Chapter 2, here we see the full effect
of the anti-colonial principles of praxis – of judgement, authorship, control
and action – to reclaim meanings and possibilities from (post)colonial
closures. When all is said and done, it will be for the peoples of Palestine as
a totality, encompassing all faiths, Muslim, Jew, Christian and all else that
call the land home, to define, in real and material terms, anti-colonial futures

making this argument with a view towards a particular political solution: I refrain from
making such an argument as an academic dwelling in the luxury of an elite New York
academic institution and not in a position to dictate to Palestinians 'on the ground' what
their political desires should be. I am making an analytical point. To produce a symmetry
of logic here – even if not a symmetry of power – is to fail to understand the ways in
which for Palestinians and as a historical fact (dare I venture), this was and is a project of
colonial settlement, even if one born as part of a long history of European antisemitism
and realized in the wake of Nazi genocide.
Nadia Abu El-Haj, "Racial palestinianization and the Janus-faced nature of the Israeli state", *Patterns of
Prejudice*, 44(1), 2010, 27-41, at 34-35. My intention is exactly to argue for an assertion of the anti-colonial
repudiation of the enforced norm-ality of *Zionist-Israelism* without this assumed need for qualification.
As long as this threat persists, we remain fully colonised, and this is precisely the intention of the weaponisation of 'anti-Semitism' by the *White*-philosophers of *Zionist-Israelism*. It is time we say, no longer.

that remain still unforetold. And towards this end, the One Democratic State Campaign launched in 2018, and its '10-Point Programme Manifesto' provides a framework for action.[70] What I offer here, as something that still need be said, is simply an anti-colonial reaffirmation of this cause of struggle, and a repudiation of the 'anti-Semitism' of *Zionist-Israelism*.

70 At 'One Democratic State Campaign: Manifesto', One State Campaign', available at: <https://ones-tatecampaign.org/all/en-manifesto/> (accessed 28 November 2023).

6

On 'Violence',
Concerning the Encounter

It is often heard, this demand, framed as a question along these lines: "Will you condemn these atrocities of the *terrorists?*"[1] This, the opening to any discussion on matters of 'violence' deemed perpetrated by those without *Right*, without, that is, the perceived author-ity to wield the *sword* – oh, and how lethal and cunning the 'swords' of today have become – in the making of the *World*. Such a question demands the appropriate answer, this is the point of its asking. And it is the answer, after all, that signifies a proper suppli-cation to the *order* of *norm-ality*; if otherwise, an irredeemable offence. To this, 'their' question, it is expected that 'we' must always affirm, along with them, unreserved condemnation. Then, 'we' might begin to 'argue' about 'violence',[2] not before, not otherwise. This is as expected.

What implication a different response to this 'question'? Not a negative one that asserts a non-condemnation, but a different response altogether: "Who dares ask? By what arrogant assumption of *Right* this presumed authority to ask the question, to define the events for, and terms of, judge-ment, forget the expectation of an answer?" By this 'unexpected' response we open to clear view the assumption that underpins the very asking of the

---

1 This has become incessant in this current time as I make final revisions to this manuscript, every 'inter-view' of a commentator perceived as being on the side of the Palestinian cause, or less that, even slightly critical of the actions of the 'State of Israel' as they undertake their righteous massacres of the peoples of Palestine, being demanded a response to this question from the start. The arrogance is stupendous.
2 I borrow this notion of 'arguing' about 'violence' from from Michael Walzer, *Arguing About War* (New Haven: Yale University Press, 2004). As we shall see, there is much loaded meaning in this assumption of discursive *Right*.

question. The question, we see, is significant precisely because its asking affirms, as non-negotiable, the *norm-ality* of the (b)orders of the *World*. It is *expected* that from this *norm-ality,* the question of 'violence' is considered. This is not where I want to begin.

Throughout this work I have utilised the frame of anti-colonial *front-lines* to assert particular positions that stand counterposed to the assertions of (post)colonial (b)orders, that is, to what exist as prevailing norm-ality.[3] Any call to alter this actuality of the *World* is not merely an appeal for a 'negotia-tion' or 'resettlement' of 'arguments' regarding the ascriptions of 'subject-Be-ingness'. It is not, therefore, an argument for the equal 're-cognition' of 'Black' lives, of the diversity of 'post-colonial subjects' now fully 'Human', of Palestinian 'self-determination' as prescribed by the 'State of Israel', none of these are the outcomes imagined by the positions advanced here. All such accommodations into the *World* are but manoeuvres of the 'post-colonial deceit'. Against *(b)orders* of norm-ality, therefore, *frontlines*: a point of depar-ture for thought and action that unavoidably, and unapologetically, point to an incommensurable *encounter* between the assertion of (post)colonial *Right* and the assertion of anti-colonial repudiation. Much of this might appear as overtly provocative to those less familiar with sentiments from the 'other' side of the (post)colonial (b)order. Indeed, some might regard these specific posi-tions I have adopted as provocations to 'violence', too disturbing to contem-plate, better to simply point out the 'injustice', or appeal for more generalised 'resistance', 'our' critical work thereby done. This would be simpler. We might adopt a clearer, less complicated 'moral' code; we might simply assert a condemnation of *all* 'violence'. This would be more convenient. But inad-equate. The question remains: how are we to think about the problem of 'violence'? How are we to respond to the question of 'violence'? These ques-tions warrant attention.

A Preliminary Note on 'Arguments' and Distractions

As I write this chapter, *Europe* – that is the global conglomeration of self-as-cribed 'civilisational' *White*-ness – is again in the grips of pontificating about the rights and wrongs of 'war'. Daily reiterations of voyeuristic outrage at Russia's 'invasion' of Ukraine are registered.[4] The brutality and evil of

---

3 Recalling Enrique Dussel, the work of anti-colonial philosophy in this way is to precisely repudiate the 'legality of perversion' that regulates and enforces the global '*proyecto* of domination'; Enrique Dussel (trans. Aquilina Martinez and Christine Morkovsky), *Philosophy of Liberation* (Eugene: Wipf & Stock, 2003), 54-58.

4 As attention has shifted from Russia-Ukraine to 'Israel-Gaza/Palestine', the shift in tone, from speedy

Vladimir Putin is widely and repeatedly declared with certainty, exemplified by his utter disregard for the 'civilised norms' of international law that prohibits – so we are reminded – the use of force against a 'sovereign' state.[5] 'Crimes against humanity', even 'genocide', have been sanctimoniously asserted, Russian misdeeds demanding of immediate action by the 'International Community'.[6] These are the terms of the current discourse, at least in the outraged centres of *Europe*. How assuring for those adherents of *Europe* to possess such philosophical, political and moral resources to judge on all matters pertaining to 'violence'.[7] I mention this specific instance of the hysteria over killing-dying (and most importantly, profiteering) – named 'war' – only by way of passing.[8] I am not so interested in the particular fixations of rights and wrongs as asserted by the politicians and philosophers of *Europe* as if Russia's incursions is a novelty to the prevailing system of reality that structures the (post)colonial *World*.[9] The pervasiveness of, and the profiteering from, warmongering serves *Europe* well, and this we see in all its

and unequivocal judgements of 'violation' to that of much considered circumspection, is stark and noteworthy. If it were not so despicable, this dance of hypocrisy might simply be dismissed as being laughable. The very real cost to life and the impunity with which it is regarded doesn't allow us this luxury.

5 Unsurprisingly, the matter has received quick attention by the international law community with a clear judgement of 'illegality'; see for example, James A. Green, Christian Henderson and Tom Ruys, 'Editorial: Russia's attack on Ukraine and the jus ad bellum', *Journal on the Use of Force and International Law*, 25 March 2022, available at <https://www.tandfonline.com/doi/full/10.1080/20531702.2022.2056803> (accessed 5 May 2022). We note a very different tone of nuance when the actions of the military adventurisms of the United States are considered; see for example, Christian Henderson, 'The 25 February 2021 military strikes and the 'armed attack' requirement of self-defence: from 'sina qua non' to the point of vanishing?', *Journal on the Use of Force and International Law*, 25 January 2022, available at <https://www.tandfonline.com/doi/full/10.1080/20531702.2022.2029022> (accessed 5 May 2022); and Simona Ross, 'U.S. justifications for the use of force in Syria through the prism of the Responsibility to Protect, *Journal on the Use of Force and International Law*, 8(2), 2021, 233-276.

6 'Situation in Ukraine', International Criminal Court, 2 March 2022, available at <https://www.icc-cpi.int/ukraine> (accessed 25 June 2022). / Becky Morton, 'Ukraine: Russia faces war crimes investigation, BBC, 3 March 2022, available at <https://www.bbc.co.uk/news/world-60597751> (accessed 25 June 2022).

7 To cite some possible political and philosophical approaches to the question, perhaps Michael Walzer might be sufficiently moved to regard this indeed a 'just war' based on Russia's claims of their legitimate cause? Perhaps Victor Tadros might argue that, even if the Russian 'invasion' was 'unjust', this was an occasion in which 'unjust wars are worth fighting for', and that the Ukrainians, as 'resisters, are acting 'unjustly' in defending themselves in that their 'resistance' leads to more deaths? Perhaps Saba Bazargan-Forward might consider that it is, on this occasion, right to 'aid and abet' Russia's actions in perpetrating their 'unjust war'? See, Michael Walzer, *Just and Unjust Wars* (New York: Basic Books, 1977); Victor Tadros, 'Unjust Wars Worth Fighting For', *Journal of Practical Ethics* (4(1), 52-78; Saba Bazargan-Forward, 'The Permissibility of Aiding and Abetting Unjust Wars', *Journal of Moral Philosophy* 8(4), 2011, pp. 513-529.

8 For an important decoupling of the idea of 'War' from its 'Eurocentric' framing, see Tarak Barkawi, 'Decolonising War', *European Journal of International Security* 1(2), 199-214.

9 An important correction to this purported abhorrence to aggression and 'violence' is Derek Gregory's apt expression 'everywhere war', describing the pervasiveness of imperial violence; 'The everywhere war', *The Geographical Journal* 177(3), 2011, 238-250.

vulgarity in the present situation. Simply, while the unnecessary lives lost and suffering inflicted are as always, everywhere, deplorable, there is nothing new, or exceptional, in this situation of lethal aggression when observed through anti-colonial lenses.

Let us not prevaricate. The wantonness of killing-dying is pervasive; as an actuality of the (post)colonial totality that is the *World* as it is (b)ordered, it remains the organising fact that structures *this* 'World'.[10] Importantly, this is not a problem awaiting resolution through the assertions of philosophers, even as they assume this their vocational calling. Frankly, neither 'philosophers of war' who deliberate over some abstracted moral postulates as if 'violence' and 'war' were games of hypotheticals,[11] nor those more inclined to (critical) revisitations of the metaphysics of 'the political' from which judgements on legitimacy, limits and accountability are sought to be established, have any handle on the actual ways of the *World*.[12] Both, as far as I see, examples as they are of philosophy considering philosophy, do not satisfy; at

10 The most celebrated meditation on the 'Modern' structure of 'violence' as a 'political' fact, and assumption, at least with regard to the situation of *Europe* is Hannah Arendt's, *On Violence* (San Diego: Harvest, 1970). Arendt's concern was to situate 'violence' in contradistinction to power, and thereby to disavow its pervasive hold on imagination and policy. While we know that Arendt has a deep understanding of violence as a formative experience of global (post)coloniality, and precisely of this legacy in its horrific turn to its extreme as she feels it, Arendt is a thinker of and for *Europe*; there is little in Arendt that demonstrates a concern for the anti-colonial situation as one from which thoughts on 'violence' should originate. As an example, Arendt quite explicitly positioned herself, we might say, on the side of *White*-(b)order against 'Black Power', as she denounced the US academic establishments' "curious tendency to yield more to Negro [student] demands, even if they are clearly silly and outrageous" (*ibid.*, 20); for Arendt, this tendency to violence amongst militant students is quite the fault of the influence of Franz Fanon. I see Arendt, notwithstanding her sensitivities to colonial pasts and antecedents, at core, as a philosopher anguishing over the shameful demise of a reified *Europe*. For this reason, perhaps students interested in *Europe's* mythologies might find Arendt of use. I find little that speaks to an anti-colonial situation. Differently, we might regard Achille Mbembe's examination of the deep implications of 'the relations of enmity' in his *Necropolitics*, trans. Steven Corcoran (Durham: Durham University Press, 2019), as exactly an attempt to address, from a very different vantage point, the pervasiveness of violence within the *Postcolony*.

11 I take this term 'philosopher of war' from 'Victor Tadros, 'Punitive War', in Helen Frowe and Gerald Lang (Eds), *How We Fight: Ethics in War* (Oxford: Oxford University Press, 2014, 18-37, at 18. The 'philosopher' here purports to engage in a profound consideration of matters pertaining to the rationalisations of violence – "all things considered" as Tadros absurdly and repeatedly assures the 'reader' – to disguise predetermined preferences and biases. In such 'considerations', there is no concern with any 'philosophy' that emanates from locations and perspectives of those on the other side of this turn to 'war', clearly such are matters entirely 'unconsidered' in the philosopher's ruminations. In the guise of serious 'moral' reflection, all is a game. This is a doing of 'philosophy' that I find utterly odious, devoid of life, unaccountable and inhuman, by which I mean, absent a consideration of the very real human contexts and consequences of such thought.

12 See, for example, Etiene Balibar, *Violence and Civility: On the Limits of Political Philosophy* (New York: Columbia University Press, 2015); Vittorio Bufacci, *Violence and Social Justice* (London: Palgrave Macmillan, 2007). An exception, interestingly from an earlier time of thinking critically before the rise to fashion of 'critical theory' in its variously branded orientations, is Robert Paul Wolff, 'On Violence', *The Journal of Philosophy* 66(19), 1969, 601-616.

best they are distractions that operate under the delusion that the *World* is the outcome of a contest of deliberative dignity and equality, at worst, they serve, to borrow from Michael Walzer, as 'excuse and apology'.[13]

Walzer is a useful foil to demonstrate what I mean. The context of the following insights of his is not pertinent – he was writing here on the 'threat' of 'Islamic terrorism' post September 11, 2001 – but the light it sheds on the assumption of discursive priority, and supremacy, is worth our pause:

> Secular and religious intellectuals, scholars, preachers, and publi-cists, not necessarily in any organized way, but with some sense of shared commitment, have to set about delegitimizing the culture of excuse and apology, probing the religious and nationalist sources of terror, calling upon the best in Islamic civilization against the worst, defending the separation of religion and politics in all civilizations. This sort of thing is very important; argument is very important. It might sound self-serving for someone who makes his living making arguments to say this, but it is true nonetheless. For all their inner-di-rectedness, their fanatical commitment and literal-minded faith, terrorists do rely on and the terrorist organizations rely even more on, a friendly environment – and this friendly environment is a cultural/intellectual/political creation. We have to work to transform the environment, so that wherever terrorists go, they will encounter hostility and rejection.[14]

Walzer is correct. The work of 'argument' is certainly essential in constructing the necessary environment of hostility and rejection against (terrorist) 'violence'. But my position on 'argument' is radically other to Walzer's, it originates from a location which, I dare say, the majority of the peoples that populate this much abused category of 'Humanity' experiences *this* World. We might invite Walzer to join us here. He might then choose to replace the word 'Islamic' in the above extract with 'Christian' or '*European*'. Then he might ponder the many ways in which the 'terrorism' of *Europe*, based on its 'fanatical commitment and literal-minded faith', has been supported by the 'cultural/intellectual/political creation' of the necessary 'friendly environ-ments' for its perpetration. He might thus, perhaps, realise that, indeed, a culture of 'excuse and apology' has defined the global (post)colonial project.

---

13 See Walzer, *Arguing About* War, 52.
14 Walzer, *ibid.,* 140-141.

Of course, Walzer, as he writes and 'argues', does not realise this; he cannot understand that he, as "someone who makes his living making arguments" is utterly complicit in creating the environment of 'excuse and apology'. Frankly, the fact of the situation is that he does not need to be so encumbered by such truths; his assumptions of *White-fantasy* suffices, the accompanying *Right* to discursive/judgemental priority and supremacy entirely the ground of his confidence.

I make reference to Walzer in order to make the following point clear. Walzer addresses the *World* as (b)ordered *norm-ality*. For Walzer, therefore, the question of 'violence' is a question of *exception* to *his/White*-norm-ality. I begin from a perspective of *frontlines*. To engage in the question of 'violence', from this vantage-point is a matter of encountering the *World* as a material reality, not simply a philosophical assumption. I do not argue for the sake of it, as an intellectual pastime of academic 'philosophers of violence'. From an anti-colonial location, we see that fully, *worlds* are at stake.[15] And this we must understand; when we are invited to argue about 'violence', fully, it is the *World,* in such 'arguments', that is obscured, the perversity of its *norm-ality* hidden from view, the absurdity of its pervasiveness disguised. To 'argue' about 'condemnations' or otherwise, 'proportionality' or otherwise, 'justified military targets' or otherwise, 'ceasefires' or 'humanitarian pauses' or otherwise, all such 'arguments' serve as philosophical seductions to abide by the 'post-colonial' deceit, to abide by that most insidious *White-Lie* that life, as such, matters, that 'violence' is as *exception* in the *World*. No, I begin with a clear-eyed view. There is nothing *exceptional* about 'violence', no essential prohibition on its infliction. Indeed, I do not take the naming of 'violence', as in and of itself, as a given, or meaningful; precisely the ambiguity of the term lends itself to its malleable utility and deceitful operation. This is more than simply an argument over 'legitimate' or 'illegitimate', 'lawful' or 'unlawful' violence. I want instead to discard this assumption of meaning, to make evident two assumptions that appear to define most 'arguments' on 'violence': 1) on its presumed *known-ness*, and 2) on its presumed *exceptionality*. To capture this openness, and to open to view matters properly of *routine* and *exception* in the *World*, I adopt, accordingly, the contingent, even if clumsy, term 'un/violence' in this discussion. My reasons will soon become clearer.

---

15   For a recent collection of essays that undertakes such an analysis, see, Randolph B. Persaud and Naren-
     dran Kumarakulasingam (eds.) 'Special Issue: Empire to Globalisation: Violence and the Making of
     the Third World.', *Third World Quarterly* 40(2), 2019. But once again, analysis and critique aside, the
     question remains as to what, by way of response, is suggested?

So, what of this? On what grounds my 'arguments' on 'violence'?

It is often the case that Frantz Fanon provides the backdrop to 'post/decolonial' discussions 'concerning violence'.[16] Fanon's is an important statement, and I will return to Fanon later in the discussion. For present purposes, Walter Benjamin provides a more useful point of departure. The 'argument' I make in this chapter might be understood as following from the insight contained in Thesis VIII of Benjamin's 'Philosophy of History':

> The tradition of the oppressed teaches us that the 'state of emergency' in which we live is not the exception but the rule. We must attain to a conception of history that is in keeping with this insight. Then we shall clearly realize that it is our task to bring about a real state of emergency, and this will improve our position in the struggle against Fascism. One reason why Fascism has a chance is that in the name of progress its opponents treat it as a historical norm. The current amazement that the things we are experiencing are 'still' possible in the twentieth century is *not* philosophical. This amazement is not the beginning of knowledge – unless it is the knowledge that the view of history which gives rise to it is untenable.[17]

This is a well-known passage, the first line especially much repeated.[18] I cite it here as a powerful, succinct, statement of truth seen clearly and without illusory filters.[19] I fear most of us 'post/decolonial' thinkers – I do not mean

16 It might be noted that in most of these discussions much of the potency of Fanon's anti-colonial statements are diluted, addressing little the materiality of 'violence' or of the encounter that is entailed in any situation of actual 'resistance'. Instead, we see much 'ontological' investigations of 'colonised' beingness and 'decolonisation'; see, for example, Joy James, '"Concerning Violence": Franz Fanon's Rebel Intellectual in Search of a Black Cyborg', *The South Atlantic Quarterly* 112(1), 2013, 57-70; Oladipo Fashina, 'Frantz Fanon and the Ethical Justification of Anti-Colonial Violence', Social Theory and Practice, 14(2), 1989, 179-212

17 Walter Benjamin, *On the Concept of History: Theses on the Philosophy of History*, available at <https://www.sfu.ca/~andrewf/CONCEPT2.html> (accessed 26 March 2022).

18 Most consideration of the *Theses* are however preoccupied with the question, as such, of the 'philosophy of *History*', a particularly *Europe*-ean fixation. See, for example, Ronald Beiner, 'Walter Benjamin's Philosophy of History', Political Theory, 12(3), 1984, 423-434; Matthew Calarco and Steven Decaroli (eds), Giorgio Agamben: Sovereignty and Life (Stanford: Stanford University Press, 2007), 238; Francois Debrix and Mark Lacy (eds), The Geopolitics of American Insecurity: Terror, Power and Foreign Policy (New York: Routledge, 2009), 173; Jeffrey R Leo and Peter Hitchcock (eds), The New Public Intellectual: Politics, Theory, and the Public Sphere, (London: Palgrave Macmillan, 2016), 107. An exception is Mark Neocleous, 'The Problem with Normality: Taking Exception to "Permanent Emergency"', *Alternatives: Global, Local, Political* 31(2), 2006, 191-213. And for an important correction to the assumption of *History*, see, Ashis Nandy, 'History's Forgotten Doubles', *History and Theory* 34(2), 1995, 44-66.

19 Benjamin provides an elaboration in his 'Critique of Violence', particularly in his statements on 'justice', that is of 'divine', 'revolutionary violence' as enacted in the human realm to destroy the 'mythic violence' of the State; see, Marcus Bullock and Michael W. Jennings (eds.), *Walter Benjamin:*

here those whose thinking is materially grounded in experiences of frontlines but those of us engaged in so-called (self-proclaimed) 'border thinking' – have rather shied away from the uncomfortable implications of this insight, our attentions more focussed on rearticulations of 'amazement' rather than on the 'philosophical' questions that might enable a different knowing of the *World*. Benjamin is right. Our constantly expressed anguish at the prevalence and pervasiveness of 'violence' is of little purpose; our 'amazement' is only useful if it generates a different knowing, to bring about, as Benjamin put it, 'a real state of emergency'. I suggest we take this injunction to know differently seriously.

This said, one final observation is necessary, to conclude this preliminary contextualisation of 'argument' in the matter of un/violence. As we contemplate the implications of un/violence, therefore, it is imperative to understand that subjugated peoples with experience of the (post)colonial situation do not cease to audaciously *think*, and from this, to assert action.[20] (B)order/frontline, we see, is a situation of opposing protagonists; the 'encounter' precisely the situation that makes explicit the incommensurable positions of anti-colonial praxis against (post)colonial norm-alisation. What this means is significant. In a *World* defined and regulated through the (post)colonial *Reason* of un/violence, to reclaim a philosophy of frontlines includes the reassertion, as a prerogative of anti-colonial praxis, of 'repudiatory violence'.[21] This is not necessarily to suggest an advocacy for such action; we might equally regard 'repudiatory non-violence' in this connection.[22] Of significance is the

---

Selected Writings, Volume 1, 1913-1926 (Cambridge, Mass: The Belknap Press of Harvard University Press, 1996), 236-252. But this preoccupation of an all-encompassing explanation is of little concern to me. My arguments are not so ambitious to extend to a total philosophical account of the problem of 'violence'. Mine is rather more concerned with addressing the more profane problem of 'violence' as a specific relationality of the (b)order/frontline 'encounter'.

20 Recall the 'principles' of anti-colonial praxis asserted in Chapter 2: judgement, authorship, control and action. James C. Scott's remains one of the most detailed accounts of these principles in operation in encounter between subjugation and repudiation; see, *Weapons of the Weak: everyday forms of peasant resistance* (New Haven: Yale University Press, 1985).; and *Domination and the Arts of Resistance: Hidden Transcripts* (New Haven: Yale University Press, 1990). Also, Partha Chatterjee, *The Politics of the Governed: reflections on popular politics in most of the world* (New York: Colombia University Press, 2004).

21 Enrique Dusssel called this 'legitimate compulsion' in the construction of 'power from below'. I prefer to be more explicit in acceptance of the semantics of 'violence', as 'repudiation', to focus attention on the reappropriation of this *Right* in the anti-colonial situation both as a matter of philosophy and of action; see Enrique Dussel (trans. George Ciccariello-Maher), *Twenty Theses on Politics* (Durham: Duke University Press, 104-106.

22 There is, I think, real worth in considering the full implications of what I am calling repudiatory non-violence in thinking about possible human futures. Indeed, to 'repudiate' violence as an assumption of onto-epistemological human-beingness may well be the fullest expression of 'decolonisation'. But this is a different work, one that I can't undertake here. My concern is the anti-colonial encounter

encounter this implies; the repudiation of norm-ality, this is the crux of the matter. As such, my advocacy, or preference, matters little. I simply suggest we see things as they are, and this fundamentally requires that we abandon the 'post-colonial' assumption/*Lie* that 'violence' is *exception* to *norm-ality*. Many might regard this still an 'ideal' to be insisted on, a view that would regard such normative injunction as a limit to the desires of *Might*. I understand it differently. This assumption, and assertion of *exceptionality*, and the normative injunction to 'non-violence' that purportedly follows, operate, literally, to 'disarm' the violated; as the lethal enforcement of norm-ality remains wholly rationalised and unrestrained by any injunction to 'non-violence', so is any reciprocal response by the violated vehemently claimed to be a violation of the *norm*. Simply, as those with *Right* kill, those without are, it seems, obliged to do little but endure. This is absurd.

My 'argument', therefore, for now, is this: (b)orders/frontlines present a situation of encounter entirely open to the *normative equality* of reciprocal violence from which the opposing and incommensurable assertions of *subjection-desubjectification* stand opposed. All subsequent judgements – moral, legal, metaphysical – depend then on the self-assigned locations of thought on either side of this encounter, *(b)order-frontline*.

All this I elaborate below.

Registers (and the Registering) of *Knowing-Un/Violence*

In asking the question of 'violence', what do we mean by it? How do we understand the place of 'violence' in the *World*? How do we *see* it, and *speak* it? In asking the question, who defines its meaning? What is it that we are to 'condemn' or not 'condemn'? What moment, what 'event', what experience, what suffering, triggers this demand for 'condemnation', if so? Who assumes this *Right* to know? It seems we (must) 'know' the answer to these questions; surely, this *knowing* must be the precursor to any meaningful discussion. I begin differently.

'Violence' is quite the malleable category for (post)colonial philosophies. Its deceptive power as a discursive category – of and for 'argument' – lies in its apparent *known-ness*, its apparent knowability. Precisely this assumption requires examination.

---

confronted with the assertion of colonial violence as norm-alised. My argument is thus limited to the simple affirmation of reciprocal violence as a matter of praxis. I do not have the confidence to make any greater assertion in judging the actions of those in struggle, I take no outright stand on actual *frontline* judgements, be they grounded on tactical/strategic concerns or deeper moral/spiritual convictions; contra, see Judith Butler, *The Force of Non-Violence: An Ethico-Political Bind* (London: Verso, 2020).

I have already stated that I do not regard the meaning of 'violence' as in any way fixed; the precise implications of 'violence' can only be understood as a matter of relational encounter and its effects in experience. There is a further aspect of 'knowability' that is important in this connection. 'Violence' is itself a *naming*, the words used to specifically describe it – war, terrorism, (anticipatory/preventive) self-defence, humanitarian intervention, targeted killing/assassination, sexual crimes, collateral damage, public order, poverty, accident, competition etc – already infused with *meaning*;[23] it is a matter of *judgement* asserted upon the *World* that is made known and knowable through enforced and normalised regimes of language-knowledge. Simply, without judgement, itself dependent upon regimes and technologies of (in)visibility and speech/silencing, it is meaningless to speak of 'violence' in any substantive and definitive sense. Consider this spectrum, or 'registers', of 'experience'; we might regard this indeed as a register of 'suffering':

Invisibility – Misfortune – Injustice – Violation

We are familiar with these ascriptions of situations. But what do these situations of experience actually mean? Do they 'exist' as such? How do they arise? How might we 'see/know' them to be? By what normative judgements do they acquire their named 'status'? As we contemplate the *World*, by what contingencies are determined, or defined, the discursive register upon which an experience of being-suffering is to find 're-cognition' as one of the above categories of (non)relational (non)encounter? Why are some (made-)invisible, some simply deemed unfortunate, their suffering devoid of relational attributability, accountability, simply ontologically as such? Why are others named as inflicted either by reason of 'injustice' or 'violation', as 'atrocities'

---

23 How we choose our words is therefore fundamental to the ways in which we see and speak the *World*, especially so as we confront the *Words* of (post)coloniality. In this connection, there is a danger of fetishization, of 'violence' and its Words, of the apparent 'exceptionalism' of the 'violence' of *this* time. The quest deemed urgent and necessary, for new and novel descriptors, points to this fetishization. As an example, see, Adriana Cavarero, *Horrorism: Naming Contemporary Violence* (New York: Columbia University Press, 2011). For all its richness, I also include in this tendency Achille Mbembe's *Necropolitics*, which is infused with a presumption of exceptionalism, of a marked and significant departure in the nature of contemporary violence. Mbembe asserts the following: "[In] the wake of decolonization, war (in the figure of conquest and occupation, of terror and counterinsurgency) has become the *sacrament of our times*, at this, the turn of the twenty-first century" (2, emphasis, mine) While it might be true that recent rationalisations of lethality appear to conform to the logics of *pharmakon* – of a medication that acts as both remedy and poison, as Mbembe reminds us – and while it is necessary to expose the work of terminologies of normalisation, I see little utility in such fetishization of the present. 'War', as 'terror', 'horror', remains a *naming*, and the work of its invocation certainly requires investigation. But, this said, the apparent need to make exceptional the novelties of the present in this regard, is in my view, more distracting than it is useful. We will return to the work of *war* as a naming of encounter later in the discussion.

committed by 'terrorists' requiring 'condemnation'? Why is it that some instances of 'suffering' given meaning as a condition of beingness that is relationally significant, as a subjects-of-violence, warranting normative attention of varying immediacy?[24] Who's *Right* to prescribe the answers to these questions? By what *Right*? There is much here for 'argument', clearly.

The problem, as I see it, is not one of the contested *fact* of 'violence' and of its inflicted suffering. Neither the perpetration of 'violence', nor the selective and partial adjudications of abhorrence, are questions of 'fact', known and knowable as such. Quite the opposite, 'violence', as known/knowable, is a matter of assertion and infliction of discursive privilege, the re-cognition of un/violence along the spectrum that ranges from unknowability to spectacle – from the ignominy of 'invisibility' to the dismissiveness of 'misfortune', to the calculated accounting of 'injustice' to the sanction of 'violation' – entirely dependent on the contingent and calculated *registering* of 'violence' in each particular instantiation in the *World*. This is simply as it is, the way of the *World* as constituted, a way of *Right*.[25]

---

24 John Reynolds and Sujith Xavier ask similar questions:

> So why is the victim of child soldier recruitment constructed as more deserving than the child victim of structural adjustment? Why is socially produced mass starvation or grotesque inequality less odious a scourge or more imaginable an atrocity than the crimes currently being prosecuted? The production of law in this way is not a neutral process but reflects choices and historical patterns in the development of international legal practice and *have tended to relegate* the significance of socio-economic inequality and marginalise global South voices and interests.

John Reynolds and Sujits Xavier, 'The Dark Corners of the World: TWAIL and International Criminal Justice', *Journal of International Criminal Justice* 14, 2016, 959-983, 981 (reference omitted, emphasis, mine). It is not quite clear what is meant by 'global 'South voices' in this statement; do these correspond to the 'voices' and 'interests' of 'post-colonial' State functionaries or are those some other voices? How might we understand conflicts of 'South voices' in this connection? This aside, as Reynolds and Xavier see it, the necessary response to this tendency of 'choice' and 'historical patterns' is greater TWAILian vigilance to point out such oversights, to provide expanded substantive content to 'crimes' and its corrections, to seek recognition for South epistemologies in the development of International Criminal Law, to correct, in short, these perceived 'tendencies' of neglect and disregard. I do not share their faith for the reasons I explain

25 Judith Butler is right to observe that, "[c]ertain lives will be highly protected, and the abrogation of their claims to sanctity will be sufficient to mobilize the forces of war. Other lives will not find such fast and furious support and will not even qualify as "grievable.""; *Precarious Life: The Powers of Mourning and Violence* (London: Verso, 2004), 32. Also, *Frames of War: When is Life Grievable* (London: Verso, 2009). Butler's is an impassioned appeal against the pervasiveness of human disposability. But, contra Butler, it is not that such lives that are deemed 'ungrievable' are not regarded as 'human' or that they are 'unreal' lives, it is not that there is a lack of 'recognition' that might be improved by a more egalitarian understanding of 'precariousness' and 'vulnerability'. All of this are not the effect of a 'lack' but precisely the proper operation of the *World*. Certain 'lives' are 'ungrievable' fully as 'human' lives, understood as thus; it is simply that they are *disregarded*. The error is to fall for the (Colonial-)Modern *Lie* that 'Human' life is sacred, and for that equally so. The contempt for certain lives, the infliction of disposability to those lives, these are all actions in full recognition of their 'humanity'. It is precisely their humanity that is treated with disregard, with disdain. I return to this point later in the chapter.

There is no *a priori* truth to be known, therefore; all is naming – *seeing/ speaking* – and judgement. And this the work of (post)colonial philosophy to labour upon, to undertake those weighty mediations of ontologies, epistemologies, and, indeed, the 'political' exigencies of being-in-the-*World* such that precisely those judgements of situatedness – perhaps as made by Walzer's heroic figure of the 'morally strong leader' – may be conferred normative authority.[26] Thereby are the actuality of situations of encounter brought into the fold of the *World* through the intervention of (post)colonial philosophy, thus is the experience of *subjection* entrenched. It is in this manner, and through such registers, that we are accustomed to recognise the norm-ality of populations of 'misfortune' (if not invisibility), or, differently, to have brought to prominence 'injustice' or 'violation' as aberrations to norm-ality necessitating action, correction, accountability.[27] Through the assumption of precisely such power, such author-ity to *name*, to *register*, is the 'question of violence' presumed to be asked by those with *Right*, is the response of unequivocal condemnation demanded of those without.

So, we see, 'violence' *is* a most malleable category of (b)ordering and subjection. The assumption, and repeated assertion, of the purported 'prohibition'

26 Walzer imagines a 'heroic' figure indeed, carrying such heavy burden:

> "[M]any, perhaps most, of the political leaders who figure in the history books or in our own memories of twentieth-century history seem to Have had no difficulty killing innocent people. They had no sense of the guilt involved; they were simply criminals. A morally strong leader is someone who understands why it is wrong to kill the innocent and refuses to do so refuses again and again, until the heavens are about to fall. And then he becomes a moral criminal ... who knows that he can't do what he has to do – and finally does.";

Michael Walzer, *Arguing About War*, 45. It is interesting to note that Walzer appreciates that much of the 'leaders' of history and recent memory, as he put it, are nothing more than criminals. This must presumably be an acknowledgement fully of *White-European* culpability, including that of recent US Presidents. And yet, he is content to abide still by the assumption of such burdens of judgement on 'Western' leadership as the 'violence' of 'terrorism' in the *World* is contemplated. This perplexes. Talal Asad, giving Walzer's argument rather more serious substantive attention than it deserves, provides a critical response in, *On Suicide Bombing* (New York: Columbia University Press, 2007); See also, Talal Asad, 'Reflections on Violence, Law, and Humanitarianism', *Critical Inquiry* 41(2), 2015, 390-427. For a very different judgement upon the general 'argument' about 'war', 'terrorism', and violence in general, based on a very different conceived 'Principle of Humanity', see, Ted Honderich, *Humanity, Terrorism, Terrorist War: Palestine, 9/11, Iraq, 7/7...* (London: Continuum, 2006)

27 This the central point of argument relating to what is quite ridiculously named 'global justice'. For lengthy discussions on such judgements upon 'suffering' and its implications, see for example, Thomas Pogge, 'Real World Justice', *The Journal of Ethics*, 9 (2005), 29-53; Thomas Nagel, 'The Problem of Global Justice', *Philosophy & Public Affairs*, 33 (2005), 1-19; Richard Falk, 'Reparations, International Law and Global Justice: A New Frontier' in Pablo De Greiff (ed), *The Handbook of Reparations* (Oxford: Oxford University Press, 2006), 478-503; Mathias Risse, *On Global Justice* (Princeton, Princeton University Press, 2012); Harpreet Kaur Paul and Tatiana Gravito, 'The burning case for climate reparations', *Global Justice Now*, 30 June 2022, available at <https://www.globaljustice.org.uk/blog/2022/06/the-burning-case-for-climate-reparations/> (accessed 16 November 2022).

of 'violence', of its apparent exceptionality even in its manifest ubiquity in the affairs of the *World*, central to its operation and utility. This assumption has taken firm root in the 'post-colonial' imagination, proof precisely of the successful penetration of the manoeuvres of (post)colonial philosophy in 'colonised' minds. And the proof? That we still seriously believe that the abject lives of immiseration, if not the mutilated corpses of inconsequence that are mostly invisible to the *World* – their measure of disposability dependent only on the exigencies of norm-ality – that these are all 'lives that matter' in the *Reason* of the (post)colonial *World*. Notwithstanding all the evidence and experience to the contrary, we want to believe still that the 'promise' of the essential care for 'life', as such, holds true, that the lives lost, and the sufferings inflicted, could not have been intentional, or merely incidental, in the affairs of the *World*. We see the evidence again and again repeated and, with that, we too repeat our protestations, time and time again. Understandably so, perhaps. But in so doing, we miss the point entirely. It is not *exception* that is at issue, but its exact opposite. To understand the *World* differently, it is necessary to see *un/violence* as essentially *routine*.

On *Routine*[28] and *Exception*

The *World* is as it is. 'Life', as such, matters little. There is no 'universal' and 'equal' concern for any purported 'dignity of life' in the calculations of *Europe-Postcolony*; it is as Talal Asad stated it, "human life has differential exchange value in the marketplace of death".[29] Let us understand that these are the basic foundational tenets of (post)coloniality. As a consequence of the everyday routines of the *World*, the so-called 'global poor' are made-subject as such in numerous *postcolonies*, they amass surrounding the protected enclaves of the 'transnational elite classes' residing in corresponding *Europes*. This is the *World* largely unnoticed, where death is indeed a source of productive 'market' value.[30] In *this* World, the deadly calculations of enrichment and impoverishment, the unseen everyday killings and dyings, the terror of life constantly in an encounter with the fickle whims of the *decisions* by intimate 'sovereigns', the disregard or disdain over those deemed insignificant and disposable, all these are 'natural', 'unfortunate' perhaps, but natural all

---

28 I borrow this term, albeit with modified meaning and implication, from Gyanendra Pandey, *Routine Violence: Nations, Fragments, Histories* (Stanford: Stanford University Press, 2006).

29 Asad, *On Suicide Bombing*, 94

30 In addition to Mbembe's *necropolitics*, for a discussion of 'necroeconomics, see Warren Montag, 'Necro-Economics: Adam Smith and Death in the Life of the Universal', *Radical Philosophy* 134 (11-12), 2005, 7-17; Fatmir Haskaj, 'From biopower to necroecomies: Neoliberalism, biopower and death economies', *Philosophy and Social Criticism* 44(10), 2018, 1148-1168.

the same. If and when observed, such experiences of 'suffering', are mostly acknowledged as the ordinary operation of 'states', 'markets', 'international organisations' and 'corporations', of the 'environment', of 'insecurity, 'disease' and 'malnutrition', perhaps of 'culture' and 'religion', open to, even perhaps necessary of, improvement, but all within the fabric of the 'normal'. When visibilised as 'spectacle', they make either for the projections of 'violence' as exception, either invested with burdens of urgent 'interventions',[31] or less severely, for descriptive reporting and perhaps prospective policy-formulations, the work of 'experts' to consider and accomplish, 'progressively', we might say. We are familiar with this sphere of life as generally understood and spoken about in professionalised communities of knowledge/power: 'development', 'security', 'health' etc.[32] There are, of course, so many ways to fill in the details of this rough description; there is abundant accumulated 'data' on these manifold situations of the 'routine'. It is the *World* as it is, ubiquitous and banal, as structures and relations of the enforced (b)ordering of the *routinised un/violence* of the *World*. Fully, 'regulated' as such.

Of course, we have now different, critical, understandings of these actualities; indeed, we have and expanded our conceptual frames and accumulated new *words* to describe 'violence', as we seek recognition for the truth that much of the perceived conditions of depravity and destitution in the *postcolonies* is the outcome of human ingenuity, not natural providence, that it is the enforced conditions and processes of 'subjugation' and 'impoverishment', and not the natural state of 'poverty', that sustains in these circumstances of deprivation and suffering.[33] We know that such 'normalities' of the enrichment and impoverishment have long histories that are well examined and documented. And so, Paul Farmer, using the frame of 'structural violence', tells us:

---

31 See Brad Evans and Henry Giroux, *Disposable Futures: the seduction of violence in the age of spectacle* (San Francisco: City Lights Publishers, 2015).

32 See, for example, Kyle Grayson, 'Human security as power/knowledge: the biopolitics of a definitional debate', *Cambridge Review of International Affairs* 21(3), 2008, 383-401; Trevor Parfitt, 'Are the Third World Poor Homines Sacri? Biopolitics, Sovereignty, and Development', *Alternatives: Global, Local, Political* 34, 2009, 41-58; Mark Duffield, 'Global Civil War: The Non-Insured, International Containment and Post- Interventionary Society', *Journal of Refugee Studies* 21(2), 2008), 145-165; Mark Duffield, 'The Liberal Way of Development and the Development-Security Impasse: Exploring the Global Life-Chance Divide', *Security Dialogue* 41(1), 2010, 53-76.

33 As examples of such conceptual expansion, take 'structural violence', 'epistemic violence', 'emotional/ psychological violence'; see, Johan Galtung, 'Violence, peace, and peace research', *Journal of Peace Research* 6(3), 1969, 167-191 / Johan Galtung, 'Cultural Violence', Journal of Peace Research, 27(3), 1990, 291-305; Boaventura de Sousa Santo, *Epistemologies of the South: Justice against Epistemicide* (London: Paradigm Publishers, 2014); J.J. Degenaar, 'The Concept of Violence', *Politikon: South African Journal of Political Studies*, 7(1), 1980, 14-27.

Structural violence is the natural expression of a political and economic order that seems as old as slavery. ... And this economic order has been crowned with success... Indeed, one could argue that structural violence now comes with symbolic props far more powerful—indeed, far more convincing—than anything we might serve up to counter them; examples include the discounting of any divergent voice as "unrealistic" or "utopian," ...

Exploring the anthropology of structural violence is a dour business. Our job is to document, as meticulously and as honestly as we can, the complex workings of a vast machinery rooted in a political economy that only a romantic would term fragile. What is fragile is rather our enterprise of creating a more truthful accounting and fighting amnesia. We will wait for the "glitch in the matrix" so that more can see clearly just what the cost is—not for us (for we who read the journals or engage in the social analyses are by definition shielded)—but for those who still set their backs to the impossible task of living on next to nothing while others wallow in surfeit.[34]

This about sums it up, the routine pervasiveness of structures that inflict differentiated-beingness, not merely as fact but as norm-ality. The proof of its 'colonising' power lies in its apparent naturalness and inevitability. Like Farmer we might persist with the 'dour business' of documentation; 'anthropologies' and 'sociologies' of 'inequality' are necessary records of actually-existing 'Humanity'. They tell us of the nature of the (post)colonial *World*, its contours and features, its (b)orders and frontlines. But, differently to Farmer, I don't regard the problem as one amenable to correction, when there appears a 'glitch in the matrix', as if it is better knowledge of suffering that enables a different 'seeing-knowing', as if this is the essential lack. The point about 'structural violence', however vociferously we might shout its *name*, is that it is fundamentally norm-alised as *unviolence* – intentional, programmatic, fully *Reason*-able – sustained as such with the organised might of more explicit and direct modalities, and technologies, of enforcement. Indeed, structural violence is precisely the normative rationality that makes routine the coordinated operation of what Tom Burgis aptly calls the global 'looting machine'.[35] Quite, this is *Europe-Postcolony* structured.

34 Paul Farmer, 'An Anthropology of Structural Violence', *Current Anthropology*, 45(3), 2004, 305-317, 317.
35 Tom Burgis, *The Looting Machine: Warlords, Tycoons, Smugglers and the Systematic Theft of Africa's*

As I have maintained, of significance here is not the experiential fact, as such, of 'suffering'. There is no dearth of 'data' on the suffering of the 'wretched'. Such information, accumulated as they are by diverse 'disciplines' of 'fieldwork', are indeed of instrumental value, open to the contingent determination of normative significance. Contingency is precisely at issue; *routine un/violence* is wholly a matter of a 'norm-alised' determination to ensure that 'suffering' is correctly registered as appropriate to each circumstance of visibility. And this is no easy work. Immense investments are necessary, both in terms of discursive and material resources. With respect to the former, this is the work of the philosophoscape, work done through the *Words* we have been schooled into familiarity, the *Words* of 'regulation', open to much room for contestation and debate, of course, but framing of the '(im)possible', nevertheless. And from the philosophoscape to the *Worldscape*; from the power of *words* to their materialisation in the *World* – War, Humanitarian Intervention, Self-Defence, Policing, Order, National Security, Development, Sedition, War on Terror – these are the real *Word-World* outcomes of such investments enforced as 'policy', as *Law*. Words, coupled with hard cash and personnel, in schools and universities and 'think-tanks', with the weaponry of 'police', 'security' and 'military' forces, by the manoeuvrings of financial, regulatory and adjudicatory institutions, through the policies of governmental and non-governmental agencies, all these, continually reviewed and modified, all these in combined force and effect fully the technologies of '(global) governance'. Each of these we understand to be vast geographies and architectures of social, political and economic reproduction, each, fields of 'knowledge-power' in their own right. But this is exactly the point; this immense architecture of 'government' and 'governance' serves to regulate and enforce the 'structure' that defines and creates the quality of 'routine' (and 'exception') to the 'un/violence' of the *World*. Make no mistake, the 'structure' of the *World* is strongly founded, philosophically and militaristically.[36] And we think we might alter this totality by our 'critical' interjections of indignation?

Wealth (London: William Collins, 2015). See also, Jasmin Hristov, *Paramilitarism and Neoliberalism: Violent Systems of Capital Accumulation in Colombia and Beyond* (London: Pluto Press, 2014).

36 An important 'indicator' of this militarism as 'structure' is the 'Global Militarisation Index':

> the GMI understands militarisation as a description of the relative weight and importance of a state's military apparatus in relation to its society as a whole as well as a process that records the increase or decrease in the level of militarisation.

Markus Bayer, Rolf Alberth, Stella Hauk and Max Mutschler, *Global Militarisation Index: presentation, codebook and reflexion. (BICC Working Paper, 3/2021),* (Bonn: Bonn International Center for Conversion (BICC), 2021), 5, available at <https://gmi.bicc.de/publications/WP_3_2021_GMI_Codebook_english.pdf≥ (accessed 4 June 2023). Also, for an 'economic' analysis of the foundations and motivations of U.S. militarism, see Mason Gaffney, 'Corporate Power and Expansive U.S. Military Policy', *American Journal of Economic and Sociology* 77(2), 2018, 331-417.

To know the facts of '(structural) violence', in and of itself, means little. To name 'violence', in and of itself, and to make visible and recognise suffering, as such, will not do to disrupt, let alone rupture, the norm-ality of the *World*. All this is grist to the mill of (post)colonial philosophers, all a matter of 'arguing' about un/violence. To focus on 'suffering', as a matter purportedly of an aberration, is to be diverted from the central actuality. What is critical to see clearly is not the exception of 'violence', but precisely its *norm-ality*, its pervasiveness as *routine*. Un/violence, as relational actuality and structure *is* the consequence of (post)colonial *Reason* that enforces the (b)orders of *licence, containment, and abandonment*. No 'terrorism' witnessed here in the normal accounts of the *World*. No 'condemnations' demanded or expected. This reality of the everyday, everywhere, of the *routine* of inflicted cruelty and suffering, of the profiteering from this *routine* of cruelty and suffering, this is the fundamental organisation of sociality in what has come to be taken as the given, as *political-legal norm-ality*. It is as it is.

And so, what is it that a protagonist for a philosophy of the 'anti-colonial' against 'violence' obliged here to do? To make an argument for 'justice'? Addressed to whom? Using whose *Words*? The words of '*Europe's* archive', as Achille Mbembe calls them?[37] We know these *Words* well, these words that purportedly institute the *World* that entice with their 'promise', of (universal) care, of emancipation/liberation, of and for 'Humanity'. We also know of the many 'betrayals' of these *Words*. But, like Mbembe, many of us remain seduced nevertheless, with faith in some possible redemption of their 'truth', now the 'archive' understood as being of universal inheritance and legacy.[38] Such claims to universality appeal, no doubt. But, on this, I fear Mbembe, wrong. *Europe's* 'archive' serves *Europe's* desires; it has little relevance to any real aspiration of those subjected to the situation of the *Postcolony*.

---

37 See Mbembe, *Necropolitics*, 188. For a very different reflection on the 'archive', here both as a space of 'documents' and as an institution of imperial imaginaries, of destruction and invisibilisation, see Azoulay, *Potential History*, Chap. 3.

38 "... Europe, which has given so much to the world and taken so much in return, often by force and by ruse, is no longer the world's center of gravity. ... But does saying it has ceased to be the world's center of gravity mean that the European archive is exhausted? For that matter, was this archive only ever the product of a particular history? As the history of Europe has been confounded over several centuries with the history of the world, and the history of the world in turn has been confounded with Europe's own, it follows, does it not, that this archive does not belong to Europe alone?"; Mbembe, *ibid*, 188. *A* similar urging, for a rescue of *Europe* no less, for *Europe* to be true to its promise, for all Humanity, is made by Mbembe in *Out of the Dark Night: Essays on Decolonization* (New York: Columbia University Press, 2021). I understand Mbembe's intention, indeed it might be taken as a variant of my argument that 'Europe' is not 'theirs'. My disagreement with Mbembe is that in his telling, 'Europe' remains a coherent imagination, even if *her* 'archive' is infused with the genius of *Europe's* 'Others'. In my thinking, *Europe* is precisely the perversion that appropriates the genius of worlds onto its *name*.

Underpinning the *Words* of *Europe's* 'archive' (now purportedly 'post-co-lonial') is the unrelenting *Reason* of *licence*, of the *Right* to appropriation at any cost, this contrary to what "Europe has always claimed [that] the goal of this promise really is the future of all humanity".[39] We might innovate, indeed we are invited to, and many have tried, but there is little in these 'Words' that are sufficient to overcome the *Worldscape* of un/violence, that is, to overcome the underlying *Reason* of coloniality that has never ceased defining the actual-ities of *Europe's World*-making. Such efforts to recover some presumed 'Real' in the *Ideas* of *Europe* have only ever resulted in an adaptation of 'words' that aspire still to *Europe's* imaginaries of the *World*. We see this in the many attempts to reinsert the damned into philosophical re-cognition through such inventions as the 'Event', 'dissensus' and such like, whereby 'the subject' is sought to be reclaimed for *Being* in the so-called sphere of 'the political', now, purportedly, returned to some philosophical authenticity.[40] As a matter of philosophical creativity, these efforts might be regarded as elegant and appealing innovations to rescue the 'subject' as a philosophical category, to recover the 'subject' to the possibilities of human flourishing as opposed to the immiserations witnessed in the *World* as actuality. Noble, the cause, but misguided. In this fixation with what is only ever an abstraction – 'the subject-in-the-political' – what is missed, obscured from view, is the founda-tional ontological violence central to the (post)colonial system of reality; it is fully in the 'political' transmogrification of human-being-ness that 'violence' as a relationality of alienation and estrangement inheres.

Recall, we understand 'colonisation' – which exceeds the fact of conquest – as a totalising project of *subjection*. We have seen that this means the trans-mogrification of human-beingness in its manifold cosmologies and social forms into the prescribed and enforced categories of 'subject'-beingness in 'civil/polit-ical-society' as variously imagined by (post)colonial philosophies. By this *subjec-tion* are the (b)orders of 'political-legal' *belonging-separation* norm-alised. Thus, the genius of the 'declaration of independence' as a manoeuvre of method-ological 'post-colonialism', entrenching a particular, parochial understanding

---

39 See Mbembe, *Out of the Dark Night*, 76.
40 See for example, Alain Badiou (trans. Bruno Bosteels), *Theory of the Subject*, (London: Continuum, 2009); Jacques Ranciere (trans. Steven Corcoran), *Dissensus: On Politics and Aesthetics*, (London: Continuum, 2010); Slavoj Zizek, *In Defence of Lost Causes* (London: Verso, 2017); Sergei Prozorov, *Theory of the Political Subject: Void Universalism II* (Abingdon: Taylor & Francis, 2013).This, as I see it, is an internal argument, for the soul of 'Europe', as it were, as *Idea* and possibility, conducted in the imaginaries and vocabularies of *Europe*. The *Other*, all the others of *Europe*, have little say in this discussion save as illustrations of *Europe's* promise enacted in identified circumstances of revolu-tionary, 'political' emergence/becoming.

of 'human-being-ness' one with another – human and other-wise – into a purportedly secular and 'universal' condition of 're-cognition'. All of (post) colonial philosophoscape can, therefore, be summarised as the enforced and violent *manufacture* of the reified 'Human-subject-in-the-political' made to be contained now within a totalised (post)colonial *Worldscape*. Under this Idea of the exemplary *Human* as the 'subject' and agent of civilisational 'progress', all manner of cruelty has come to pass. We know all this, of course. But I want to stress the following point pertaining to what is *routine* and what is *exception*. Indeed, from the time of early 'colonial' extension, it remains the very beingness of the variously encountered *Other* – named 'savage', 'native', 'Black' etc – that is deemed *exception*, warranting correction through first, the 'Christian', then the secular, 'developmentalist' charity of righteous cruelties. As a matter of *History*, there is no dearth of public acknowledgement, even 'regret' over such errors of *Europe's* past. Less repentance however is manifest in *Europe's* contemporary civilisational imaginations; it is as Ashis Nandy cautioned, "[c]olonialism may have vanished from the world scene but its smile lingers in the air."[41] The 'smile' in question is that which entices, it is the 'promise', the 'becoming', the 'emergence' out of 'colonial' subjugation into, now, equally civil-ised, 'political society', the 'beingness' purportedly portended by the imagination that is *Europe*, now the promised future that beckons the *postcolony*. The 'smile' lingers the *World* over; this now is a 'smile' on the face of all 'post-colonial' state-regimes, intent, still, on spreading the toll of *Humanity* upon the 'uncivilised' requiring enforced induction into the ways of 'citizenship' as dispossession and compliance. All this is 'progress', 'development', from the aspirations of 'decolonisation' this now the responsibility of 'becoming/being-post-colonial' imposed on those now newly initiated into 'full-Humanity'. Speaking on India, Arundhati Roy's description is, as ever, pointed:

> The Indian Constitution, the moral underpinning of Indian democracy, was adopted by Parliament in 1950. It was a tragic day for tribal people. The Constitution ratified colonial policy and made the State custodian of tribal homelands. Overnight, it turned the entire tribal population into squatters on their own land. It denied them their traditional rights to forest produce, it criminalised a whole way of life. In exchange for the right to vote, it snatched away their right to livelihood and dignity.

41 Ashis Nandy, 'Shamans, Savages and the Wilderness: On the Audibility of Dissent and the Future of Civilizations', *Alternatives* 14(3), 1989, 263-277, 276.

Having dispossessed them and pushed them into a downward spiral
of indigence, in a cruel sleight of hand, the government began to use
their own penury against them. Each time it needed to displace a
large population—for dams, irrigation projects, mines—it talked
of "bringing tribals into the mainstream" or of giving them "the
fruits of modern development". Of the tens of millions of internally
displaced people (more than 30 million by big dams alone), refugees
of India's 'progress', the great majority are tribal people. When the
government begins to talk of tribal welfare, it's time to worry.[42]

What Roy describes is not the failure of the 'post-colonial' state to make-
real the promise of citizenship, it is the actual meaning of 'citizenship' in the
(post)colonial situation. The brutality and cruelty of the 'political' sphere,
brought into operation by the convergent 'National' and 'International'
regulation of licence-containment-abandonment, this is the foundation of
the architecture of un/violence, *routine* in every way. From this, through the
language and discursive conventions of 'Sovereignty' and 'Rights', of 'Law',
'National' or 'International', public or private, all is justified and justifiable
to enforce the identified exigencies of (b)orderings.[43] This is the 'post-colonial' *World*, the domain of the 'political' proper, of 'Sovereignty' as sheer
brutality even as it is performatively festishised and cast as a spell, the fact of
the 'post-colonial' International state-system' far more profoundly integrated
and entrenched, by intent and capacity a coherent and efficient global technology of extraction, appropriation and subjection; a 'looting machine':

> [The] looting machine has been modernized. Where once treaties
> signed at gunpoint dispossessed Africa's inhabitants of their land,

42 Arundhati Roy, 'Walking With The Comrades', *Outlook* 29 March 2010, 24-59, 26, available at
   <https://www.outlookindia.com/magazine/story/walking-with-the-comrades/264738> (accessed 4
   February 2023)
43 On the 'indeterminacy' of legal argumentation in this connection, with the focus on the so-called
   'Iraq War' (notably, seldom referred to as the 'invasion' of Iraq) of 2003, see Mieville, *Between Equal
   Rights*. In this light, we see the utter meaninglessness of earnest assertions of 'illegality' or 'limits' in
   relation to actions of 'intervention', weapons systems, and such like; for example, Frederic Megret,
   'The Humanitarian Problem with Drones', *Utah Law Review* 5, 2013, 1283-1320; Arshed Tanwir,
   'The US Drones and Their Legality in the Present Humanitarian World', *Indian Journal of Law and
   Justice* 5(2), 2014, 152-166; Kirsten McConnachie, 'Camps of containment: a genealogy of the refugee
   camp', *Humanity: an international journal of human rights, humanitarianism, and development*
   7(3), 2016, 397-412; Fernando Tesón and Bas van der Vossen, *Debating Humanitarian Intervention: Should We Try to Save Strangers?* (Oxford: Oxford University Press, 2018); Faine Greenwood,
   'Drones and distrust in humanitarian aid', ICRC, 22 July 2021, available at <https://blogs.icrc.org/
   law-and-policy/2021/07/22/drones-distrust-humanitarian/≥ (accessed 16 November 2022); Alexander Leveringhaus, 'Beyond Military Humanitarian Intervention: From Assassination to Election
   Hacking?', *The Philosophical Journal of Conflict and Violence* 5(1), 2021, 109-128.

gold and diamonds, today phalanxes of lawyers representing oil and mineral companies with annual revenues in the hundreds of billions of dollars impose miserly terms of African governments and employ tax dodges to bleed profit from destitute nations. In the place of the old empires are hidden networks of multinationals, middlemen and African potentates. These networks fuse state and corporate power. They are aligned to no nation and belong instead to the transnational elites that have flourished in the era of globalization. Above all, they serve their own enrichment.[44]

I repeat, this is not some perversion, or 'corruption' of regulation, although a great deal of corruption indeed provides the necessary lubrication for its operation. This is norm-ality. Routine. Little in this picture is the embodied beingness of the 'citizen' central, even as the reified figure of the 'subject/citizen' provides the ideal philosophical alibi; the 'post-colonial deceit' is precisely that the 'subjects' of the *Postcolony* are invited to appeal for 'inclusion' into the 'political' domain for the benefits of 'citizenship' now (purportedly) juridically equal to all, to fixate on the promise of 'equality' even as the conditions of their embodied beingness in the material actuality of the *World* are routinely violated. Outside the fantasies of the 'post-colonial' philosophoscape, however, the 'subject' has little room to manoeuvre in the material (post)colonial *Worldscape* of the 'political', her fate here, fully ontologically so, situated precariously within the (*b*)*orders* of un/violence. Giorgio Agamben (and all those who have since followed with this preoccupation with 'the exception', 'bare life', the 'camp' etc), therefore, got it exactly wrong; a(ban)donment is a situation fully and routinely within the embrace of (sovereign) norm-ality, 'rights-less-ness' precisely the corresponding condition of subject-beingness in this the

---

44 Burgis, *The Looting Machine*, 8. In this connection, also significant, and seldom explicated in discussions on 'violence' and 'security', is the commonplace of the 'privatisation' of violence. As James Cockayne reminds us:

> There is nothing either timeless or natural about the way that violence is organized in today's world. Yet the system of public territorial states, recognized and constituted by international law, is so central to our lived experience that it is very difficult to imagine how violence might otherwise be organized. Likewise, the law we know – a law of, within and between states – is so central to how we "imagine the real" that we can hardly conceive of law without states. But the global organization of legitimate violence appears to be changing. Private actors operating through global networks – whether pursuing profit or power – now rival states in their ability globally to mobilize and project violence. In some cases, these actors may attract aspects of legitimacy allowing their privately organized violence to rival or even resemble law.

James Cockayne, "The global reorganization of legitimate violence: military entrepreneurs and the private face of international humanitarian law", *International Review of the Red Cross*, 88(863), 2006, 459-490; at 459-460 (reference omitted).

(b)ordered structure of *Europe-Postcolony*.[45] Nothing exceptional here as the experience of 'subjected' peoples of the material actuality of 'Modernity', of *Europe-Postcolony*, clearly testify. 'Bare(d)-life' is entirely routine; thus understood, the 'slave ship', the 'plantation', the 'camp', the off-shore 'detention centres', all these are not the emergent spaces and situations of the 'exception' but the very basic places, the very foundational 'institutions', of the (post) colonial *World*.[46] Seen from this vantage-point of norm-ality, the situation of the *exception* is quite the opposite; it is the audacity of being-otherwise that is perverse, the assertion of a possibility that is fundamentally, ontologically, otherwise than subjected precisely 'violence' against 'Humanity' as rationalised by the philosophies of *European-Whiteness*. To be thus refusing of assigned abjection, 'out-of-Law', we might say, is to be fully warranting the infliction of unabated, illimitable 'correction'. To question the *routine* of the *World*, to materially challenge *Europe-Postcolony*, this is exactly what is forbidden as *exception* to the *norm*: this is 'violence', 'terrorism' even, absolutely prohibited, unequivocally to be condemned.

Look again at the *World;* we might see it clearly. For the 'global poor', the *Black*-ed, the 'occupied' Palestinians, all those wretched 'subjects' of abjection for whom rightlessness and (ever regretted) disposability are indeed the routine of norm-ality, for them, it is their encounters with the desires of *Europe-Postcolony*, it is their audacity to assert refusal and repudiation – of *frontlines* in the face of (b)orders – that always serve as the instigation for elimination, especially so now with the discursive reinforcements of 'the war on terror' and the unlimited licence this unleashes for the 'policing of

---

45 For a corrective to this dominant trend in critical theoretical work; see Mark Neocleous, 'The Problem with Normality'; and Mark Neocleous, 'The Police of Civilization: The War on Terror as Civilizing Offensive', *International Political Sociology* 5(2), 144-159.

46 In this connection, Azoulay's understanding of the true meaning and implication of the 'institution' as imperial technology of violation is to point:

>   [I]mperial institutions do not put something in motion, and their foundation is not the beginning of something new. Imperial institutions rather seek to put an end to existing activities, formations, and structures. They seek to impose their own principles and structures as the foundation of transcendental forms that have no history other than their concrete instantiations. Hence, in the context of imperialism, rather than relying on common dictionary definitions of the verb institute – starting something new, putting something in motion – I use a different verb, violate, which captures with greater accuracy the constitutive irreverence and disrespect of imperial institutions toward what exists ... The verb violate is not foreign to the discourse of institutions, but rarely if ever refers to institutions' mode of operation; rather, it refers to those who refuse to be complicit in its violence or recognise its authority. Imperial institutions violate peoples' right to preserve their worlds and pursue their activities, and by doing so they authorize themselves to declare those people "violators" while exonerating themselves of responsibility and accountability for their deeds against them.

Azoulay, *Potential History*, 170-171 (emphases in original).

civilisation'.[47] To be 'other-wise' than subjected, this properly is *exception*. hilosophers of the 'Post-Colonial Constitutional State', of 'just war theories', of 'humanitarian intervention', of the 'duty to protect', of all such reasser-tions of the right/responsibility to 'civilise' and regulate the *World*, would of course refute such brazen representations of their position, but such brazen-ness is exactly necessary to see clearly, and to understand differently, the actual implications and material effects of the *World* norm-alised. We are invited to abide by the conceit: "Politics is a form of *peaceful* contention, and war is *organized violence*."[48] The truth, however, is quite different: it is as Mark Neocleous states it, "[w]ar as peace, peace as pacification".[49]

What might we take from this? That violence continues to define the 'post-colonial' present? That the situation now is worsening as *postcolonies* align with the brutal desires of *Europe*, the fate of the wretched of the *World* more precarious in these 'necropolitical' times? That the 'subject' stands abandoned, betrayed, requiring rescue back into the fold of the *Enlightenment*? That all this necessitates greater (TWAILian/post/decolonial) scrutiny and critique? That what is urgent is the reclaiming, fully as 'universal', *Europe's* archive? How tired these repeated discoveries and appeals; they achieve nothing to encounter the norm-ality of (post)colonial *Reason*. Recall Benjamin: what knowledge have we gained? I urge we see again all that is *routine* and all that is *exception*, truly, without any 'post-colonial' sentimentality, clearly. The regulation of disposability, of subjugation, if not outright annihilation of the 'damned', are matters of *routine*; it is the impertinence of 'their' dignity and 'their' refusal to supplicate, that is the *exception*. Within this structure of 'regulation' is defined the full spectrum of un/violence. Under this structure of enforcement, the full spectrum of un/violence is (routinely) inflicted in the *Postcolony* in the name of the many malleable *Words* of 'Europe's archive': 'governance', 'security', 'development', 'democracy', 'Humanity', all. This is what we see, the actual in the *World*; Talal Asad stated it simply, "cruelty is an indispensable technique for maintaining a particular kind of international order, an order in which the lives of some people are less valuable than the lives of others and therefore their deaths less disturbing."[50]

A different learning is necessary.

---

47 "The war on terror is thus the violent fabrication of world order in exactly the way that the original police power was the violent fabrication of social order. The war on terror, as international politics, is a form of police; civilization's return, writ large.", Neocleous, 'The Police of Civilization', 156.

48 Walzer, *Arguing About War*, ix.

49 Mark Neocleous, 'War as peace, peace as pacification', *Radical Philosophy* 159 (Jan/Feb), 2010, 8-17.

50 Asad, *On Suicide Bombing*, 94.

Therefore, Concerning *Encounters*

I earlier asserted the anti-colonial position as this: (b)orders/frontlines present a situation of encounter entirely open to the *normative equality* of reciprocal violence from which the opposing and incommensurable assertions of *subjection-desubjectification* stand opposed. I add here one further normative assertion, a prior 'principle' as such:

> *If it is not the actuality of the World that no life matters any less than any other life, then it must be that, in this World, no life shall matter any more than any other life.*

We might regard this precisely as the foundational tenet of anti-colonial praxes.

We arrive now at a point of reckoning, the point in which we are forced to make, not 'arguments', but judgements. It is here, in this point of the *encounter* that is (post)colonial *(b)order*/anti-colonial *frontline*, that the actualities of *being-anti-colonial* materialise, where anti-colonial philosophy is returned to worlds of struggle.

In the preceding chapters, I advanced the following explicitly as frontline assertions against the prevailing norm-alities of (b)ordering:

- that *White*-ness be addressed head-on such that an anti-colonial understanding of '*White*-replacement' be explicitly embraced as an imperative to eliminate the foundational, genocidal *Reason* of Colonial-Modern (b)ordering;

- that by understanding that *Europe* is not 'Theirs', that the *Postcolony* not 'Ours', the inflictions of *Europe-Postcolony*, as a norm-alised 'post-colonial' totality, be repudiated, and the assertion of anti-colonial beingness, in time and place variously lived, forcefully reclaimed. This means to fully occupy the position of 'sedition', so named by the potentates of *Europe-Postcolony*, to fully overrun the locations of 'separation' that form the material-militarised *border/frontlines* that preserve the enforced material conditions of 'post-colonial' enrichments and immiseration;

- that with respect to the situation of Palestine, the anti-Semitism of *Zionist-Israelism* and of its manifestation in the World as the 'State of Israel' be refused the absurd privilege of the so-called 'right to exist', and that the anti-colonial situation be explicitly asserted of a fully integral totality within which the diverse peoples of the land – Muslim, Jewish, Christian, and all else, Arab, Ashkenazi, Sephardi, Falasha, all – may find (re)settlement, and be recognised entirely, as peoples of *Palestine*.

These are not mere 'arguments' for debate. They are positions on, and against, the *World* as it is enforced. They are repudiations of *norm-ality*, to be advanced through the actualities of repudiatory violence if and as necessary; indeed, it is necessary to confront the reality that it is highly improbable that such violence can, in any real terms, be avoided if the actual structures of the norm-alities of *routine* and *exception* are to be substantively repudiated. I do not advance these positions lightly, they are not presented as clarion calls for 'resistance'. I do not make here any claims one way or another of what might transpire by way of either consolidation of prevailing (b)orders or of the (im)possibilies of transformation. I do however assert the persistence of the *encounter* – as (extra) ordinary struggles waged daily around the worlds of *living* – understood as the materialisation and manifestation of the *anti-colonial* that remain vital in these situations of *frontlines*. The encounter, therefore, is the philosophical situation. It is in this situation, this moment, this location, of collision between the desires of rapacious coloniality and the refusals of the anti-colonial, that the question of 'violence' is to be posed, must be posed. We cannot shy away from it.

On this point, it is necessary to make the following observation.

It is commonplace nowadays, in contemplation of 'coloniality', impe-rialism, etc, to find impassioned affirmations of 'resistance' and 'struggle' (perhaps even 'revolution'), and celebrations of those insurgent against ever abundant real-*World* brutality. There is much vigour in such claims, much enthusiasm in making them. But as I observe it, much of such 'epistemic' labours for transformation are conducted with little attention to what this might mean in actual terms, little attention, that is, to what 'resistance/ struggle' entails in the realities of the *World* of 'un/violence'. Instead, we find many an assertion that serves, substantively, as little more than slogans, perhaps this makes us feel we achieve something worthwhile by such exalta-tions. Take, as an example, Sabelo Ndluvo-Gatsheni:

> [F]rom the African side, it is clear that another world cannot be possible as long as the continent and its people are not fully decolonized and the snares of the postcolonial neocolonized world are not broken. This will require an epistemic rebellion that enables the formerly colonized people to gain self-confidence, enabling them to re-imagine another world free from Western tutelage and African dictators that enjoy Western protection. A new imagination that liberates both the colo-nizer and the colonized simultaneously is needed. ... Perspectives from the South must be given more space as they promise another world free

from Western hegemonic thought that was constructed on oppressive
and exploitative values of slavery, imperialism and colonialism. ...

The struggle must continue. Aluta continua – this time taking
the form of a committed epistemological resistance against epistemic
violence that had prevented alternative imaginations of the world and
freedom from the knowledges and cosmologies of the Global South![51]

This is, quite simply, so much nonsense. The immensity of 'coloniality', of
the histories and materialities of 'slavery, imperialism and colonialism', of the
(post)colonial, 'neocolonial' structure of the World, of the deep entrails of
violence that enforce the interests and desires of 'Western' powers and 'African
dictators', all of this is in Ndlovu-Gatsheni's sights for 'decolonisation', thus
the call to commitment, *aluta continua*, in the form of a 'committed epistemological resistance'. It is a rousing call. With little meaning. It is quite the
fashion to labour on 'resistance' and 'struggle',[52] but in much of this, there
is a notable silence. It is quite something to observe that so much talk of
'resistance' contains so little mention of the materiality and embodiments
of 'violence' as immanent in any situation of 'struggle', that is to say, of the
material and corporeal substance of the 'epistemic' situation. Such, as celebrated by Ndlovu-Gatsheni, is 'resistance', 'struggle', without an 'enemy',
without the *encounter*, without relational substance in all the bloody possibilities intrinsic to the situation. Without content, such verbiage is merely useful
for ruminations that end in pompous self-congratulatory platitudes, useful
for the echo-chambers of professionalised 'critical' scholarship, perhaps, but
little else. A greater intellectual responsibility, and humility, is required of
those who profess a stance of 'resistance' against coloniality.

Epistemology matters, of course. It is a matter of knowing the *World*
differently. This not simply a question of cosmologies absent materiality,
absent the messy earthiness of actual 'living' in the world. Epistemological
and cosmological reaffirmations are, therefore, central to any reorganisation of
social-beingness and of social relations – that is, of the organisation of material
(re)production and distribution and of the relationalities of care – to be--
otherwise than imagined by the ontologies of *Europe-Postcolony*. And it bears

---

51 Sabelo J. Ndlovu-Gatsheni, *Coloniality of Power in the Postcolonial Africa: Myths of Decolonization* (Dakar: CODESRIA, 2013), 263-264.

52 For fuller theoretical elaborations on matters of 'epistemic delinking', but with little added clarity in terms of material implications, see the following two examples: Walter D. Mignolo, 'Delinking: The Rhetoric of Modernity, the Logic of Coloniality and the Grammar of Decoloniality', *Cultural Studies* 21(2-3),2006, 449-514; and Boaventura De Sousa Santos, *Epistemologies of the South: Justice Against Epistemicide* (Abingdon: Routledge, 2014).

remembering, it is precisely diverse cosmologies of beingness-in-the-world that were sought to destroyed by slavery, colonialism, imperialism, and that which remains under 'post-colonial' attack still, both materially and philosophically. Put differently, epistemology, if it means anything beyond the meaningless preoccupations of academic 'critical' philosophers, is intimately *material*, essentially of the worlds of living and dying. As such, 'epistemological decolonisation' is fully the transformation of the *World*, that is *this* World, as desired by 'Western' powers and 'post-colonial dictators'. I wonder what is actually meant by a "committed epistemological resistance against epistemic violence" in this connection. If it were only that the *World* were so easily transformed.

To be 'epistemologically' committed to 'alternative imaginations of the world' is to be fully immersed in the bloody and brutal contexts that are unavoidably involved, to be prepared to fully encounter the "violence that had prevented alternative imaginations of the world and freedom from the knowledges and cosmologies of the Global South." This violence remains ready to be unleashed in the face of any 'resistance', often involving the everyday routines of state-sponsored indiscriminate killings, rape and mutilations, the torching of villages, etc, examples of which Arundhati Roy chronicles in the context of the 'Government of India' who name these specifically as 'encounters' against 'the Gravest Internal Security Threat'.[53] There truly is no accounting for the creativity of 'post-colonial' purveyors of cruelty in the face of the seditious audacity of peoples to survive, let alone to resist. This is what is at stake if we dare imagine such grandiose aims as 'decolonisation' and 'liberation', to assert a beingness as such against (b)orders as they are. This is what is involved in a situation of the *frontline* that is the everyday reality of those who do, as a matter of living, struggle. I have picked on Ndlovu-Gatsheni here, but only as an example of a common tendency in 'post/decolonial' writings. The point I want to make is this: 'resistance', against the norm-ality of global coloniality, these are matters of grave, and often fatal, consequence. We must be clear, as we use these 'dangerous' words – resistance, struggle, decolonisation, liberation – that we are willing to abide by their material significance and implications.

No, we cannot shy away from the 'discomfort' in confronting the bloody materiality of the encounter: *violence*. This is a matter of taking sides – (b)order/

---

53 Roy, 'Walking With the Comrades'. See generally, Arundhati Roy, *My Seditious Heart* (London: Haymarket Books, 2019) Roy's is a particularly sharp commentary on the violence of the powerful against the dispossessed, her focus pointed on India but also with a wider lens on the violence of imperialism more generally. I cite Roy as I am familiar with her work. No doubt so many other chroniclers of suffering and struggle may equally be relied on.

frontline – in *encounter*, to be on one side or the other. 'They' will insist that 'we' are clear. Condemn the 'atrocities' of the 'terrorist', they demand precisely so 'we' make clear we stand on their side, the only side deemed permissible. We might 'argue'. And by arguing in these terms, they affirm their *Right*. So, let us indeed be clear, that this is not in their *Right*, not in their 'author-ity' to presume they can make such demand. Let us ask our own questions. What is the 'atrocity' that demands condemnation? What moment, event, of suffering initiates this 'provocation' to necessary judgement? Who are deemed 'terrorist'? By what original experience, act, this ascription of irredeemable-beingness? Who are *they* to so judge? We see, the question of what is 'condemned' and 'who' condemns becomes clear as entirely being questions of *encounter*.

My position is this. The praxis of anti-colonial repudiation, be it that it may manifest in the form of repudiatory violence in the face of the terrorism of norm-ality, is not dependent upon the normative sanction of philosophers who serve as apologists for (post)colonial (b)orderings. But to affirm this is not to pretend that the 'normative' weight of the *routine* violence of (post) colonial potentates will in any way be diminished by the truths of consequent suffering we might demonstrate. This is to fall into the trap of assuming that the actualities of (b)ordering-violence are determined by an equal contest of moral or normative platitudes, in other words, that there might be some settlement possible, a commensurable resolution of 'conflict'. By my 'arguments', I do not seek to 'persuade', I simply clarify the situation.

The responsibility to return the anti-colonial to philosophy begins by reclaiming the author-ity of thinking-being. It is to assume and assert, therefore, the 'unthinkable', precisely that which is prohibited by the philosophers of (post)colonial norm-ality. It is a matter of 'perspective' and judgement, incommensurable, irreconcilable, perhaps, inevitably violent, a matter for the encounter to make actual. It does not end there, however, for the very imperative of the labours of thinking the 'unthinkable' is to act the impermissible, the forbidden, the 'illegal'.[54] Here, we might usefully turn to Fanon; after Benjamin's insight, Fanon's unequivocal teaching:

---

54 In this, I depart from Lindahl and his attempts to overcome the perceived closure of the 'legal/illegal' duality and find instead the 'alegal' space as an opening of 'political agonism', thus opening up a critical opportunity for understanding struggle against the asserted, assumed, finality of the 'legal'; see Hans Lindahl, 'The Opening: Alegality and Political Agonism', in Andrew Sharp (ed.) *Law and Agonistic Politics* (London: Routledge, 2009), 57-70; and 'A-Legality: Postnhationalism and the Question of Legal Boundaries', *The Modern Law Review* 73(1), 2010, 30-56. My argument is that it is precisely the explicit affirmation of illegality that renders visible and incommensurable the situation of frontline against the assertion of (b)orders. Alegality falls short; it merely disturbs the apparent fixity of the encounter, not its underlying coloniality.

Decolonization, which sets out to change the order of the world, is, obviously, a programme of complete disorder. But it cannot come as a result of magical practices, nor of a natural shock, nor of a friendly understanding ... Decolonization is the meeting of two forces, opposed to each other by their very nature... ... The naked truth of decolonization evokes for us the searing bullets and bloodstained knives which emanate from it. For if the last shall be first, this will only come to pass after a murderous and decisive struggle between the two protagonists.[55]

Fanon was not speaking metaphorically.[56] He simply spoke a truth. Regardless of any affirmation, irrespective of the discomfort of those of us more accustomed to 'epistemological resistance' as a question of 'post/decolonial theory', rather than one pertaining to the materiality and spirituality of life in its messy wholeness, the fact of refusal and repudiation in the face of violent subjection will persist, sometimes in 'subterranean spaces', and sometimes in manifest irruption.[57] It is not for any 'philosopher of violence', tempted as we might be, to prescribe what is or is not morally universally 'just', as a matter of abstracted pontification, on these matters of the *encounter*. What we can do, indeed, what we must do, is to decide on the side of the *encounter* from which we see and speak of the *World*.

Recall the foundational assertion made in the Introduction. I repeat it here:

> The 'global poor' - the violated, subjugated, impoverished 'subjects' of (post)colonial norm-ality who were previously dignified by the names and hopes of anti-colonial struggle - owe this World, (b)ordered through the 'post-colonial settlements of contemporary global colo-niality, Nothing!

To take this assertion seriously is fully to dismantle the *World*. To assert that 'the global poor' owes this *World* nothing is to radically overturn the

---

55 Fanon, *Wretched of the Earth*, 27-28.
56 This is not to say that Fanon 'glorified' violence. He simply made explicit its place in the inevitable encounter that is involved in 'decolonisation'. Hannah Arendt is right to point to the caution that Fanon understood the heavy burdens of this transformation; Arendt, *On Violence*, 14. But this said, the burden remains intact. Perhaps this is a radical relationality that might be achieved through radical 'non-violence', but that is a different discussion. What is certain however, is that the most brutal violence will be the response, at the *border/frontline*, of those that preserve the norm-alities of *Europe-Postcolony*. Fanon understood this and did not shy away from it.
57 See Scott, *Hidden Transcripts*.

assumption and assertion of the 'post-colonial settlement', that is, the resettlement of coloniality which enforces the perverse norm-ality that *they* – the
'Global Poor' – owe *this* World, everything, their subjection, their subjugation, their immiseration, their abjection, all. Against *(b)order, frontline*. This,
properly, 'decolonisation' as Fanon means it. This is not an appeal to make us
'critical' types feel good. No redemption is necessarily envisaged; loss, sacrifice
and suffering always the companion of any 'resistance'. I simply intend to
explicitly assert the situation of the encounter and of the anti-colonial credentials of its normative claim. Enough with so much false piety, of 'high-minded
principles' of 'universality'.

For the abject 'subjects' (b)ordered within the norm-alities of the *World*,
contained or made-'disposable' within the global *Postcolony*, to abide by the
'promise' that the 'post-colonial' condition is one of 'violence' eschewed,
even prohibited, is precisely to be denied praxiological-beingness, that is to
be confiscated of the dignity to think/act otherwise than 'subjected', and
thereby, to remain simply in their 'naturalised' wretchedness as 'the global
poor', as abject-subjects of (un/violent) norm-ality of the (post)colonial
present, nothing else. Here we see the full effect of the deceit; the 'promise'
of the repudiation of 'violence', as some purported aspiration towards a
'universal Humanity', erases completely any prior 'autonomy' of beingness,
prior that is to 'discovery' and 'subjection' into the (post)colonial philosophoscape and *Worldscape*, from which the audacity of anti-colonial refusal in the
'post-colonial' present may emanate. This is a high price paid by those who
were once dangerously *anti-colonial*, now demanded to be 'post-colonial'.
And so, they remain, dangerous; we see them on frontlines still, taking their
suffering, their dignity, their happiness, their sacrifices, seriously.[58] No, the
'post-colonial' cleansing of 'philosophy' from its (post)colonial *worldliness*
will not do. The 'post-colonial state', and its 'International' support-system,

---

58 It is of course commonplace, in making *exception* those who refuse subjection, to describe them exactly
   as 'brutes', monsters', without 'humanity'. A very different description of humanity of struggle and
   'happiness' can be found in Roy's account of the 'Maoist' rebels in the forests surrounding Danda-
   karanya; 'Walking With the Rebels'; a very different account of sacrifice and love and poetry can
   be found in Abufarha's descriptions of the humanity of the 'suicide bombers' of Palestine; Nasser
   Abufarha, *The Making of a Human Bomb: An Ethnography of Palestinian Resistance* (London: Duke
   University Press, 2009); a very different account of suffering, courage and dignity can be found in
   Ajour's understanding of the humanity of Palestinian 'hunger strikers'; Ashjan Ajour, Reclaiming
   Humanity in Palestinian Hunger Strikes: Revolutionary Subjectivity and Decolonizing the Body,
   (London: Palsgrave Macmillan, 2021). Abufarha's and Ajour's works do employ the categorical frame
   of 'subjectivity' in their analyses which, I have argued, is to fall into ontological traps of 'becoming-be-
   longing' but this, in this context, does not diminish the significance of their work. It is their narrative
   accounts that are more compelling as articulations of anti-colonial repudiations.

possesses no absolute, or unconditional claim to 'sovereign' *Right* in the face of anti-colonial reappropriation of imagination and action. The assumption of the 'authority' of the *Postcolony* – of its claimed 'legitimate' monopoly of violence under extant political-legal philosophy and enforcement – poses no valid defence against the 'just force' of anti-colonial expression. Under such conditions of subjection-subjugation as a global systemic totality, of the continuities of the violent and forced dispossession of the materials and spaces of livelihoods and the violation of physical and psychosocial worlds, there is no prohibition on the resort to 'repudiatory violence' by the 'global poor' in the encounter with the agents of (post)colonial (b)ordering. 'Theirs' is not the burden to prove otherwise. Inconvenient as it may be, 'brutes' will continue to preserve their judgements, their wisdoms of beingness, their dignity otherwise than subjection, and from all of this, their refusal 'to be exterminated'.[59]

So, what implications the assertions I have made in the preceding chapters?

I cannot know the details of any specific anti-colonial response or outcome. I have stated my positions, my understanding of the implications of returning (post)colonial settlements of cruelty and subjugation to anti-colonial repudiations. I realise fully that these are serious assertions. They might be easily articulated in a work such as this one, but they will not come easily.

---

59 I simply add this affirmation to Sven Lindqvist (trans. Joan Tate), *Exterminate all the Brutes'* (London: Granta Publications, 2018). Roy provides the following reflection in 'Walking With The Comrades', 55:

> I think of what Comrade Venu said to me: they want to crush us, not only because of the minerals, but because we are offering the world an alternative model.
>
> It's not an Alternative yet, this idea of Gram Swaraj with a Gun. There's too much hunger, too much sickness here. But it has certainly created the possibilities for an alternative. Not for the whole world, not for Alaska, or New Delhi, nor even perhaps for the whole of Chhattisgarh, but for itself. For Dandakaranya. It's the world's best-kept secret. It has laid the foundations for an alternative to its own annihilation. It has defied history. Against the greatest odds it has forged a blueprint for its own survival. It needs help and imagination, it needs doctors, teachers, farmers.
>
> It does not need war.
>
> But if war is all it gets, it will fight back.

We might read and understand the many 'communiques' of the 'Zapatistas' as similar articulations of an 'alternative', theirs perhaps enriched with the experience of a greater consolidation of territory and the organisation of communities both in terms of cosmologies and material (re)production; see; Subcomandante Marcos, *Our Word is Our Weapon* at <https://theanarchistlibrary.org/library/subcomandante-marcos-our-word-is-our-weapon.pdf> (accessed 17 November 2022); Gustavo Esteva and Madhu Suri Prakash, *Grassroots Post-Modernism: Remaking the Soil of Cultures* (London: Zed books, 2014) 182-83; Walter Mignolo, 'The Zapatista's Theoretical Revolution: Its Historical, Ethical, and Political Consequences', *Review* 25(3), 2002, 245-75; Marcos, 'Between Light and Shadow', *Enlace Zapatista*, 27 May 2014, available at: <http://enlacezapatista.ezln.org.mx/2014/05/27/between-light-and-shadow/> (accessed 17 November 2022).

Indeed, there is no escaping the full brutality of (post)colonial violence that will greet any challenge to *norm-ality*; we witness the teaching of this 'lesson' now with regards to the situation of Palestine. I know this. But I do assert a position. And this is unequivocal.

We might perhaps agree with Arendt that "[t]he practice of violence, like all action, changes the world, but the most probable change is to a more violent world."[60] With this insight, we might wish it different, that the *encounter* – as a praxis of frontlines – in any particular and given situation adopt radical repudiatory 'non-violence' instead; we might proffer judgement that no other action may be deemed to be in the cause of 'justice'. But to be blunt, these assumptions and judgements are not for *us*, as 'philosophers' on 'violence' however noble our intentions may be, to prescribe from a distance our preferences for an imagined *World*. I trust these are fully the 'arguments' about struggle, about life, about 'violence' and its implications, about love and sacrifice and duty, that those at the frontlines of struggle everyday understand and address. On this we can have no doubt, the 'subalterns' do think, dream, speak, act, even kill. *Rightly* so. They might also, forgive, compromise, tolerate, even succumb, from time to time. Whatever their judgement in the face of the *World*, I think it imperative we affirm the location of the frontline in this encounter, whether perceived as 'violent' or otherwise. This, if at all we situate ourselves on the side of 'anti-colonial' struggle, must be unequivocally so. Anything less is fraudulent.

We pause and consider this statement. Consider the location of thought from which it is voiced:

> I feel that it is my duty to explain to you why we did what we did. Of course, from a liberal point of view of thinking, I feel sorry for what happened, and I am sorry that we caused you some trouble during the last two or three days. But leaving this aside, I hope that you will understand, or at least try to understand, why we did what we did. Maybe it will be difficult for you to understand our point of view. People living different circumstances think on different lines. They cannot think in the same manner, and we, the Palestinian people, and the conditions we have been living for a good number of years, all these conditions have modeled (sic) our way of thinking.

---

60 Arendt, *On Violence*, 80. But against this assumption, we might heed Honderich: "It may also become evident in the end, less comfortingly, that violence *would* be justified in these situations if it worked. That is, it may become evident that ... violence which *did* end wretchedness would be preferable to no violence and no change.", *Terrorism for Humanity*, 41 (emphases in original).

We cannot help it. You can understand our way of thinking when you know a very basic fact. We, the Palestinians, for 22 years, for the last 22 years, have been living in camps and tents. We were driven out of our country, our houses, our homes, and our lands, driven out like sheep and left here in refugee camps in very inhumane conditions.

For 22 years our people have been waiting in order to restore their rights, but nothing happened. Three years ago, circumstances became favorable, so that our people could carry arms to defend their cause and start to fight to restore their rights, to go back to their country, and liberate their country. After 22 years of injustice, inhumanity, living in camps with nobody caring for us, we feel that we have the very full right to protect our revolution. We have all the right to protect our revolution. Our code of morals is our revolution. What saves our revolution, what helps our revolution, what protects our revolution is right, is very right and very honorable and very noble and very beautiful, because our revolution means justice, means having back our homes, having back our country, which is a very just and noble aim. You have to take this point into consideration. If you want to be in one way or another, cooperative with us, try to understand our point of view.[61]

After 22 years? Make that now 75 years and see clearly, the situation. These words, how powerful still today. Against the pompous and self-righteous pronouncements of 'philosophers' of violence, against the discomforts of those of us wo might prefer imaginations of 'non-violence' to prevail, these are true words of 'justice', if at all this means anything. This is an understanding of 'Humanity' in its relational messiness, articulated nevertheless with deep compassion and moral strength. Properly asserted is the anti-colonial 'code of morals' as Habash put it, utterly reasonable, rational, justifiable and more than all of this, necessary.[62] Indeed, they are the words exactly of a

---

61 George Habash, *Our Code of Morals is Our Revolution: Selected Speeches and Interviews 1970-1984* (Amsterdam: International Centre for Palestine Studies, 2021). The words spoken, as leader of the Popular Front for the Liberation of Palestine, in a speech delivered to hostages taken from hijacked planes at the Jordan International Hotel in Amman, on June 12, 1970.

62 The assertion was valid in 1970 when Habash made it. It is all the more so presently. This a more recent articulation, now in terms of the meaning and implications of *jihad* in the situation of Palestine, Khaled Mesha'al, when Chairman of the Hamas Political Bureau:

   I would like first to explain how the people of this region feel and think, because the distorted stereotypes of Palestinians, or Muslims, or Hamas, that is presented in the West prevents you from seeing reality. We have two states of mind that go together: they may seem contradictory but they complement each other; and both are very human. One is 'morally strong leader'; they state what is explicitly a matter of position and judgement expressing, 'the whole of our duty to uphold the rights of the inno-cents.' Philosophers of *European-White-ness* will utterly dismiss this absurd and dangerous proposition, no doubt. They will rationalise and enforce the *World*. They will demand 'condemnation' of such words and actions. But they mistake *their* Words for truth; theirs, equally absurd to those who look upon the *World* from frontlines, theirs the savagery of 'terrorism' that bears no humanity for the lives of others, theirs the inhumanity of lust and profit over compassion, all duly rationalised as 'natural' and 'good' by their philo-sophies stained by the blood of 'History'. This is what the *World* looks like from the other side of the *border/frontline*. Fully violent already, little need here for Arendtian worry. The 'discomfort', the anxiety over a *World* more 'violent', this is 'ours', as we presume our 'comfort' in this *World*, on *this* side of the (b)order.

This a final point I want to make, regarding our purported abhorrence of 'violence', concerning our 'horror' that is assumed to 'rightly' originate the demand for 'condemnation'.

Much of the concern with 'terrorism', with 'horrorism' even,[63] is premised on a particular revelation of 'vulnerability', of 'precarity', as Judith Butler eloquently elaborates.[64] For Butler, it is the solidarity of universal vulnerability, of our 'precarious lives', that make human-beingness uniquely a possibility of conscious concern. It is this shared social ontology that neces-sitates for Butler the normative imperative, that "there ought to be a more inclusive and egalitarian way of recognizing precariousness."[65] And yet, as Asad's observation makes clear, and as Butler is fully cognizant, 'vulnera-bility' is not quite a value equally shared, its unequal distribution precisely

---

a state of compassion and love towards people who are not hostile or aggressive towards us – to all people, including the poor and those of a different religion or race. The other is of strength and steadfastness, courage and defiance in facing those who attack us. This is what it means to be human ...

This is where the concept of struggle, of jihad, of resistance comes in. This is not our attitude to everyone; we engage in struggle, jihad, resistance against the enemy who steals our land and destroys our houses, commits sacrilegious acts against our holy places, assaults children and women and kills people. It is our normal, natural right to resist, to struggle against them. All the laws given by God, and by international law, give us this right. So, jihad is a response to aggression; it does not itself initiate aggression.

Quoted in Alistair Crooke, *Resistance: The Essence of the Islamist Revolution* (London: Pluto Press, 2009), 203-204. Crooke provides an excellent discussion of the Palestinian perspective of armed resis-tance in terms of 'profound human values'.

63 See Cavarero, *Horrorism*
64 See Judith Butler, *Precarious Lives*; and *Frames of War*
65 Judith Butler, *Frames of War*, 13

the perverse *norm-ality* of *this* 'particular international order'. I say this not to repeat the complaint, but to shift our attention to the assumption that follows. We might consider it a rebuttal of 'innocence' in the light of a reframing of 'vulnerability'.

We are familiar with the 'un/violence' of the *World*; we might be disturbed by it, but we are not, in Cavarero's terms, 'horrified' by its perversity and prevalence. Simply, we are accustomed to suffering as *routine*, 'violence' here unregistered, 'just' *norm-ality*. But not so the 'violence' registered as 'terrorism', as 'horrorism', this we register as *exceptional*. Such naming of an *event* of suffering evokes a different response, a different normative judgement. Why so? Here operates, the assumption of 'innocence', of 'helplessness':

> the "helpless one" ... is he who does not bear arms and thus cannot harm, kill or wound. ...[T]he term "helpless" tends to designate a person who, attacked by an armed other, has no arms with which to defend himself. Defenceless and in the power of the other, the helpless person finds himself substantially in a condition of passivity, undergoing violence he can neither flee from not defend against. The scene is entirely tilted toward unilateral violence'. There is no symmetry, no parity, no reciprocity.[66]

We might begin by acknowledging that this description fully corresponds to the routine experience of wretchedness of the 'global poor'. It is not that we lack a cognizance of their 'helplessness'; indeed, where such suffering has passed the threshold of 'invisibility' and made 'spectacle', then there is much documentation of their experience, recognition, perhaps, of their 'misfortune', even, on rare occasions, on the 'injustice' of their situation. Notwithstanding such attention, no *horror*. Just matters for 'argument', a re-settlement of *norm-ality*, perhaps. Nothing new to see here, to know here, *their* 'vulnerability' simply the ubiquitous way of the *World*. Their 'innocence' counting for little, mostly not counting at all for, perhaps, they are themselves culpable for their wretchedness, for their lack of ambition, lack of effort, to survive in their respective wretched, damned places. Un-*horrific* helplessness.

But in *our* places, a very different assumption. Our places are presumed 'secure', as of *Right*, expected to be made-secure by every means, policed to be secure. Here the assumption of *innocence* is supreme, and *helplessness* in the face of 'violence' fully registered, its materialisation as suffering beyond

---

66 Cavarero, *Horrorism*, 30

imagination, utterly un-*Reason*-able. Hence the 'horror'. Hence the demand for condemnation. It is, we see, all a matter of the *World* framed, *subjection*, ontologically differentiated, 'suffering', epistemologically regulated.

No, we must take seriously Asad's observation; I repeat it: "cruelty is an indispensable technique for maintaining a particular kind of international order, an order in which the lives of some peoples are less valuable than the lives of others and therefore their deaths less disturbing." These words fully capture the perverse absurdity of 'post-colonial' norm-ality. We cannot plead 'innocence'. We are not helpless. *Europe-Postcolony* operate as a totality. I am not so concerned here to extol the virtues of responding, by way of 'responsibility', towards 'distant *suffering*';[67] we have enough of that. And we have seen that this is simply to valorise the 'saviour'. It is more pertinent to focus, contra *innocence*, on our complicities in the perpetuation of *distant violence*. This is more to point, and indeed, more pointed in its implications. Cruelty, is not simply an 'indispensable technique of a particular international order' as if this was a structure devoid experience, it is an indispensable technique that preserves differentiated lives in the intimacy of belonging-separation, both the lives of splendour and of squalor fully the Human lives of this 'order', 'our' lives of 'security' precisely the effect of the same *norm-ality* as 'their' lives of wretchedness.[68] This properly is the operation of *terror-ism*. 'We' on this side of the (b)order, are not *subject-ively* innocent whatever our self-regard on the matter of the commission or omission, of 'violence'.

With this correction to the much Self-centred fixations with precarity, vulnerability, helplessness, innocence, established, we might consider the deep implications of anti-colonial praxes. As a philosophical situation, the anti-colonial marks a rupture in the *World* as norm-ality, it overturns the underlying *Reason* of coloniality, variously described in the preceding chapters. Thus

---

67 See for example, Andrew Linklater, 'Distant Suffering and Cosmopolitan Obligations', *International Politics* 44, 2007, 19-36; Maria Kyriakidou, Imagining Ourselves Beyond the Nation? Exploring Cosmopolitanism in Relation to Media Coverage of Distant Suffering", *Studies in Ethnicity and Nationalism* 9(3), 2009, 481-496.

68 Ted Honderich is correct:

The terrorists, when they are taxed with what will be called the irrelevance of their claim that our ordinary conduct is wrong, can maintain the strong truth that our two kinds of conduct are connected. It is not that the terrible circumstances of misery and injustice, against which violence is directed, come about by chance. They have not come about through historical passages in which we and our predecessors have played no particular part. The circumstances of distress of every kind, rather, are as good as our own work. We contribute to them essentially by our wrongful conduct. It is not that there is no connection between violence and our omissions, but rather that there is the connection that our omissions are essential contributions to the misery and injustice against which terrorism for humanity is directed. – Honderich, *Terrorism for Humanity*, 146.

we have seen, whether it be in the structure of *White-Reason* that regulates *Black-ed* lives as matter for extraction, appropriation, subjugation, or in the global (b)ordering of *Europe-Postcolony* as a coherent regulatory totality of differentiated subjection, of *licence, containment* and *a(ban)donment*, or in the colonial consequences in Palestine of the genocidal and anti-semitic assertion of *Zionist-Israelism*, the operation of the foundational assumption (and enforcement) of (post)colonial norm-ality that *the lives of some peoples are less valuable than the lives of others and therefore their deaths less disturbing*. When all else is said and done, this simple philosophical postulate defines the (post) colonial as a totalising situation that regulates, as norm-ality, *un/violence*. Against this, the repudiation, the rupture of the anti-colonial as a recovery of *frontlines*, as praxis of *encounter*. This then to conclude my 'argument', as a response to any demand for a condemnation of 'terrorism' so named by (post)colonial potentates, the following foundational assertion I repeat:

> *If it is not the actuality of the World that no life matters any less than any other life, then it must be that, in this World, no life shall matter any more than any other life.*

It cannot be otherwise. In the face of the *World* that is fully a (post)colonial artefact, in the face of the absurd perversities of *this* World, we must begin here, this the knowledge that continues the burdens of bringing about a 'state of emergency', of 'decolonisation', of *being anti-colonial*. We are all involved. And we will all, in one way or another, be implicated.

www.ingramcontent.com/pod-product-compliance
Lightning Source LLC
Chambersburg PA
CBHW071740270326
41928CB00013B/2743